The Enchanted Broccoli Forest

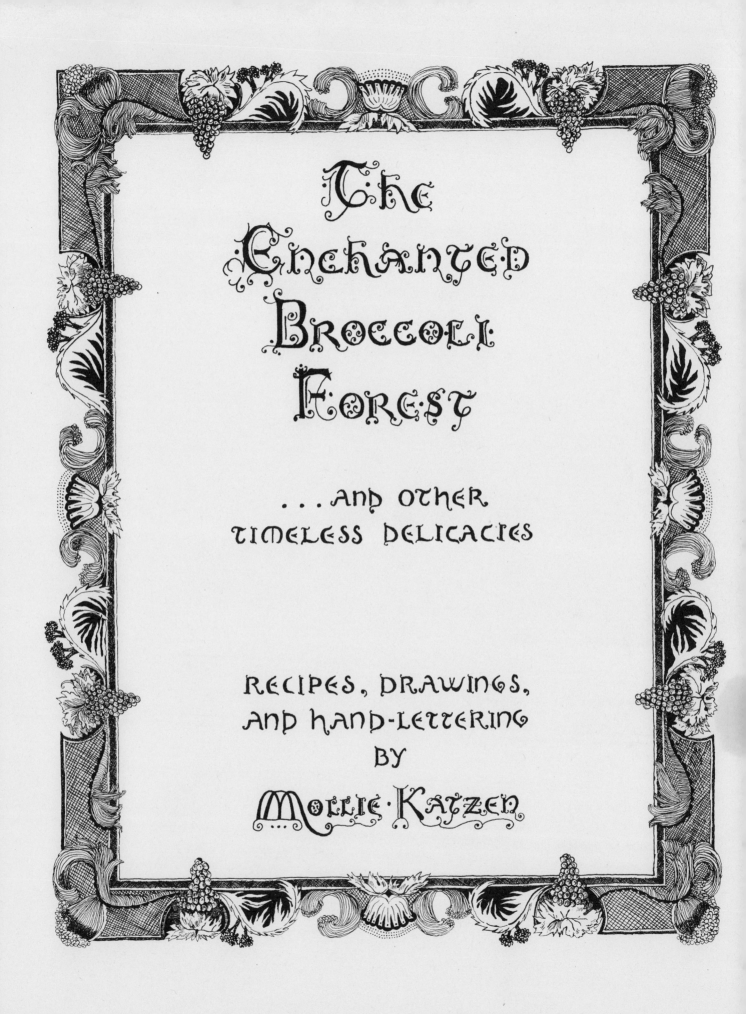

The Enchanted Broccoli Forest

...and other Timeless Delicacies

Recipes, Drawings, and Hand-Lettering by

Mollie Katzen

1☺

TEN SPEED PRESS
P.O. Box 7123
Berkeley, California 94707

You may order single copies prepaid direct from
the publisher for $11.95 (paper-bound) or $16.95
(cloth-bound), plus $.50 for postage and handling.
(California residents add 6% state sales tax; Bay
Area residents add 6½%.)

Library of Congress Catalog Number: 82-050667
Cloth edition ISBN: 0-89815-079-5
Paper edition ISBN: 0-89815-078-7

Cover Design by Mollie Katzen

10 9 8 7 6 5 4 3 2 1

Printed in the United States of America

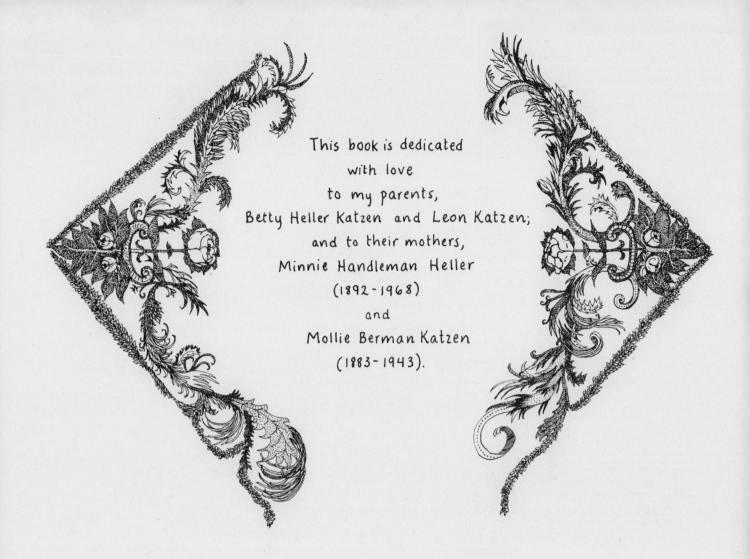

This book is dedicated
with love
to my parents,
Betty Heller Katzen and Leon Katzen;
and to their mothers,
Minnie Handleman Heller
(1892-1968)
and
Mollie Berman Katzen
(1883-1943).

✦ ACKNOWLEDGEMENTS ✦

It is a joy for me to acknowledge the people who have enabled me to begin, sustain, and complete this project:

Hal Hershey ~ friend, mentor, office-mate, and seasoned book-designer, whose balanced, honest feedback on every aspect of this book has helped to clear my vision, and whose detailed assistance has been indispensible to the production of this book; Jeffrey Black ~ whose love, patience, and enthusiasm fed me steadily during the final year of intense work on this project, and whose companionship has greatly lightened up my heart; Ezra K. Katzen ~ brother to me, and special counsel, literary agent, and godfather to this book; Buffalo ~ my step-dog, whose sunny presence kept me going on many foggy days; Meredith Barchat, Patricia Dustan, Sarah Gowin, Susan Ostertag, and Sarah Sutro ~ extraordinary friends, each of whom has had a special relationship with ~ an influence upon ~ The Enchanted Broccoli Forest; Brenton Beck (of Fifth Street Design, Berkeley) ~ whose graphic work has inspired me, and who has given me invaluable assistance in the production of the cover; Jane Rockwell ~ who took time away from her own

Acknowledgements, continued.....

book-design work to assist me with some of the final production, and whose quiet, steady support has been a constant comfort; **Leggity Rockwell** ~ Jane's dog, unofficial mascot of our shared office; **George Young** ~ of Ten Speed Press, who has been especially supportive and understanding; **Martha Ellen Katz** ~ author of The Complete Book of High-Protein Baking (Ballantine, 1975), who generously advised me on the bread chapter. (Note: The Ballantine edition is presently hard to find, but it's worth seeking. Look in libraries and ask friends. Meanwhile, Martha plans to do a new, revised edition, which I eagerly anticipate.); **Jackie Wan** ~ who proof-read these pages several times through, presenting her helpful findings with tact, taste, and consistency; **Frances Bowles** ~ who cheerfully and most impressively prepared the index, offering many helpful suggestions along the way; **Carolly Erickson, Elizabeth Fishel, Jeremy Joan Hewes,** and **Linda Williams** ~ writers and friends who are my co-members of a small group that meets regularly to share encouragement for books-in-progress (and for many other aspects of life). These women have been a blessing to me — and my best resource for laughter.

Further, I would like to thank: **Tara Gwyneth Blau,** for her strong support during the initial stages of this project; my brothers, **Joshua W. Katzen** and **Daniel T. Katzen** for their gifts of exuberance and humor; my cousin, **Rachel Katzen,** a graphic designer, for giving me my earliest lessons in layout technique; **Christine M. Blai,** for teaching me a great deal about vegetarian cooking when we worked together at the Shandygaff Restaurant (San Francisco ~ 1971); **Louis Bardenstein,** for generously donating his Blintz Soufflé recipe; **Donna Lee McCabe** for giving me the idea for Poached Eggs on a Bed of Vegetables; **Cathy Costanza** and **Dale Peters,** office-workers at Ten Speed Press, who spent many hours at the copy machine on my behalf; **R. Pieper,** for photographing my hands as I kneaded bread dough, so I could draw from the photographs; **Kathy Heavey,** for helping me get this book started.

During the course of this four-year project, there have been people whose presence in my life, whether directly related to this work or not, contributed strength and inspiration. I would like to acknowledge: **Carol Betsch; Nancy Carrey; Julie Elson; D.G. Gowin; Anne** and **Don Karr; Amelia W. Katzen; Julie K. Katzen; Molly F. Katzen; Reuben Katzen; Ida, Morty,** and **David Katzen; Edith** and **Norman Lank; Kathy Morris; Joan Hammerman Robbins; Bernice Rubin; M. B. Ryan; Susan, Joel, Max,** and **Jacob Savishinsky;** and **Rachel Josefowitz Siegel.**

Finally, I want to express my gratitude to all the people who have sent me letters of appreciation for The Moosewood Cookbook. I have tried to answer each one, but the volume has been overwhelming, and there have been more letters than I could respond to. I apologize for the unanswered mail, and here is my reply (not as personal as I would like, but heartfelt nevertheless): Your warm, loving feedback has provided much of the motivation needed to prepare The Enchanted Broccoli Forest. Thank you!!! ♥♥

Welcome to
The Enchanted Broccoli Forest!

This is a collection of recipes reflecting many different ethnic cooking styles, and containing a fairly wide variety of ingredients. Many of these dishes are products of my own imagination and experimentation, and some were generously shared with me by people whose cooking I admire (my mother, certain friends, a caterer, etc.). You will find recipes for light dishes and for hearty ones; some are spicy, others are subtle. The common trait linking all these recipes is their meatlessness. Yet, this book is by no means an exclusive message for vegetarians. Meat-eaters can use these recipes, too — for occasional meatless meals and/or as accompaniments to meat dishes. The vegetarian aspect of this cookbook is not intended to promote any style of living over any other. Rather, its purpose is merely to provide more options for enjoyable eating.

How does an original recipe come into existence? All it really takes to become an improviser is a love of food, an awareness of what you love about it, and the curiosity to experiment. How did I come up with these particular recipes? Ten years of restaurant experience, an ongoing interest in creative cookery (and eatery), many life-loving friends with whom to share that interest, a tendency to daydream about food combinations (plus a tendency to write down and then actually try the daydream ideas) — all these experiences have fueled this book. The Enchanted Broccoli Forest took me four years to visualize, realize, and complete. These four years saw countless long walks (mind full of flavor-fantasies), hundreds of recipe tests, and many quiet hours of drawing. All of this has been a pleasure for me.

This book is organized into six chapters: SOUPS, SALADS, BREADS, ENTRÉES, LIGHT MEALS FOR NIBBLERS, and DESSERTS.

The soup chapter contains recipes for both hot and cold soups. All of them are made from scratch, without bouillon or prepared mix. Most are quite easy.

The salad unit has a variety of cold vegetable and fruit dishes, some pre-cooked, some raw; some marinated, others stuffed. It also offers a pep-talk for wilted saladmakers, an introduction to three lesser-known vegetables, and a page of salad smorgasbord menus (ideal for hot-weather meals).

The bread section takes you step-by-step through the process of yeasted bread-baking, with a comic strip of diagrams, commentary, and a few sound effects. This is followed by a question-and-answer article, going into more technical detail. After this methodology come a basic bread recipe and a series of yeasted breads of various flavors and forms (including rolls and filled coffeecakes). You are also provided with quick breads, muffins, biscuits, homemade graham crackers, and chappatis (Indian flatbread).

Since "entrees" is such a general term, I have divided this chapter into seven sub-units: MAIN-DISH PASTRIES (quiches, vegetable pies, strudels, calzone, piroshki, enchiladas, blintzes); PASTA (homemade noodles, sauces, lasagna, and more); EGG DISHES (soufflés, omelettes, quick egg suppers, etc.); TOFU DISHES; CASSEROLES; BEANS & GRAINS; and "VEGETABLES AS THEMSELVES" (including, among other things, some vegetable-chopping diagrams and wok technique).

"Light Meals for Nibblers" is a small chapter featuring dips and hot cheeses. It contains a message for solo eaters, plus some encouragement for people who prefer to eat more simply.

The dessert chapter contains a representative sampling of sugar-sweetened, honey-sweetened, fruity, chocolaty, cheesy, crispy, and gooey offerings. It aspires to respond to as many preferences as reasonably possible.

Sample menus are distributed throughout the book, posted on scrolls for easy visibility. There are some menu-planning notes at the back of the book, plus a page of additional menus. Many people, after discovering that they love to prepare individual vegetarian dishes, find it confusing to plan an entire meatless menu. If this is true for you, I hope the menus provided within these pages will be useful, and that you will soon be encouraged to create your own.

Mollie Katzen

Berkeley, California
July 1982

CONTENTS

Continued on Next Page........

TWO NOTES OF INTERPRETATION:

(1) There is an approximate preparation time posted at the top of each recipe. These are <u>estimations</u>, representing the average pace of an average cook. It is recommended that you read through each recipe before you begin to cook, so if necessary, you can adjust the preparation time to your own pace.

(2) The average yield of these recipes is about 4 servings. I kept amounts to a minimum, figuring that it is usually easier to multiply recipes than it is to divide them. The number of servings posted at the top of each recipe refers to <u>main-dish-sized</u> portions. So, if you are serving many different dishes together, you will get a greater yield (also, if you are a meat-eater, and you are serving these on the side).

General Pantry Notes

EGGS
Grade A "Large" eggs were used for all the recipes in this book.

BUTTER
"Lightly salted" butter was used for all the cooking and baking in this book. However, once something is all cooked or baked, and you want to spread something on it, sweet "unsalted" butter is very nice. (If you use sweet "unsalted" butter in the cooking or baking of these recipes, you might want to slightly increase the salt.)

MARGARINE
If butter is beyond your budget, you can substitute all or part margarine. Try to find one with good, real ingredients, preferably made with safflower oil.

MILK

Low-fat milk can be used in all the recipes calling for milk. Low-fat evaporated milk can often be used in place of cream, especially in soups. Other compromises can be made to minimize butterfat content. For example, use part half-and-half and part milk instead of cream, etc. Experiment to find what works for you.

SOUR CREAM, YOGURT, SOUR HALF-and-HALF
These are all pretty much interchangeable. I have found sour half-and-half to be a perfect substitute for full-fat sour cream. Sour half-and-half is available in most grocery stores, usually in the same vicinity as the sour cream. Yogurt and sour cream (or half-and-half) can be mixed, providing a rich taste, but a less-rich butterfat content.

FLOURS
It is hard to know what to buy these days, when the supermarket shelf seems to confront one with 16 different types of flour. This issue is explored in some detail on p. 91. For the purposes of this book, use unbleached white flour (Brit. "strong, plain white"), unless another kind is specified.

HONEY

How to shop for it: see p. 257

How to store it: Ideally, it should be kept at room temperature, so it remains syrupy and clear. If it gets too cold, it gradually hardens and turns opaque, sometimes causing your spoon to break in half when you try to serve it (so you get discouraged and put it back on the shelf for another 6 months, where it hardens further...). KEEP HONEY IN A TIGHTLY-LIDDED JAR. Keep the jar clean, so it will not attract ants. Keep the rim of the jar clean, so you can actually open it when you need to. If the honey solidifies, place the whole jar in a saucepan of water, and heat it gently until it liquifies.

CANNED FOODS

These are the few cases in which canned foods are used, sometimes, in place of fresh, frozen or dried:

(1) tomato products (whole tomatoes, purée or paste)
(2) green chilies (available in grocery stores near Mexican items)
(3) water chestnuts
(4) pineapple, if packed in its own unsweetened juice. (Canned pineapple is actually recommended over fresh, for cooking or baking.)

OILS

For the recipes in this book, you should have on hand:

(1) olive oil, for salads and some sautéing;
(2) peanut oil (Planter's is fine) for wok-work;
(3) vegetable oil (generic, refined) for deep-frying; and
(4) Chinese sesame oil (really more a seasoning than an oil) for specialty seasoning.

TAMARI SAUCE/SOY SAUCE

Tamari sauce _is_ a soy sauce, a Japanese soy sauce. I prefer it over more common, less expensive Chinese soy sauce, because I think it has a better, richer flavor. Tamari is available in "natural foods" stores and in many groceries, but you can use a more familiar, more accessible brand of Chinese soy sauce, if you prefer.

More detailed pantry notes, p. 286.......

Soups:
Table of Contents

HOT SOUPS

COLD SOUPS

Here is a chapterful of meatless soup recipes, both hot and chilled, from Basic and Wholesome (Vegetable Soup, Potato-Leek Soup, Corn Chowder) to Exotic and Also Wholesome (Curried Peanut Soup, Galician Garbanzo Soup, Pumpkin Rarebit Soup, Green Gazpacho). Between the Basic and the Exotic is a range of tasty and personable combinations, suiting a variety of moods and seasons.

The average yield of these recipes is 4-5 servings, enabling a smaller household to enjoy a given soup without having to continue trying to enjoy it for 4 consecutive dinners. These quantities are easily doubled for larger households. Just be sure you use a large enough kettle.

These soups are fairly highly-seasoned, and it is not necessary (nor is it desirable) to influence their flavors with any vegetable bouillon product. Plain water will work very well. However, if you wish to make real stock from scratch, go right ahead. This is a fine way to get more mileage out of old, limp vegetables and/or scraps, and it can give your soups a deeper Essence of Vegetable.

TO MAKE STOCK FROM SCRATCH:
  Collect skins (cleaned!) of onions, garlic, potatoes, carrots, etc. (A wonderful flavor item: mushroom stems!) Avoid strongly-flavored vegetables, such as cabbage, broccoli, cauliflower or celery. Or, at least, go lightly with these. Also collect limp-but-still-okay vegetables, like tired, old zucchini, carrots, potatoes, etc. Boil your collection in lightly-salted water for anywhere from 30 minutes to an hour. Cool, strain, and taste. If you like the flavor, use the stock for soup.

ANOTHER KIND OF STOCK:
  Leftover water from steaming vegetables or boiling potatoes.

A GOOD STOCK FOR IMPROVISING:
  (Good, because it is very flavorful, and therefore gives you a head-start on Substance for your improvisation): leftover bean-cooking water.

A broad soup repertoire can give one's menu-planning a tremendous boost. Most of these soups are substantial and interesting enough to be served with bread and salad as an entire meal. Cold soups are a good solution to the problem of Dinner in hot, muggy weather. They can be prepared in advance, so the preparer doesn't swelter through last-minute cooking. Cold soups are also an elegant second course for dinners any season of the year.

Vegetable Soup .....

Preparation time:
45-50 minutes

4-6 servings
Freezable (in basic form)

1 large potato, diced into ½-inch cubes
4 cups water or stock
a dash of salt

> Boil together, covered, in a kettle, until the potatoes are just tender.

2 Tbs. butter
1 Tbs. olive oil
1 cup chopped onion
1 large clove of crushed garlic
3/4 tsp salt
1 stalk chopped celery
1 large, diced carrot
½ lb. chopped mushrooms
½ tsp. each- thyme, dill,
    marjoram, basil
freshly-ground black pepper

> Heat a heavy skillet. Add butter, oil, onions, garlic and salt. Sauté over medium heat, stirring, for 5 minutes. Add remaining ingredients; continue cooking and stirring. When all is tender (8-10 minutes) add the entire skilletful, liquid and all, to the potatoes and their water. Simmer an additional 20-30 minutes.

3/4 cup dry white wine
1 Tbs. tamari sauce
1 cup raw peas (fresh or frozen)

> Add these when there are 20 minutes left to simmer before serving time.

Freshly-minced scallions ·············~ Sprinkle these on top of each serving.

NOTE: This is one of those convenient soups which actually improves with a little standing-around-before-serving time. You can assemble it in the morning to serve it at night. Just do everything but the final simmering, and let the soup stand at room temperature (keep it covered). Simmer just before serving.

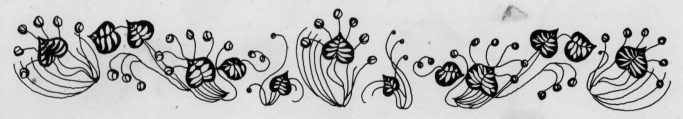

..... & Its Many Variations

1) **Multi-Vegetable Soup:**   Lots more different kinds of vegetables (broccoli, zucchini, peppers, cauliflower, etc.) will blend in well. Pre-cook everything except tomatoes or spinach. Leftover cooked beans and/or grains are also welcome. Add all of these just before the final simmering. As simmering progresses give it a taste test. You may want to adjust seasonings to accommodate these extras.

2) **Zuppa Alla Pavese:**   The same soup, but with a different presentation. As the soup simmers, toast thick slices of bread ~ one per serving. When the bread is toasted, fry it in butter on both sides until it is very brown. (Optional: you can add a clove of crushed garlic and a few dashes of oregano to the frying butter.) Place one of these "croûtes" in each bowl. Break a raw egg onto each piece, and sprinkle in a little parmesan cheese. Ladle hot soup onto each of these still-lifes, and serve.

3) **Hearty Vegetable:**   Add an extra potato to the first stage of basic vegetable soup. When the potatoes are soft, strain them, saving their cooking water for broth. Mash the potatoes, adding a few dashes of salt and 1 Tbs. butter, and return them to the soup. Add a spoonful of sour cream to each bowl, as you serve it. Don't forget the scallions on top.

4) **Vegetable~Tofu:**   Add one half pound (2 cakes, usually) diced tofu to the soup just during the last 10 minutes of simmering.

5) **Vegetable~Eggdrop:**   Beat 3 large eggs together with a tsp. of tamari sauce. When the soup has 5 remaining minutes to simmer, turn up the heat, until the soup reaches a gentle boil. Using a long chopstick, stir the soup briskly in a circular direction with one hand as you slowly drizzle in the beaten egg with the other. After all the egg is in, keep stirring for 2-3 more minutes. Remove from heat and serve immediately.

6) **Alphabet Soup:** Cook one cup raw whole wheat or white alphabet noodles in plenty of boiling, salted water, until <u>al dente</u> (just tender). Drain, rinse with cold water (this helps prevent clumping) and distribute them among the serving bowls. Drizzle a little olive oil into each bowl, mix the alphabets gently, and ladle in the hot soup.

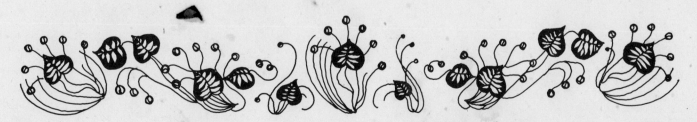

SESAME·EGGDROP SOUP

preparation time: 30-40 minutes   4 servings
→ You can make the soup ~up to Step 4~ ahead of time.

OPTIONAL
Soak ½ oz. dried black mushrooms in 1½ cups boiling water for 15-20 minutes. Strain through cheesecloth, and reserve the water to use as part of the stock. Remove and discard the mushroom stems; slice the caps into strips. (This addition is optional, because black mushrooms are expensive. Although they're very delicious, the soup will also be fine without them.)

1 Tbs. peanut or soy oil
3 thin slices fresh ginger root
2 Tbs. Chinese sesame oil
2 Tbs. sesame seeds
1 large carrot, cut into matchsticks*
6 minced scallions (separate greens & whites)
2 large, beaten eggs

a few dashes of salt & pepper
4 Tbs. soy or tamari sauce
4 cups stock or water
3 medium-sized tomatoes, chopped
1 Tbs. wine vinegar
1 cup steamed green peas

* See cutting diagram on page 236.

1) In a kettle or a large saucepan, quickly sauté ginger slices in peanut or soy oil for several minutes. Remove and discard the ginger.

2) Add the sesame oil, sesame seeds, carrots and scallion whites (save the greens). Salt the mixture lightly, and grind in some fresh black pepper. Sauté over medium heat for 5 minutes, stirring frequently.

3) Add the soy or tamari, stock or water, and chopped tomatoes. Cover, and let it cook over medium heat about 10 minutes more. At this point, the soup is ready to rest until just before serving time.

4) About 10 minutes before serving time, add the vinegar, peas, and optional black mushrooms. Heat the soup to a gentle boil. Stir the soup in a circular direction with a long chopstick, and drizzle in the beaten egg in a thin, steady stream. Continue stirring the simmering soup for about 5 more minutes. Serve topped with minced scallion greens.

DILLED VEGETABLE-BARLEY SOUP

preparation time (including barley-cooking): 2½ hours

4-6 servings

This soup improves with age. It tastes best on the 2nd day. As it sits around, however, the barley continues to expand, so it usually needs additional water when reheating. Adjust the seasonings, if necessary.

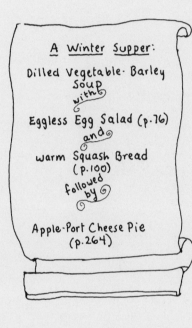

A Winter Supper:

Dilled Vegetable-Barley Soup
with
Eggless Egg Salad (p.76)
and
warm Squash Bread (p.100)
followed by
Apple-Port Cheese Pie (p.264)

½ cup raw pearl barley
1 cup water

1 Tbs. butter
½ cup minced onion
1 tsp. salt
1 bay leaf
1 medium carrot, diced small
1 medium stalk celery, chopped
4 cups stock or water
¼ lb. chopped mushrooms
6 Tbs. dry white wine
1½ tsp. dried (2-3 Tbs. fresh) dill weed
fresh black pepper
1 tsp. tamari sauce

Toppings:
Sour Cream
Toasted sunflower seeds
Grated hard-boiled eggs
Freshly-chopped parsley

Use all or some
or one
or none

I. Place barley and 1 cup water together in a small saucepan. Bring to a boil, cover, and lower heat to a simmer. Cook about 20 minutes, or until tender.

II. In a soup kettle or saucepan, sauté the onion, salt, and bay leaf in butter until the onion is soft and clear. Add the carrot and celery, and cook over medium heat, 5 minutes. Add all remaining ingredients (except optional toppings) and the cooked barley.

III. Lower the heat to a quiet simmer, cover the soup, and let it bubble peacefully for about 1½ hours. The soup will thicken, and additional water might be necessary. Use your own judgment. Some people might prefer to approach their barley soup with a knife and fork. As far as I know, there are no rules about this one way or the other.

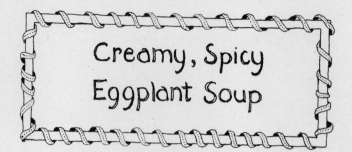

Creamy, Spicy Eggplant Soup

preparation time: 1¼ hours

4 rich servings

1 1½ lb. eggplant
(a little olive oil)
2 cups water or stock
1 Tbs. olive oil
3 medium cloves crushed garlic
2 cups chopped onion
1 tsp. salt
freshly-ground black pepper
¼ cup dry sherry
3 Tbs. sour cream
2 Tbs. tahini
¼ tsp. cayenne (more, to taste)
¼ cup freshly-minced parsley

Serve
Creamy, Spicy
Eggplant Soup
with
↓ ↓ ↓ ↓
Spinach Borek
(p. 139),
a green salad
with Buttermilk-Cucumber
dressing (p.78),
and Ricotta-Cherry Mousse
(p. 273).

Topping: extra yogurt and finely-minced tomato & bell pepper

I. Preheat oven to 375°F.

II. Slice the eggplant in half lengthwise. Lightly salt each open side, and let it sit about 15 minutes to sweat away its bitter juices. Rinse, pat dry, and brush the cut sides with olive oil. Bake 30-40 minutes, face-down on a tray. Cool until handle-able. Scoop out the pulp; discard the skins.

III. Sauté the garlic and onions in 1 Tbs. olive oil with 1 tsp. salt —until the onions are soft and translucent. Grind in some fresh black pepper.

IV. Purée together (use a blender or a food processor with steel blade) the eggplant pulp, water or stock, and onion-garlic sauté. Return the purée to a heavy saucepan. Add sherry, cover, and heat gently.

V. When the soup is hot, whisk in tahini, sour cream and cayenne; keep whisking until the mixture is smooth. Cover, and keep warm until serving time. Stir in parsley right before serving. Top each bowlful with yogurt, and minced tomatoes and peppers.

Mediterranean Lemon Soup

Preparation time:
30 minutes, after
grains are cooked.

4 servings

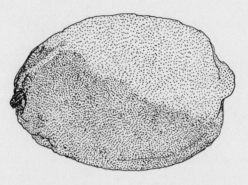

Good hot .... or cold.

2 Tbs. butter
1 cup finely-minced onion
1 tsp. salt
a few grindings of fresh, black pepper

1 cup cooked brown rice or barley*
½ cup fresh-squeezed lemon juice
2 cups stock or water

2 beaten eggs ~ at room temperature
1 tsp. dried, crushed mint

freshly-minced parsley
freshly-minced chives
yogurt, sour cream or heavy cream
grated hard-cooked eggs

toppings

1) In a soup-sized saucepan, sauté the onion in butter with salt and pepper, until the onion is soft and translucent.

2) Add the rice or barley * (make sure the grains are cooked first. You need one cup cooked, so that's ½ cup raw, in slightly less than twice as much water.) Also add the water or stock and the lemon juice. Heat it, covered, over a low flame until it boils gently.

3) Stir the soup rapidly as you drizzle in the beaten egg. Add mint; remove from heat.

4) A nice way to serve this soup is to place small dishes of the different toppings on the table, condiment-style, and to pass these around.

Fresh Corn Chowder

Preparation time:

about 50 minutes.

3-4 servings

2 Tbs. butter
1 cup chopped onion
$\frac{1}{2}$ cup minced celery
1 sweet red bell pepper, minced
4 cups fresh sweet corn
(approximately 4-5 cobs'-worth)

$\frac{1}{2}$ tsp. salt
freshly-ground black pepper
$\frac{1}{4}$ tsp. thyme
$\frac{1}{2}$ tsp. dried basil
1 cup stock or water
1 cup evaporated milk* (or regular milk)

* <u>About evaporated milk</u>: I like to use this as often as possible in place of cream, as it imparts a deep, rich flavor with much less butterfat. Low-fat evaporated milk is also available, and also good. This reduces the butterfat level even further.

1) In a medium-sized saucepan begin cooking the onions in the butter over medium-low heat, stirring. After about 3-5 minutes add celery, and keep cooking. Five minutes later add peppers and corn.

2) Add seasonings, stir well, and cover. Reduce heat; let it cook 5 minutes.

3) Add stock. Cover and simmer about 10 minutes. Using a blender or food processor, purée about half the solids in some of the soup's own liquid.

4) About 10 minutes before serving time, add the milk. Don't actually cook the soup any further; simply heat it — gently! — to Eating Temperature.

❀ Curried Apple Soup ❀

Preparation time: 2½ hours, including stock·making.

I. THE STOCK:
~ peels and cores from the apples (II)
~ skins (cleaned) from onions & garlic (")
~ 2 cinnamon sticks
~ 2½ cups apple juice
~ 2½ cups water

Combine everything in a kettle.
  Boil gently, partially-
  covered, about 45 minutes.
  Remove from heat, let stand 1 hour.
  Strain and discard solids.

II. THE SOUP:
  3 Tbs. butter
  ½ tsp. fresh-grated ginger root
  2 medium cloves minced garlic
  1½ cups chopped onion
  4 heaping cups peeled, chopped apple
    ↳ (any kind but delicious)
  1 tsp. salt
  juice from 1 lemon

mixed together {
  3 Tbs. flour
  1 tsp. each : dry mustard, turmeric,
    ground cumin, ground coriander
  ¼ tsp each: ground cloves
    cayenne pepper (more, to taste)
}

  2 cups mixed yogurt & sour cream
    ↳ (any proportion. Or One. Or the Other.)

Topping: slivered, toasted almonds

(1) Make the stock. Take out yogurt & sour cream, to come to room temperature.

(2) Heat a heavy skillet. Add butter, ginger, garlic, and a dash of salt. Stir and cook over moderate heat a minute or so, then add onions. Sauté another 5 minutes, then add 1 tsp. salt and apples, stirring well. Add lemon juice, and sprinkle in the pre-combined flour and spices, stirring constantly. Cover and cook 8-10 minutes over low heat, stirring occasionally. Turn off the heat, and let it rest about 10 minutes. Heat the stock.

(3) Purée the stock and sautéed mixture together, bit-by-bit in a food processor or blender. Make sure the result is very smooth. Transfer it to a kettle or heavy saucepan, and whisk in the yogurt/sour cream. → AT THIS POINT THE SOUP SHOULDN'T BE COOKED ANY FURTHER. Just heat it over low heat right before serving time. (The soup can be made a couple of hours ahead and heated just before it's served.)
  ~ Serve topped with toasted almond slivers.
  ~ Also good cold.

Variations on a Cream of Tomato

Each of these variations calls for precooked tomatoes. You can use fresh ones (just cut them into chunks, remove cores, and stew them over medium heat without adding water ~ 15-20 minutes, covered) OR, you can substitute canned tomatoes. The preparation time suggestions assume your tomatoes are ready.

I.

Preparation Time for each variation is about 1 hour.

4 servings apiece

1 Tbs. butter	½ tsp. dried rosemary	3 Tbs. dry sherry
1½ cups chopped onion	½ tsp. dried basil	¼ tsp. honey
1 large clove crushed garlic	freshly-ground black pepper	4 oz. cream cheese
½ tsp. salt	3½ cups cooked tomatoes	fresh parsley

1) In a saucepan or kettle, cook the onions and garlic in the butter with the salt until the onions are soft and translucent. Add the herbs and pepper, and sauté a few minutes more.

2) Add tomatoes, sherry, and honey. Cover and simmer 30-40 minutes.

→ NOTE: The purpose of the honey in this recipe, and of the baking soda-plus-honey in the following one, is to neutralize the acidity of the tomatoes. In case you wondered.

3) Cut the cream cheese into small cubes and add these to the hot soup. (Continue cooking and stir until smooth (the cheese will take a little while to melt thoroughly).

4) Serve topped with freshly-chopped parsley.

II.

2 Tbs. butter	½ tsp. celery seed	¼ tsp. baking soda
1½ cups chopped onion	½ tsp. allspice or cloves	¼ tsp. honey
2 bay leaves	2 Tbs. flour	2 Tbs. dry sherry
½ tsp. salt	3 cups cooked tomatoes	½-1 cup light cream
fresh black pepper		(or, Half & Half)

1) In a saucepan or kettle, cook the onions in the butter with salt and seasonings. Use medium heat, and stir frequently. When onions are limp (about 5 minutes), sprinkle in flour. Continue stirring and cooking about 5-8 minutes more.

2) Add tomatoes and baking soda. Cover and let it simmer 30 minutes. Stir from the bottom from time to time, as it simmers. Take the cream out of the refrigerator, so it can come to room temperature.

3) Add honey and sherry. Cover and simmer another 10 minutes. Fish out the bay leaves so nobody chokes on them.

4) Drizzle in the cream just before serving. Heat until just hot enough to serve (don't cook the soup any further once the cream is in there).

III.

1 Tbs. butter	½ tsp. salt	¼ tsp. thyme
1 cup chopped onion	1 stalk chopped celery	2½ cups puréed,
1 cup thinly-sliced potatoes	½ tsp. dill weed	cooked tomatoes
2 cloves crushed garlic	½ tsp. dried basil	1 tsp. honey
		1½ cups milk

1) Place butter, onion, potatoes, garlic, salt and celery in a large saucepan. Cover and cook over very low heat, stirring occasionally, until potatoes are tender. (If necessary add a little water or stock to avoid sticking.)

2) Add all remaining ingredients, except milk (have the milk out, so it can come to room temperature). Cover and simmer about 30 minutes.

3) Add milk just before serving. Heat gently.

OPTIONAL GARNISH: Small cubes of <u>Swiss Cheese</u> added to each bowl.

Chinese Mushroom Soup

Preparation Time: 40 minutes   3-4 servings

1 oz. dried black mushrooms
2 ½ cups boiling water

6 healthy scallions   lots of freshly-grated black pepper
1 1-inch piece of ginger root, grated   1 Tbs. cornstarch
1 medium clove of crushed garlic   1 cup water or stock
1 Tbs. peanut or soy oil   1 tsp. honey or sugar
½ lb. fresh mushrooms, cleaned & sliced   1 Tbs. wine vinegar
2 Tbs. tamari sauce   ½ cup thinly-sliced water chestnuts
¼ cup dry sherry or Chinese rice wine   Chinese sesame oil

PRELUDE: Rinse the dried mushrooms, and place them in a bowl. Pour 2½ cups boiling water over them, cover the bowl with a plate, and let it stand for 30 minutes while you prepare other ingredients. Drain the mushrooms in a strainer lined with cheesecloth, and save all the water! Squeeze all the excess moisture from the mushrooms; rinse and squeeze again. Remove and discard the stems; thinly slice the caps.

1) Remove the scallion tops and set aside. Chop the whites coarsely. Sauté these with the ginger and garlic in the oil, in a saucepan or kettle. Stir-fry for several minutes over medium heat. Add the sliced, fresh mushrooms, and stir-fry a few minutes more. Add the prepared black mushrooms, and sauté 2 more minutes.

2) Add all the remaining ingredients except the scallion tops and sesame oil. (Include the black mushrooms' soaking water.) Cover, and let simmer 15 minutes, stirring occasionally.

3) Finely mince the scallion greens. Top each individual serving with a few of these and a drizzle of sesame oil.

Green, Green Noodle Soup

45 minutes to prepare.   4 servings : Very Green.

Three ♫ Notes:

1) Make this soup right before serving, to get the fullest color.

2) This soup needs <u>pesto sauce</u> (recipe on p.161). The making of the pesto has <u>not</u> been included in the above preparation time estimate.

3) This soup also requires green (spinach) fettucine noodles. These are available in most grocery stores, but if you prefer to make your own, the recipe is on p.159. Preparation time assumes you are already equipped with noodles.

1 Tbs. olive oil
1 Tbs. butter
2 medium cloves crushed garlic
½ cup minced onion
½-1 tsp. salt (to taste. Start with less.)
pinch of each: <u>thyme</u> & <u>oregano</u>
1 7-inch long, 1½ inch diameter zucchini,
    cut like this: (⅛" thick)

½ lb. fresh spinach (finely-chopped)   ¼ lb. green (spinach) fettucine noodles (raw)
fresh black pepper   3 Tbs. pesto sauce
4 cups stock or water   freshly-grated parmesan (topping)

1) In a saucepan or kettle, sauté onions, garlic, salt and herbs in combined oil and butter, until the onions are clear and soft.

2) Add zucchini and spinach. Continue to sauté another 5 minutes over medium heat, stirring frequently. Grind in some black pepper.

3) Add water or stock, bring to a boil, cover, and lower heat to a faint glow. Simmer just 5 minutes, or until Bright Green. (At this point, put up noodle water.) Remove from heat.

4) In a blender or processor, purée approximately half the green mixture, and return it to the unpuréed half. Cover, and let it sit while the noodles cook.

5) Cook the noodles in plenty of rapidly-boiling water until <u>al dente</u> (just tender). Drain, and toss immediately with the pesto. Divide the noodles among the serving bowls, and ladle the soup over. Sprinkle in some parmesan, and serve right away.

Potato, Cheese & Chili Soup

About
50 minutes
to prepare.

4 medium (3" diameter) potatoes
3 cups water

4-6 servings.

1 Tbs. butter
1 Tbs. olive oil
1 ½ cups chopped onion
1¾ tsp. salt
1 tsp. cumin
1 tsp. basil
2 medium cloves of garlic, crushed
lots of freshly-ground black pepper
1½ cups diced green bell pepper
1 cup diced canned green chilies

¾ cup sour cream
1 cup milk
¾ cup (packed) grated jack cheese
2 scallions, finely-minced (whites and greens)

(1) Scrub the potatoes, cut them into small chunks, and cook them in the water, partially-covered, until tender (about 20 minutes). Cool to room temperature.

(2) Meanwhile, begin sautéing the onions in combined butter and olive oil in a large, heavy skillet. After several minutes, add salt, cumin, basil, garlic, and black pepper. Continue to sauté over medium heat until the onions are soft (5-8 minutes). Add chopped green bell pepper, and sauté a few minutes more.

(3) Purée the potatoes in their cooking water. (Use a blender, or a food processor fitted with the steel blade.) Return the purée to a kettle or a large, sturdy saucepan, and add the sauté, plus the diced green chilies, sour cream, and milk. Whisk until well-blended, and heat over a slow flame. When it is hot, stir in the cheese and scallions, and serve.

Potato~Leek Soup

1 hour to prepare.

4-6 servings.

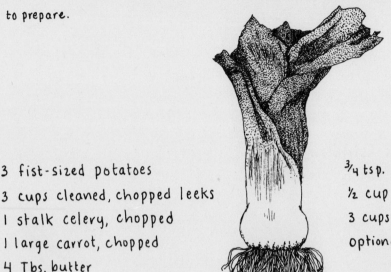

3 fist-sized potatoes
3 cups cleaned, chopped leeks
1 stalk celery, chopped
1 large carrot, chopped
4 Tbs. butter

¾ tsp. salt
½ cup stock or water
3 cups milk
optional: snippets of fresh herbs
        (thyme, marjoram, basil)

freshly-ground black pepper

(1) Scrub the potatoes, and cut them into 1-inch chunks. Place them in a saucepan with the leeks, celery, carrot and butter. Add salt. Cook the vegetables, stirring over medium heat, until the butter is melted and all the particles are coated (5 minutes).

(2) Add the stock or water, bring to a boil, then cover, and reduce heat to a simmer. Cook until the potatoes are soft (20-30 minutes). Check the moisture level occasionally. You may need to add a little extra stock or water, if it gets too low.

(3) When the potatoes are tender, remove the pan from the heat, and purée its contents in the milk (use a blender, or a food processor fitted with the steel blade). Make sure the mixture is utterly smooth. Return it to the saucepan.

(4) Add optional herbs (or not). Grind in some black pepper. Taste it to see if it wants more salt.

(5) Heat the soup gently, covered, until <u>just</u> hot. Try not to let it boil. Serve right away.

The Pumpkin Tureen

Minutes to prepare
~ 1½ to 2 hours to bake

Preheat oven to 350°F.

4 servings

    You don't need a kettle for this soup. The soup gets baked right inside the pumpkin, and the whole tureen can be brought to the table as an edible centerpiece.

1 sincere, 3-4 lb. pumpkin
1 Tbs. butter
¼ cup finely, finely minced onion
1 tsp. prepared horseradish } increase, to taste
1 tsp. prepared mustard

1 13 oz. can lowfat evaporated milk
2 slices rye bread (w/ caraway seeds)
a few dashes of each: salt, pepper, cayenne, nutmeg
½ cup (packed) grated Swiss cheese

1) Prepare the pumpkin as though you were going to make a Jack-O-Lantern, and stop at the point where you would normally make the face. (For those of you who have never made a Jack-O-Lantern: Cut off top. Scoop out seeds and stringiness.)

2) Rub the interior of said pumpkin with 1 Tbs. soft butter.

3) Add all remaining ingredients (cut the bread into little cubes 1st), replace the top (you may wish to put tin foil under it, in case it shrinks a little), and place Pumpkin Tureen on a tray and place the tray in the oven.

4) Bake until the pumpkin becomes tender (about 2 hours). Tenderness test = Remove the lid, and stick a fork gently into one of the sides. You should feel scant resistance on the pumpkin's part. TO SERVE: Scoop deeply to bring up some pumpkin pieces from sides & bottom.

Pumpkin Rarebit Soup

50 minutes
to prepare

4·5 Servings

4 cups cooked pumpkin
1 cup stock or water
1½ cups light beer or ale
1 heaping cup chopped onion
2 Tbs. butter
¾ - 1 tsp. salt
2-3 medium-sized garlic cloves, crushed
1 Tbs. worcestershire sauce
freshly-ground black pepper } to taste
cayenne pepper
1 packed cup grated cheddar cheese

optional toppings { chopped toasted walnuts
croutons

1) Using a blender or a food processor, purée the pumpkin in the stock. Combine with beer or ale in a heavy saucepan. Heat just to boiling point. Partially cover, and let it simmer while you:

2) Sauté the onions and garlic with salt in butter. Keep these cooking until the onions are very well done, just this side of Brown. (Keep the heat low, and let the onions render gracefully and gradually.)

3) Add the onions (scraping the pan well) to the simmering pumpkin purée. Add remaining seasonings and cheese. Stir well, and let it simmer, partially covered, another 20-30 minutes.

4) Serve topped with croutons and/or walnuts.

a
Very
Simple
Supper

PUMPKIN RAREBIT SOUP
A plateful of fresh Apple Slices
Some good, dark, moist Bread
A simple Spinach Salad

Galician Garbanzo Soup

Preparation time: 2½ hours
(<u>after</u> garbanzos are soaked.)

6 Servings.
Freezable.

<u>2 cups dry garbanzo beans</u> (also known as chickpeas)
~ soaked in plenty of water at least 4 hours; drained & rinsed.

1 Tbs. olive oil
1 heaping cup chopped onion
1 large clove crushed garlic
1 small, diced potato (about ½ cup diced)
1 medium carrot, diced
1 stalk celery, diced
1 tsp. salt

actual size of
diced whatever

5 cups stock or water
1 bay leaf
1 tsp. dry mustard
1 tsp. ground cumin
¼ tsp. crushed saffron
1 tsp. dried basil
fresh black pepper
cayenne pepper

½ cup <u>steamed green peas</u>
<u>fresh or frozen</u>
1 Tbs. red wine vinegar
1 medium-sized fresh tomato, chopped

1) Place the soaked garbanzos in a large kettle with 5 cups stock or water. Bring it to a boil, then turn the heat way down to simmer, covered, until the beans are soft. Using a blender or a food processor, purée about ⅔ the beans in their cooking water. Return the purée to the kettle, with the remaining whole beans and stock.

2) In a skillet, sauté the onions, garlic, potato, carrot, and celery with salt in the olive oil. When all are tender, transfer the sauté into the garbanzo kettle.

3) Add all the remaining ingredients except the peas, vinegar and tomato. Stir to mix well. Cover, and simmer gently about 1 hour.

4) Add the peas, vinegar, and tomato not more than 10 minutes before serving.

→ If the soup seems to be getting too thick, thin it to taste with stock or water. Adjust the seasonings, if necessary, to accommodate the thinning.

Almond Soup

Preparation Time: 40 minutes   3-4 rich servings

1¼ cups chopped blanched (skinless) almonds
2 Tbs. butter
½ cup chopped onion
1 large clove garlic, crushed
½ tsp. freshly-minced ginger
½ tsp. salt

1¾ cups water or stock
1½ cups fresh-squeezed orange juice
1-2 Tbs. dry sherry

½ tsp. fresh orange rind
black pepper   } to taste
cayenne pepper   }

Assorted Delightful Toppings

☆ slivered toasted almonds
☆ finely-minced chives
☆ thin rounds of fresh orange

(1) In a heavy skillet, cook the almonds in butter, with onion, garlic, ginger, and salt over a low flame, stirring, until the almonds are toasty and the onions are soft (8-10 minutes). Remove from heat.

(2) Using a blender or a food processor fitted with a steel blade, purée the sautéed mixture in combined water (or stock) and orange juice. Add sherry to taste. Make sure the purée is very smooth. Transfer it to a kettle or a saucepan.

(3) Stir in the orange rind and the black and cayenne peppers. Heat the soup gently (just heat it - don't cook it). Serve it as soon as it's hot, and garnish each serving with Assorted Delightful Toppings.

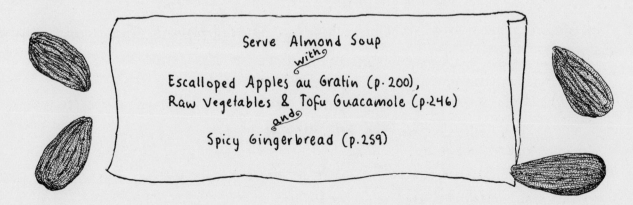

Serve Almond Soup
with
Escalloped Apples au Gratin (p. 200),
Raw Vegetables & Tofu Guacamole (p. 246)
and
Spicy Gingerbread (p. 259)

Cream of Fresh Green Pea Soup

Preparation Time:
35 minutes

4 Servings

Fresh herbs are the essential magical element of this soup. Use all or some of the list below (or experiment with your own substitutions).

1 Tbs. butter

1 cup minced onion

½ tsp. salt

2 cups fresh, raw, sweet peas

1½ cups water or stock

1 cup milk or half-and-half

freshly-ground black pepper

FRESH: Basil
           & Dill
           & Thyme
           & Tarragon
           & Parsley
           & Chives

1) In a saucepan, cook the onions with salt in butter until the onions are soft.

2) Separately steam the peas until they are bright green and just tender.

3) Add steamed peas and stock or water to sautéed onions. Cover and simmer about 10 minutes.

4) Purée about ⅓ of the soup in a blender or processor; return purée to saucepan. Add milk or cream. Don't cook any further.

5) Heat carefully just before serving. Snip in desired amounts of fresh herbs. (It's fun and convenient to use scissors for this.)

Swedish Cabbage Soup

Preparation Time:
1¼ hours.

6 Servings.

5 Tbs. sweet butter
2 cups chopped onion
2 tsp. whole or ground caraway seed
2 tsp. salt
8 packed cups (approx. 1 medium head) shredded green cabbage
6 cups vegetable stock, potato water, or water
lots of freshly-ground black pepper

1) In a <u>large</u> kettle, begin cooking the onions (slowly) in butter.

2) After a few minutes, add caraway and salt. Cover and let cook over medium-low heat about 10-15 minutes, stirring occasionally.

3) Add remaining ingredients. Cover and simmer about 30-40 minutes.

Creamy Cabbage Soup

Preparation Time:
same as above (or maybe 5 minutes more)

About 8 Servings

The Above Recipe

2 medium-sized potatoes

½ cup milk

½ cup sour cream

1) Scrub the potatoes, cut them into chunks, and put them up to boil just before "step 1" (above).
2) Drain the potatoes when they are tender. Save the water to use as the stock.
3) Whip the hot potatoes, using your habitual method (electric mixer or processor are best), blending in the milk and sour cream. Add toward end of "step 3".

Curried Peanut Soup

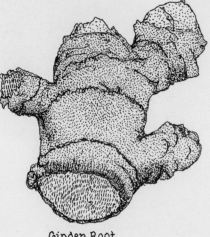

Ginger Root.

This soup is so filling and satisfying, it really should be used as the focal point of a meal. (See the menu which follows the recipe.)

You can assemble this early in the day. Put everything in except the buttermilk.

I. The Soup:

1 Tbs. butter
2 large cloves of crushed garlic
1 cup finely-chopped onion
2 tsp. freshly-grated ginger root
1 tsp. salt
1 cup chopped raw peanuts
¼ tsp. each: <u>cinnamon</u>, <u>cloves</u>, ground <u>cardamom</u> or <u>coriander</u>
½ tsp. each: <u>dry mustard</u> <u>turmeric</u>
1 tsp. ground cumin

In a large saucepan or a kettle, sauté the first 5 items together over medium heat. Add the remaining ingredients, and saute, stirring, another 8-10 minutes over medium-low heat.

Mashed together to a smooth paste {
2 cups stock or water
½ cup natural, unmolested peanut butter
a Handful of Raisins (optional)
1 Tbs. honey
¼-½ tsp. cayenne (to your tolerance/preference)

Add all of these to the above saute. Mix & cover. Simmer over sheepishly low heat 1 hour. Stir occasionally.

1½ cups room temperature buttermilk } Whisk this into the hot soup just a few minutes before serving.

II. The Topping:

2 fairly-green bananas (such as those you bought yesterday to
eat 2 days from now)

juice of 1 lemon   ¼ tsp. turmeric
3 Tbs. butter   dash of salt
¼ tsp. cinnamon   1 Tbs. sesame seeds

1) Peel the bananas and slice them thinly on the diagonal. Place them in a shallow
   bowl to bathe in fresh lemon juice. Let it stand 10 minutes.
2) Heat the butter in a heavy skillet. Add the bananas plus all their lemon juice, and
   sprinkle with salt, spices and sesame seeds (you can increase any of these, to taste).
3) Fry, gently turning and stirring, 5-8 minutes over medium-low heat. (It's okay if the
   bananas lose their shape, because they don't show up that well once in the soup anyway.)
4) Spoon the topping into each individual bowl of soup. You will not regret this seemingly
   strange taste experience. In fact, your mouth may attain enlightenment.

An Indian Dinner Menu:

1. The Above Recipe

For an added aesthetic touch, pass the topping around in a separate dish. Garnish
this serving dish with thin slices of fresh orange all around the rim.

2. A Rice & Pea Dish

Cook 2 cups of raw brown rice in 3 cups of water until tender (20-30 minutes).
Toss with ½ cup buttermilk and 2 cups freshly steamed green peas. Season to taste
with salt, black pepper, and cayenne.

3. A Cucumber & Pepper Raita

Seed and finely mince: one 6-inch cucumber. Finely mince one medium sweet
green or red bell pepper. Combine both of these with 2 cups firm yogurt. Season to
taste with salt, cumin, and garlic.

and: A Real, Good, & Expensive (Why not?) Mango Chutney (look in the Exotic Section of
your local grocery store.)

White Bean & Escarole Soup

40 minutes to prepare,
after beans are cooked.

4-5 servings

2 cups cooked white (navy or pea) beans : that's 1 cup dry beans. You needn't soak them first. Cook them in plenty of boiling water until tender, but not mushy. Drain them, if necessary. This extra water can be used as this soup's stock.   (Cooking time = 1½-2 hours.)

1 Tbs. each· butter & olive oil	1 tsp. salt
2 medium cloves crushed garlic	fresh black pepper
1 cup chopped onion	5 cups stock or water
1 bay leaf	½ lb. fresh chopped escarole or spinach
1 stalk minced celery	
1 medium carrot, diced	freshly-grated nutmeg

1) In a kettle or saucepan, cook the onions and garlic in combined butter and olive oil over low heat.

2) When onions are limp (3-5 minutes) add bay leaf, celery, carrot, salt and pepper. Stir and sauté another 5 minutes. Add stock or water. Cover.

3) Let it simmer about 20 minutes. Add cooked beans and escarole or spinach. Cover, and continue to simmer (over very low heat) another 10-15 minutes. Top each bowlful with freshly- grated nutmeg.

Serve White Bean & Escarole Soup
with

Homemade Potato Bread (p. 100),
spread with Puréed Vegetable Dip (p. 251)
and cheese omelettes (notes about
omelettes, p. 179)

and finally Apricot Streusel Pie (p. 280)

Cream of Fresh Green Bean Soup

Preparation Time: 20 minutes ..... embarrassingly simple.   3-4 servings

This soup is specifically designed for very, very fresh green beans ~ straight from a garden, if possible. The simplicity assumes that the beans are delicious in and of themselves. If you try this with frozen, French-cut beans or old, tough ones, I can't guarantee your results.

1½ lbs. very fresh green beans, stems & strings removed

2 cups milk, hot but not scalded

salt and fresh black pepper to taste

optional: small amounts of minced fresh basil and chives

1) Steam the beans until just tender and Bright Green.
2) Purée them, with the milk, until very smooth.
3) Season to taste. Heat just before serving. Don't boil or cook it!
4) OR: Serve it cold.

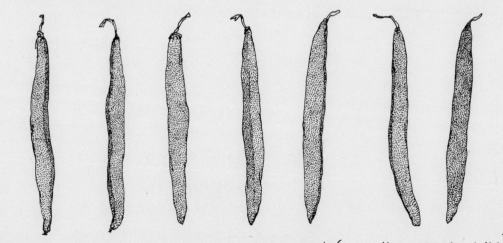

Confession: I like this soup completely unseasoned (no salt or pepper, even).

Cream of Onion Soup

Preparation Time: 35 minutes

3-4 servings
actually quite simple

2½ cups milk
3 cups thinly-sliced onion
3 Tbs. butter
½ tsp. dry mustard
1 tsp. salt
2 Tbs. flour
nutmeg (freshly-grated, if possible)
white pepper

Optional extra seasonings:

~ a few dashes of worcestershire sauce
~ ½ tsp. prepared horseradish
~ cayenne pepper

Toppings

~ Croutons (see recipe below)
~ finely-minced pimiento

1) Heat the milk very slowly in a heavy saucepan (lowest possible heat) until it <u>just</u> reaches the boiling point. Remove it from the heat before it actually boils. This is known as <u>scalding</u> the milk. (Don't cool the milk before proceeding.)

2) In another saucepan, cook the onions, with salt and mustard, in butter over low heat, until they are very limp and soft, but not brown.

3) Sprinkle the flour into the onions, mixing, as you sprinkle, with a wooden spoon. Stir and cook the mixture another 3-4 minutes over medium-low heat.

4) Add the scalded milk, stir well, cover, and cook another 10-15 minutes over lowest possible heat (use a "waffle" heat-absorption pad underneath, if you have one). Stir it from the bottom every few minutes. It will become thick and creamy.

5) Add a few dashes of white pepper, nutmeg and optional seasonings, to taste. Serve topped with croutons and/or minced pimiento.

Easy Home-Made Croutons

Preheat oven to 300°F. Cut 4 slices of delicious bread into ½-inch cubes. Heat a heavy skillet, add 2 Tbs. butter, and sauté the bread over medium heat 5 minutes, stirring. Spread the sautéed cubes onto a baking tray, and leave them in the oven 10-15 minutes. That's all, folks. (Except, don't forget to take them out of the oven.)

Brussels Sprouts Soup

Preparation Time: 45 minutes

4 servings

2 Tbs. butter
1 cup minced onion
3 cups minced Brussels sprouts
1 cup diced potato
2 cups stock or water
½ tsp. salt
½ tsp. dill weed (increase, if fresh)
black pepper
¾ cup sour cream ⎰ whisked
¾ cup buttermilk ⎱ together
Minced fresh parsley & chives

1) In a medium-sized saucepan, cook onions in butter over moderate heat for about 3-5 minutes.

2) Add Brussels sprouts. Stir and sauté another 5 minutes.

3) Add potatoes, stock or water, and salt. Cover, and simmer about 15 minutes, or until potatoes are thoroughly cooked.

4) Purée about ⅔ the mixture in blender or food processor, and return it to the kettle. Season with pepper and dill.

5) Whisk in sourcream-buttermilk mixture. Heat very slowly; serve as soon as it's hot (don't let it boil or cook). Top each serving with fresh snippings of parsley and chives.

Inspiration Soup

About 1 hour
to prepare.

1 6-oz. jar marinated artichoke hearts
1 Tbs. butter
1 cup chopped onion
1 large stalk celery, chopped
½ lb. mushrooms, sliced
1 tsp. salt
2 small (2-2½-inch diameter) potatoes, thinly-sliced
1 tsp. dried basil
1 Tbs. flour

1¼ cups stock or water
1 cup raw (fresh or frozen) green peas
½ lb. fresh spinach ~ cleaned, stemmed, and chopped
1¾ cups milk (for a richer soup, use part half & half)

4-5 servings.

(1) Drain the liquid from the marinated artichoke hearts into a saucepan. Chop the hearts coarsely, and set aside.

(2) Add the butter to the artichoke liquid. Heat it gently, until the butter melts.

(3) Add the chopped onion; sauté a few minutes.

(4) Add celery, mushrooms, salt, potatoes, and basil. Sauté 5-8 minutes over low heat, stirring occasionally.

(5) Gradually sprinkle in the flour, stirring constantly.

(6) Add water. Stir, cover, and simmer 15-20 minutes (until potatoes are tender).

(7) Add the artichoke hearts, peas, and spinach. Cover, and cook over low heat another 5 minutes.

(8) Add milk (and/or half & half). Heat just before serving. (Don't cook or boil.)

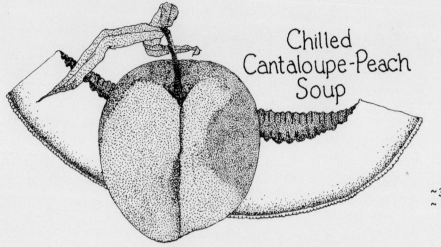

Chilled
Cantaloupe-Peach
Soup

4 servings.

~30 minutes to prepare;
~ 3 hours, minimum,
to chill.

6 medium-sized ripe peaches
¼ cup dry white wine
6 Tbs. fresh lemon juice
   (approximately the equivalent of
   juice from one large, juicy lemon)
1 Tbs. honey ⎫
¼ tsp. cinnamon ⎬ These can be increased, to taste.
dash of nutmeg ⎭

1 medium-sized ripe cantaloupe
   (5" diameter)
1 cup fresh orange juice

1. Peel, pit and slice the peaches. Place them in a heavy saucepan with everything except the cantaloupe and orange juice. Heat the peach mixture to a boil, lower to a simmer, cover, and let it stew for 10 minutes. Let it cool to room temperature.

2. Using a blender or a food processor, purée the peach mixture with all its liquid. Return the purée to a serving bowl.

3. Chop approximately 3|4 the cantaloupe (minus skin and seeds, of course), and purée it in the orange juice until smooth. Add it to the peach purée. Mince the remaining melon, and add these pieces unpuréed. Cover and chill. Serve very cold.

 Garnish with Blueberries.

✳✳✳✳ Green Gazpacho ✳✳✳✳

20 minutes to prepare,
plus time to chill.

4-6 servings.

3 green tomatoes (3" diameter)

1 medium-sized green bell pepper

1 medium (7") cucumber

4 scallions

1 medium clove garlic, crushed

¼ cup (packed) minced parsley

juice from 2 juicy limes
(about 6 Tbs. juice)

1 medium (4" long) avocado

3 cups cold water

1 tsp. salt

lots of fresh black pepper

1 Tbs. freshly-minced basil
(or, ½ tsp. dried basil)

2 Tbs. olive oil

1 Tsp. honey

optional { ~an extra avocado

~sprigs of fresh thyme,
for garnish

(1) Cut the tomatoes, pepper, and cucumber into ½-inch chunks. Mince the scallions (whites and greens). Combine these in a large bowl, along with garlic and parsley.

(2) Mash the avocado(s) with the lime juice. Add this, along with all remaining ingredients, to the cut vegetables. Mix well. (Optional: purée all or some.) Chill until very cold.

Mexican Avocado Soup

15 minutes to prepare,
plus time to chill.

4 servings.

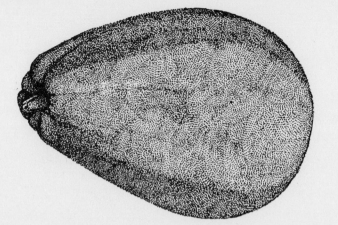

1 medium (4" long) avocado
2 cups milk
2 Tbs. dry sherry
½ tsp. salt (to taste)
¼-½ tsp. ground cumin (to taste)
lots of fresh black pepper
cayenne pepper, to taste
½ cup minced green chilies (canned)
¼ cup finely, finely-minced
red onion

Tortilla chips, for garnish

(1) Peel and pit the avocado. Cut it into 1-inch pieces. Place the pieces in a
blender jar or a food processor fitted with a steel blade, and purée until
very smooth. Transfer to a bowl.

(2) Add all remaining ingredients, and mix well. Adjust seasonings (amounts
are flexible) to suit your taste. Cover the bowl tightly, and chill until
very cold. Float a generous handful of tortilla chips on top of each
serving.

NOTE: If you wish to make your own tortilla chips, cut several corn tortillas
into wedges: . Deep-fry said wedges in very hot oil (at least an
inch of oil, at least 360°F) until crisp. Drain on several
thicknesses of paper towels. Salt, if desired.

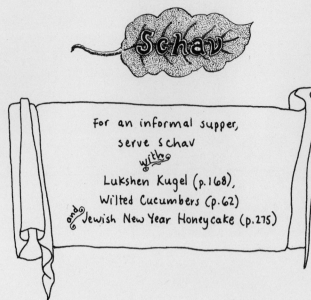

Schav

30 minutes to prepare;
at least several hours
to chill.

4-5 servings.

For an informal supper,
serve Schav
with
Lukshen Kugel (p.168),
Wilted Cucumbers (p.62)
and Jewish New Year Honeycake (p.275)

Schav is a chilled sour soup with greens, thickened with beaten egg. Traditionally, it is made with sorrel ("sour grass"), but this recipe uses spinach and lemon, as these are more accessible to more people. If you do have access to fresh sorrel, by all means substitute it for both the spinach and the lemon.

2 small (2" diameter) potatoes
3 cups water
¾ tsp. salt
1 lb. fresh spinach
2 large eggs, beaten
¼ cup fresh lemon juice
¾ tsp. dill weed
lots of black pepper
2 finely-minced scallions

sour cream, for the top

(1) Scrub the potatoes, and slice them thinly. Place them in a saucepan with the water and the salt, and cook, partially-covered until they are just tender.

(2) Stem the spinach and wash it. Chop it very fine, and cook it in a heavy skillet, covered, with no additional liquid, until it is just limp, but still bright green (3-5 minutes). Remove from heat.

(3) Place the beaten eggs in a large bowl. Whisk them, as you slowly drizzle in the hot potato water. Beat well. Add potatoes, spinach, lemon juice, scallions, and seasonings. Chill until very cold. Serve topped with sour cream.

Chilled
Cherry~Plum
Soup

4 servings

1½ lbs. ripe red or purple plums
1 lb. pitted fresh sweet cherries
¼ tsp. salt
¼ tsp. ground, powdered ginger
½ tsp. Dijon mustard
⅓ cup dry red wine

2 Tbs. honey (more, to taste)
1½ cups buttermilk
a pinch of dried crushed mint

thin, round slices of fresh lime
and/or thin slices of kiwi fruit

(1) Remove the pits, and chop the plums coarsely. Place them in a heavy saucepan with the cherries and salt. Turn the heat to low, and begin cooking them, covered.

(2) After 5 minutes of slow stewing, add ginger, mustard, wine, and honey. Cover and cook (still over low heat) 5 minutes more.

(3) Remove from heat, and let cool to room temperature. Purée approximately half the mixture in a food processor or blender, and return it to the unpuréed half.

(4) Whisk in the buttermilk and mint. Chill until very cold. Serve topped with slices of lime and/or kiwi fruit.

CHILLED CURRIED POTATO SOUP

30 minutes to prepare;
plus several hours to chill.

4-5 refreshing servings.

3 medium (4" long) potatoes
2 cups water

¾ tsp. ground cumin
¼ tsp. powdered ginger
½ tsp. turmeric
⅛ tsp. nutmeg
¼ tsp. celery seed
½ tsp. mustard seed

1 heaping cup chopped onion
1 Tbs. butter
1 tsp. salt
black pepper
cayenne
1 Tbs. fresh lemon juice

1 cup yogurt
(optional: 1 small cucumber, seeded & chopped)
¾ cup lightly toasted shredded or flaked coconut

(1) Scrub the potatoes, and slice them very thinly. Place them in a large saucepan with the water, cover, and bring to a boil. Reduce heat, and simmer until the potatoes are just tender (12-15 minutes). Remove from heat; uncover.

(2) Meanwhile, combine the spices, and mix them well. In a heavy skillet, begin cooking the onions in butter with salt over moderate heat. After several minutes, stir in the spice mixture. Add black pepper and cayenne to your taste. Keep stirring and cooking another 5-8 minutes, or until the onions are tender.

(3) Add the sautéed mixture to the potatoes. (Add some of the potato liquid to the skillet to help include all the butter and spices. Pour the liquid back into the potatoes.) Add lemon juice. Chill until cold.

(4) Stir in yogurt (and optional cucumber) shortly before serving. Top each bowlful with a generous amount of toasted coconut.

Chilled Marinated Mushroom Soup

50 minutes to prepare;
several hours to chill.

4 servings.

12 oz. mushrooms, thinly sliced
½ cup minced onion
1 large clove garlic, crushed
1 bay leaf
¾ cup dry white wine
1 cup water
¾ tsp. salt
fresh black pepper

¼ tsp. honey
½ tsp. dried basil
½ tsp. dill weed
¼ tsp. thyme
2 Tbs. olive oil
2 Tbs. red wine vinegar
¼ cup (packed) finely-minced green onions
(chives or scallion greens)

thin slices of lemon, for garnish

(1) Place mushrooms, onions, garlic, bay leaf, wine, water, salt, and pepper in a saucepan. Bring to a boil, lower the heat, cover, and simmer 15 minutes.

(2) Remove from heat. Let stand, uncovered, about 10 minutes. Fish out the bay leaf and discard it, so that nobody will eat it accidentally. (It doesn't go down too well.)

(3) Add all other ingredients, except the lemon slices. Mix well, and chill until very cold. Serve topped with delicate rounds of fresh lemon.

NOTE: If you have <u>fresh</u> thyme, garnish with a sprig of this, too.

Chilled Tomato-Egg Soup

4-5 servings

This soup is a good companion for people trying to lose weight. It is filling, refreshing, low-caloried and high in protein. It is also delicious and very easy to prepare.

4 cups tomato juice
1 medium-sized (3" diameter)
    ripe tomato, diced
1 tsp. prepared horseradish
(optional: 1 tsp. worcestershire sauce)
1 tsp. Dijon mustard
½ tsp. dill weed
salt and pepper, to taste
tabasco sauce, to taste
3 hard-boiled eggs, coarsely-grated
2 scallions, finely-minced (whites & greens)
1 small stalk celery, finely-minced

Combine all ingredients, mix well, and chill.

Serve Chilled Tomato-Egg Soup with
Vegetable Upside-Down Cake (p. 202),
a simple green salad
and a dessert of
Fresh Fruit & Cashew Shortbread (p.278)

Salads

SALADS:
Table of Contents

"SALAD"

doesn't always mean "tossed green..."
Sometimes it means a whole dishful of
one perfectly-in-season vegetable or fruit, bask-
ing in a modest amount of delicious marinade. Sometimes that vegetable is cooked, other times it is raw.
Sometimes it is grated, other times it is cut into chunks,
and occasionally it is hollowed out and stuffed with
some tasty cold filling. Sometimes the vegetable (or
fruit) is mingling with some of its colleagues, or with
cheese or eggs or tofu or nuts, and other times it
relishes having a whole bowlful of savory dressing to
itself. The main trait that makes a salad a salad is
that it is served cold.

It can do wonders for one's menu-planning repertoire
to realize that a good salad can be substantial and interesting enough to constitute the main course of a meal,
especially if grouped with soup and good bread. This
chapter features an assortment of vegetable and fruit
combinations from a variety of ethnic origins. In
addition, you are provided with salad menu ideas
throughout (and especially on page 82).

Creamy Broccoli Salad

*25-30 minutes
  to prepare;

* plus 1½ to 2 hours
  to chill.

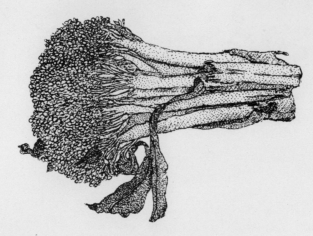

*4-6 servings.

2 good-sized bunches (about 2 lbs.) fresh broccoli
2 equally-good-sized lemons, well-juiced
½ cup mayonnaise
½ cup yogurt or sour cream (or a combination)
approximately ½ tsp. salt
½ tsp. crushed tarragon
4 finely-minced scallions (greens and whites)
lots of freshly-ground black pepper
mustard

1) Cut off the bottom few inches of the broccoli stalks and discard. Use a sharp paring knife or a vegetable peeler to trim the stalks, and to lightly shave off some of the tough outer skin. Cut these well-manicured stalks lengthwise into manageable-sized spears.

2) Steam the broccoli until it is <u>just</u> tender and bright green. Remove from the heat immediately, and rinse under cold water. Drain.

3) Combine the lemon juice with all other ingredients. Toss the still-warm broccoli with this dressing until well-mixed. Cover, and chill.

> Serve this as a luncheon entrée, with:
> * one of the Tomato Soup Variations
>   (pp. 26-27)
> * Savory Nut Bread (p. 107)
>   and
> * Peach & Rum Puddingcake (p. 258)

Chilled Marinated Cauliflower

About 30 minutes
   to prepare;
another 1½ to 2 hours
   to chill.

4·5 servings.

      This is an easy recipe, as the cauliflower is cooked right in the marinade, then the whole combination is chilled. Just before serving time, a few snippets of fresh herbs and vegetables are added, for extra touches of color, flavor, and crunch.

I.
- ¾ cup olive oil
- ¾ cup red wine vinegar
- ½ cup water
- 2 medium-sized cloves of crushed garlic
- ½ tsp. salt
- ½ tsp. whole peppercorns
- 2 bay leaves
- 1 medium (6-7 inch diameter) cauliflower, broken into bite-sized flowerettes

II.
- ½ cup minced red onion
- ½ cup freshly-minced parsley
- 2-3 fresh basil leaves, minced (or: ½ tsp. dried)
- 1 packed cup coarsely-grated carrot

(1) In a large saucepan, combine all of "I". Bring to a boil, reduce heat, cover, and simmer about 15 minutes (until cauliflower is tender).

(2) Transfer to a serving bowl and chill.

(3) Just before serving add "II". Mix well.

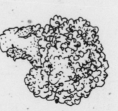
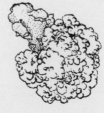

Russian Beet Salad

About 1 hour to prepare; plus time to chill.

4·5 servings.

8 healthy (2½" diameter) beets
½ cup cider vinegar
1 medium clove of garlic, crushed
2 tsp. honey

½ cup minced red onion
2 scallions, minced (whites and greens)
1 medium cucumber, seeded and finely-chopped
2 hardboiled eggs, chopped
2 Tbs. fresh dill, minced (or, 1 tsp. dried dill)
2 cups mixed sour cream and yogurt
salt and black pepper, to taste

(1) Boil the beets, whole, for about 20-25 minutes. Rinse under running water as you rub off their skins. Chop into ½-inch bits, and while they are still warm, marinate them in vinegar, garlic, and honey. Let stand 30 minutes.

(2) Add all remaining ingredients. Mix well, and chill until very cold.

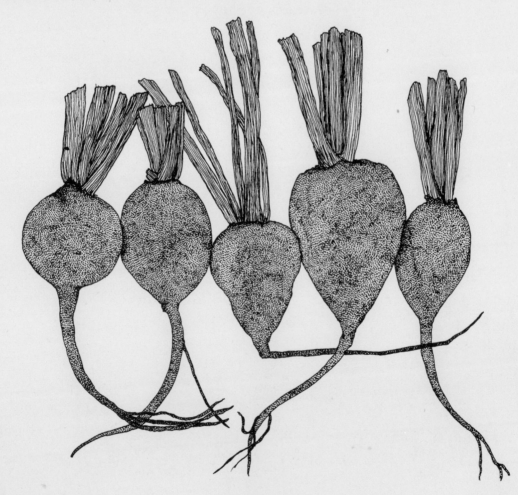

Swiss Green Beans

This salad is most delicious when made a day in advance and marinated overnight. Actual preparation time= about 30 minutes.

1½ lbs. fresh, whole green beans - cleaned and destrung

5 Tbs. fresh lemon juice
2 large cloves freshly-crushed garlic
½ cup olive oil
1 Tbs. red wine vinegar
½ tsp. crushed tarragon
½ tsp. dried dill weed
½ tsp. salt (more, to taste)
freshly-ground black pepper
2 tsp. prepared dark or Dijon mustard
½ cup (packed) freshly-minced parsley
} Dressing

⅓ lb. good Swiss cheese, in thin strips

½ cup chopped ripe olives
½ cup each: thinly-sliced green & red peppers

½ cup (or more) chopped, toasted almonds

1) Steam the beans until just tender. (Larger beans will take longer than thinner ones.) Remove from heat, and immediately rinse in cold water.
2) While the beans are cooking, combine the dressing ingredients in a large bowl. Mix well to thoroughly combine.
3) Add the rinsed (well-drained) beans to the dressing. Add Swiss cheese. Toss until dressing is well-distributed. Cover tightly, and marinate 2-3 hours, stirring about once an hour.
4) Add olives and sliced peppers. Mix well, cover, and chill overnight, or at least 5 hours. ∼ SERVE TOPPED WITH ALMONDS. ∼

Bulgarian Salad

~ It's best to make this salad in the heart of the Tomato Season. Preparation time is brief, but the salad is best when given an hour or so to marinate before it is served.

4-6 servings

4 medium tomatoes, good and ripe
½ cup thinly-sliced Spanish or red onion
1 small bell pepper - in thin strips
1 small (6-inch) cucumber - sliced
1½-2 tsp. freshly-minced marjoram or oregano leaves
 ↳(if using dried herbs, reduce amount to ½-1 tsp.)
1½-2 tsp. freshly-minced mint leaves
 ↳(same reduction as above, if using dried)
1 cup Greek olives (whole)
⅓ cup olive oil
¼ cup wine vinegar
freshly-grated black pepper
½ lb. (drained weight) feta cheese,
        crumbled.
(1 large clove crushed garlic - optional)

Cut the tomatoes into 1-inch chunks.
Combine everything in a big salad bowl, and toss gently until well-mingled.

You can adjust seasonings to taste.

❀ A Summer Supper: ❀

with Scrambled Eggs
Either of these Salads
and
Carob Pumpernickel (p.101)
or Swedish Rye Bread
(p. 103)

Israeli Salad

4-6 servings

2 young (6-inch) cucumbers ⎫
2 medium-sized, ripe tomatoes ⎬ in small cubes
½ cup sliced radishes
2 minced scallions (include green part)
1 large minced dill or half-sour pickle
1 medium-sized bell pepper - minced
½ cup sliced pimiento-stuffed green olives
½ cup minced Spanish or red onion
½ cup (packed) finely-minced fresh parsley
¼ cup olive oil
juice from 1 large lemon
salt and pepper, to taste

Toss together gently and chill.

You can make this several hours ahead of serving-time.

It's nice to serve this in a glass bowl, because it's colorful.

Optional Additions: little cubes of cream cheese
                      yogurt or sour cream on top

moroccan orange-walnut salad

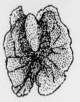

Actual preparation time is about 30 minutes, but begin an hour or two early, so the oranges have time to rest.

4-6 Servings.

{
6 large oranges
1 Tbs. honey
½ tsp. cinnamon

{
1 lb. mixed fresh greens (spinach and Romaine, combined, are best)

½ cup thinly-sliced red onion

1 cup thinly-sliced radishes

1 cup toasted walnut halves (you can chop them, if you prefer smaller pieces)

3 Tbs. olive oil

salt and pepper

1) <u>At least one hour ahead</u>: Peel and section the oranges: Using a serrated knife, cut off the polar ends of the peel, then slice the peel off the sides. If the orange is a "ready-to-eat" navel-type, it will section easily by hand. If not, use that same serrated knife to cut sections by going in one side of the membrane and out the other, releasing each orange section and leaving behind its lining. Squeeze all excess juice from the remaining membrane into the bowl of orange tidbits. Discard the membrane. Pick out seeds, if necessary. Drizzle honey and sprinkle cinnamon over the oranges-au-jus. When you are done drizzling and sprinkling, cover the bowl, and let it stand at room temperature at least one hour.

2) Clean the greens and swing or pat them dry. Combine them in a large bowl with onions, radishes and nuts. Toss well.

3) Drizzle the olive oil over the salad; toss to distribute. Season to taste with salt and freshly-ground black pepper.

4) Just before serving, add the oranges and all their liquid. Mix well.

⇒THIS SALAD GOES VERY WELL WITH A PASTA & PESTO MEAL. (SEE PAGES 158-161).

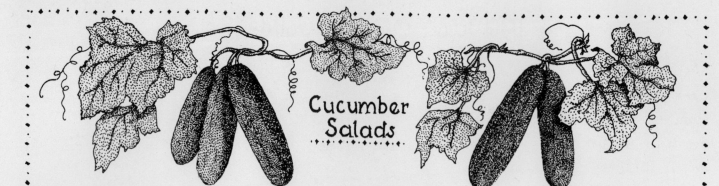

Cucumber Salads

Each of these takes only about 10 minutes to prepare, and yields 4-6 servings.

1. Wilted Cucumbers:

Make this one a day ahead, so the cucumbers can soften and absorb their dressing. ("Wilted" doesn't mean tired in this case, it means <u>relaxed</u>.)

Note: This salad contains no oil. It has practically zero calories, and it keeps for days in the refrigerator, if stored in a tightly-lidded jar.

> 1 cup red wine vinegar
> 4 tsp. honey
> 4 medium (6-7 inch) cucumbers
> 1 tsp. salt
> lots of fresh black pepper
> 1 tsp. dill weed
> ½ cup very, very thinly-sliced red onion

(1) Heat the vinegar in a saucepan, until it is hot but not boiling. Remove from heat and stir in the honey until it dissolves. Set aside.

(2) Slice the cucumbers very thinly, and place them in a bowl. Sprinkle with salt, pepper, and dill, and mix well. Add onions, and mix.

(3) Pour the still-warm vinegar solution over the mixture. Transfer to a jar, put the lid on tightly, and refrigerate.

2. Tsatsiki (Greek Cucumbers)

2 medium (6-7 inch) cucumbers
½ tsp. salt
1 cup sour cream
1 cup yogurt
2 medium cloves garlic, crushed

1) Peel, seed, and coarsely grate the cucumbers.
2) Combine everything in a bowl, and mix well. Cover tightly, and refrigerate until very cold. Serve as a salad, appetizer, or dip.

Eggplant Salads

❧ Roumanian ❧

25 minutes to prepare... & needs time to chill.
4 servings.

1 1½-lb. eggplant	¾ tsp. salt
1½ cups chopped onion	6-8 Tbs. olive oil

(1) Cut the eggplant into 1-inch cubes. Salt the cubes lightly, and cook them in a vegetable steamer over boiling water until very soft (10-15 minutes). Transfer to a bowl.

(2) Meanwhile, sauté the onion in olive oil with salt over moderate heat until very soft (but not brown)—10-12 minutes. Stir the cooked onion, plus all its oil, into the eggplant. Mix well, cover, and refrigerate until cold. Good as an hors d'oeuvre on crackers.

❧ Israeli ❧

40 minutes to prepare... & needs time to chill.
4 servings

1 1½-lb. eggplant	½ tsp. salt	juice from 1 lime
2 Tbs. olive oil	fresh black pepper	⅓ cup (packed) freshly-minced parsley
2 large cloves garlic, crushed	½ tsp. dill weed	2-3 Tbs. mayonnaise
1 cup minced onion	3 Tbs. sesame seeds	

(1) Cut the eggplant into small (½-inch) cubes.

(2) In a very large skillet, begin cooking the garlic and onions in olive oil, with salt. Stir, and cook over medium heat, gradually adding pepper, dill, and sesame seeds.

(3) After about 5 minutes, add the eggplant, and stir well. Cover, and cook over medium heat until the eggplant is soft (15-20 minutes). Add the lime juice gradually as the eggplant cooks. (If necessary, add a little water to prevent sticking.) Remove from heat, transfer to a bowl, and chill thoroughly. Stir in parsley and mayonnaise just before serving.

More ❧

~ ~ ~ ~ ~ Indian ~

About 45 minutes
to prepare;
at least 2 hours
to chill.

4 servings

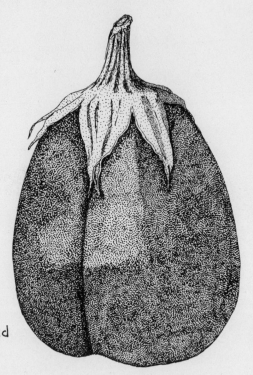

1 eggplant (1-1½ lb.)
2 Tbs. butter
1½ tsp. mustard seeds
2 Tbs. sesame seeds
1 tsp. whole cumin seeds
2 large cloves garlic, crushed

1½ cups minced onion
¾ tsp. salt
cayenne pepper, to taste
3 Tbs. lemon juice
water, as needed
optional: ½ cup yogurt

(1) Cut the eggplant into small (½-inch) cubes.

(2) In a <u>large</u>, heavy skillet, melt the butter.

(3) Add all the seeds (mustard, sesame, cumin) to the butter. Turn the heat
to medium, and cook the seeds by themselves for a few moments, stirring constantly. (This head-start helps to bring out their flavor.) Soon the
seeds will start popping from the heat.

(4) When the seeds begin to pop, add the garlic, onion, salt, and cayenne.
Stir and cook for about 5 minutes — until the onions soften.

(5) Add the eggplant, and stir well. Cover, and reduce heat to medium-low.
After about 5 minutes, stir again, and add lemon juice. Cover, and keep
cooking (stirring intermittently) until the eggplant is cooked. (Add water,
¼ cup at a time, as needed to prevent sticking.) Remove from heat, transfer
to a bowl, and chill completely. Stir in optional yogurt (or not) after
is cold.

Italian

40 minutes to prepare;
at least several hours
to chill.

4-5 servings

1 1-lb. eggplant
½ cup olive oil
¾ cup minced onion
2 large cloves garlic, crushed
¾ tsp. salt
1 stalk celery, minced
3 medium tomatoes, diced
⅓ cup red wine vinegar
2 Tbs. tomato paste
½ tsp. dried basil (or:
 3-4 fresh leaves, minced)
½ cup minced green olives
freshly-ground black pepper
¼ cup finely-minced parsley
OPTIONAL:
~ 2-3 Tbs. capers ~
~ ½ cup toasted pine nuts ~

(1) Cut the eggplant into small (½-inch) cubes. Steam the cubes in a vegetable steamer over boiling water, until they are tender (15-20 minutes). Prepare the other ingredients while the eggplant steams.

(2) In 2 Tbs. of the olive oil, sauté the onions and garlic with salt, until the onions begin to soften (5 minutes). Add the celery, and sauté another 5 minutes. Add the diced tomatoes, and cook a few minutes more. Remove from heat, and transfer to a large bowl.

(3) Add all remaining ingredients to the bowl, including the steamed eggplant (you don't need to cool it first). Mix well, and chill.

NOTE: This salad is most successful if made a day in advance, so it can marinate thoroughly.

Kind & Unusual Potato Salads

1.

Dill Pickle Potatoes

30-40 minutes to prepare;
several hours to chill.

6 servings

6 medium-sized potatoes

1 cup thinly-sliced onions
1 large carrot - sliced into thin rounds
½ cup all-purpose vegetable oil
2 tsp. whole caraway seeds
1 cup raw peas (fresh or frozen)

3 large whole dill pickles, chopped
¾-1 cup dill pickle juice (from the jar)
1½ tsp. salt
lots of fresh black pepper
cayenne pepper, to taste
3 Tbs. cider vinegar

(1) Scrub the potatoes, and chop them into potato salad-sized chunks (1-inch cubes).

(2) Place potato chunks in a large kettle, cover them with water, and bring it to a boil. Cook until the potatoes are tender (don't overcook). Drain, and rinse in a colander under cold water. Transfer to a large bowl.

(3) In a large skillet, cook the onions and carrots in oil, with caraway seeds, over medium heat for about 5-8 minutes (at which point the onions should be soft). Add the raw green peas, and keep cooking another 5 minutes - or until the peas are just barely cooked through. Add this sauté to the potatoes.

(4) Add the remaining ingredients, and mix well. Cover tightly, and refrigerate until very cold.

2.

Very-Much-Marinated Potatoes

30-40 minutes to prepare;
several hours to chill.

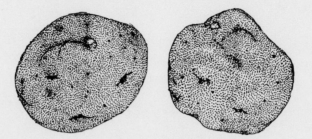

6 servings

For this salad, the potatoes are actually cooked _in_ their marinade, which gives them a very unusual flavor. (Potatoes are rarely cooked in anything but water.) The trick to this process is to get them sliced <u>seriously thin</u> (which means only a shade or two thicker than paper-thin). The ingredients for this dish are not unusual, but somehow the result equals more than the sum of its parts.

6 medium (fist-sized) potatoes
⅔ cup olive oil (or a combination of
     olive and vegetable oils)
¾ cup red wine vinegar
a generous dosage of fresh black pepper
1½ tsp. salt

3 scallions ~ whites & greens, finely-minced
1 small bell pepper, in very thin slices
¼ cup finely-minced parsley
chunks of ripe, red tomato

(1) Scrub the potatoes. Slice them in half lengthwise, then into <u>very</u> thin (less than ¼ inch, if possible. See cutting diagram on p. 235) slices.

(2) Combine potato slices, oil, vinegar, salt, and pepper in a large saucepan. Bring to a boil, then cover and lower heat to a shy simmer. Cook until the potatoes are <u>just</u> tender (20-30 minutes). Remove from heat, transfer to a bowl, and chill thoroughly.

(3) Before serving, stir in minced scallions and pepper slices. Serve garnished with minced parsley and chunks of tomato.

Alfalfa~Romaino Salad

This is a spicy adaptation of the traditional caesar salad.

Make croutons, and prepare lettuce in advance, then toss just before eating.

(20-30 minutes advance preparation.)

4-6 servings, depending on what else gets served.

3 slices good, old bread, brushed on both sides with olive oil

1 healthy-sized head of Romaine lettuce (1-1½ lbs.)

6 Tbs. olive oil
1 large clove garlic
1 Tbs. prepared dark mustard
1 Tbs. worcestershire sauce
1 tsp. prepared horseradish

1 egg
juice of 1 medium lemon
(about 3-4 Tbs.)
2-4 Tbs. grated parmesan cheese

a large handful of alfalfa sprouts   freshly-ground black pepper

1. Making the Croutons:

Cut your olive-oiled bread slices into small cubes. Toast the cubes by pan-frying – constantly stirring – in a heavy skillet over medium heat for 5-8 minutes. (No additional oil is necessary if you keep your eye on them, and keep stirring.)

2. Preparing the Lettuce:

Clean each leaf separately under cold running water. Use a salad spinner, if you have one, to get every morsel totally dry and crisp. If you don't have a spinner, dry each leaf completely with paper towels. Wrap, and keep cold until Tossing Time.

3. Tossing the Salad:

Use a large wooden salad bowl. Add the olive oil, and crush in the garlic (use a press). Beat with a fork, and gradually add mustard, worcestershire sauce, horseradish, raw egg, and lemon juice. Keep beating until you have a frothy, uniform dressing. Mix in the cheese. Break in pieces of lettuce, and turn each piece with salad-servers as you add it, so all the lettuce gets well-coated. Toward the end, add alfalfa sprouts (try to separate them, so they don't congregate in one overwhelming clump) and croutons. Grind in lots of fresh black pepper, and serve immediately.

Chilled Asparagus

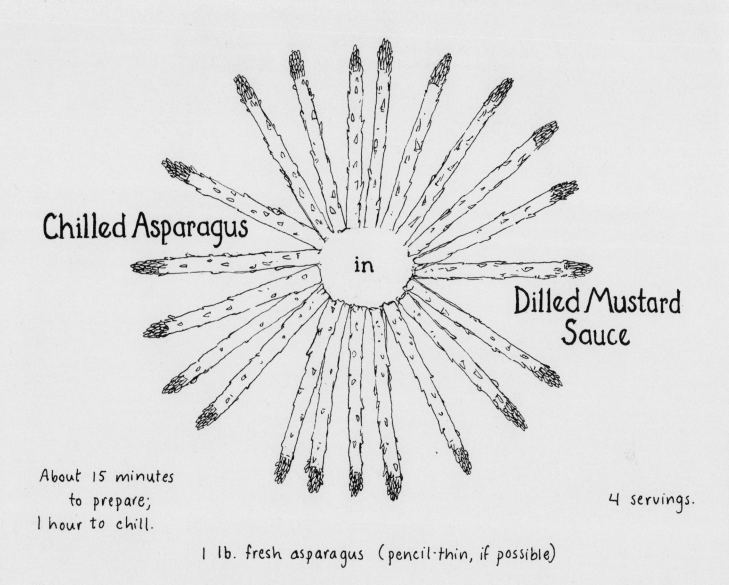

in

Dilled Mustard Sauce

About 15 minutes
   to prepare;
1 hour to chill.

4 servings.

1 lb. fresh asparagus (pencil-thin, if possible)

1 cup firm yogurt
¼ cup mayonnaise
⅓ cup Dijon mustard
2 heaping Tbs. each: freshly-minced dill
                             freshly-minced chives
salt and freshly-ground black pepper, to taste

1) Snap the very bottom-most tiplets from your elegantly thin asparagus spears. Leaving the spears whole and long, steam them until they are <u>just</u> tender (i.e., still crisp at heart). As soon as they are done, run them under cold water, and drain.

2) Combine all remaining ingredients and mix well. Place the asparagus in a long, shallow dish, pour the dressing over, and chill.   Serve on a platter lined with greens; garnish with cherry tomatoes.

Marinated Pasta Salad

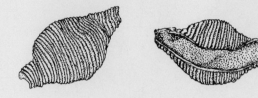

20-30 minutes
to prepare;
1½ -2 hours
to chill.

4-6 servings.

1 lb. (raw) pasta shells (above illustration=
approximate actual size, raw)

⅓ cup olive oil
⅓ cup red wine vinegar
½ tsp. salt
4-5 fresh basil leaves, minced (or, 1 tsp. dried)
1 large green bell pepper, minced
1 small, freshly-minced red onion
1 cup drained, minced pimiento
½ cup (packed) freshly-minced parsley
fresh black pepper

[Optional Additions: small cubes of fresh mozzarella cheese
a handful of toasted pine nuts]

1) Heat a very large kettleful of water to a rolling boil.

2) Add the shells, stirring with a long wooden spoon to keep water moving.
Cook the shells until <u>al dente</u> (5-8 minutes at most).

3) Drain the cooked shells in a colander. Rinse under tepid tapwater, and
shake to drain thoroughly.

4) Transfer the still-warm shells to a bowl, and immediately toss with
the olive oil. Cover and chill at least 30 minutes.

5) Add all remaining ingredients, and mix well. Serve very cold.

Fancy Stuffed Pears

½ hour
to prepare.

4-6 servings.

3 medium-sized, firm-but-ripe Bartlett pears
juice from ½ lemon

4 oz. softened cream cheese
½ cup pot cheese or firm cottage cheese
(a few drops of milk for moistening, if needed)
⅓ cup (packed) grated medium-sharp cheddar
2 Tbs. freshly-minced parsley
2 Tbs. freshly-minced scallions or chives
⅓ cup finely-chopped toasted walnuts or pecans
(optional: a few drops of worcestershire sauce)
dash of salt
a few grindings of fresh black pepper

About 6 plump & healthy dried apricots

1) Slice the pears in half lengthwise. Core them, and brush their open surfaces liberally with lemon juice.
2) Beat together the cottage, cheddar and cream cheeses. Add up to a tablespoon of milk, if needed, to reach a spreadably-creamy consistency.
3) Add all remaining ingredients, except the apricots. Mix well.
4) Spread filling over the open surface of each pear half; mound the filling generously, and smooth it with a knife.
5) Cut the apricots into thin strips, and use these to decorate the top of each filled pear with a floral petal design (see Helpful Diagram below).
6) Serve as a luncheon treat, with a leafy green salad and your favorite muffins. (Leftover filled pears can be wrapped and included in Brown Bag lunches.)

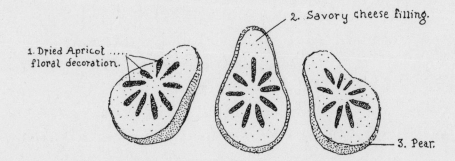

1. Dried Apricot floral decoration.
2. Savory cheese filling.
3. Pear.

✶✶✶✶✶✶ Cold Stuffed Things ✶✶✶✶✶✶

A cold, stuffed fruit or vegetable can make an oasis out of a hot summer day's lunch. Serve it on a bed of crisp, cold greens, with homemade bread & butter. Here are some ideas, in addition to the Fancy Stuffed Pears on the preceding page.

✶✶✶✶✶✶✶✶✶✶ Freshly-Herbed Cottage Cheese ✶✶✶✶✶✶✶✶✶✶✶

Cottage cheese, with fine green specks of assorted fresh herbs, is a perfect filling for raw, stuffed vegetables. Use fresh herbs only; mince them with scissors, or a very sharp knife. Start with a small quantity (maybe 2 Tbs. each herb : 2 cups cottage cheese) - and increase, to taste. Recommended: any combination of dill, basil, thyme, chives, parsley, marjoram and mint.

✶✶✶✶✶✶✶✶✶✶✶✶✶✶✶ Cold Stuffed Peppers ✶✶✶✶✶✶✶✶✶✶✶✶✶✶✶✶✶✶✶✶

& Cucumbers

Peppers and cucumbers are 2 perfect containers for herbed cottage cheese. Choose small vegetables for stuffing. For peppers, cut each one lengthwise, and just pull out the pith and the seeds. Lay each half on its back, and fill it generously (about ½ cup filling per half). For cucumbers, also slice in half lengthwise. Scoop out the seeds with a small spoon.

[Other items that can double as pepper or cucumber fillings are: the enchilada fillings on p. 144 and the mushroom pâté on p. 254.]

* * * * * * * * * * * * * * Tomato Fans * * * * * * * * * * * * * *

For 4 servings :

4 3-inch-diameter ripe tomatoes

1 medium avocado, sliced

2 hard-boiled eggs, sliced

Creamy Mustard Dressing, p.77

(1) Core the tomatoes, and make a series of parallel lengthwise slices, 2/3 of the way down, in 1/4-inch intervals.

(2) Gently insert slices of avocado and egg, alternately, in the crevasses.

(3) Place the assembled fans on individual plates, lined with lettuce leaves. Drizzle with creamy mustard dressing, and serve.

* * * * * * * * * * * * Stuffed * * * * * * * * * * * * * * * Cantaloupe

For Every 2 Servings:

1 cup firm yogurt

2-3 Tbs. honey (to taste)

1/2 tsp. vanilla extract

1 cup fresh whole blueberries or raspberries

(or sliced strawberries)

1 small (5"diameter) cantaloupe

2 Tbs. Fresh lemon juice

1/2 cup slivered, toasted almonds

~fresh mint leaves~

(1) Cut the cantaloupe in half around the equator, and scoop out the seeds. Cut a small slice from each end, so the halves can stand upright. Place each half on a plate. Drizzle the cavity with fresh lemon juice.

(2) Combine the yogurt, honey, vanilla, and berries. Stir gently, and divide this mixture between the 2 cantaloupe halves. Sprinkle the tops liberally with almonds.

OPTIONAL: Garnish with a sprig of fresh mint.

Zucchini Julienne

15 minutes to prepare;
-needs time to chill.

The eating of raw zucchini is usually associated with big spears, served on a platter with other raw vegetables around a dip.

4 servings.

Here is a different, more subtle presentation of raw zucchini - a new way to appreciate it.

Use only the smallest ones, and cut them as thinly as possible, with loving care. The delicacy of the texture will surprise you, as will the appearance of this beautiful, unusual (and simple) salad.

Serve Zucchini Julienne on a bed of butter lettuce with tomatoes AND *Provolone-Filled Calzone* (dough p.148; filling p.151) with *some Italian green olives* *a dry red wine* AND *Cherry-Berry Pie (p.265)*

4 small (5-inch) zucchini

¼ cup olive oil

6 Tbs. red wine vinegar

salt
black pepper } to taste

1 medium scallion, finely-minced

½ tsp. oregano

½ tsp. basil

OPTIONAL ADDITIONS:

~ a clove of garlic, crushed

~ finely-minced red onion

~ thinly-sliced mushrooms

~ finely-minced parsley

~ small wedges of tomato

(1) Using a very sharp knife, cut the zucchini into julienne strips by slicing them thinly lengthwise, then even more thinly widthwise. (See the diagram on p.236.)

(2) Place the zucchini in a bowl. Add all other ingredients, mix gently but thoroughly, and refrigerate until very cold.

Vegetables Rémoulade

30 minutes to prepare;
-needs time to chill.

4 servings.

1 large carrot
1 large celery stalk
1 large red or green bell pepper
1 medium cucumber

Dressing

½ cup firm yogurt
½ cup mayonnaise
¼ cup minced sweet pickle
(optional: 2-3 Tbs. capers)
2 Tbs. Dijon mustard
¼ cup (packed) freshly-minced parsley
½ tsp. dried tarragon
1 finely-minced scallion (greens & whites)
4 Tbs. fresh lemon juice

to taste {
freshly-ground black pepper
cayenne pepper
salt
}

❀fresh spinach❀

❀thin strips of Swiss cheese❀

❀wedges of tomato❀

❀slices of hardboiled egg❀

(1) Cut the carrot and celery into matchstick pieces (diagram on p. 236). Blanch them in boiling water for 5 minutes, then drain, and rinse them under cold running water. Drain again, and place in a bowl.

(2) Mince the bell pepper. Seed and mince the cucumber. (Seed it by cutting it down the center lengthwise, and scooping the seeds out with a spoon.) Add these to the carrot and celery.

(3) Combine all dressing ingredients and mix well. Pour the dressing over the vegetables, cover tightly, and refrigerate until very cold.

(4) Serve on a bed of spinach, garnished with cheese, tomato, and egg slices.

Eggless Egg Salad (made with Tofu)

4 Servings.
Preparation Time: about 15 minutes.

(I. THE SALAD:

3 firm cakes (³/4 lb) tofu
3 minced scallions (whites and greens)
1 medium carrot, coarsely-grated
1 stalk celery, finely-minced
1 small bell pepper, finely-minced
⅓ cup toasted sunflower seeds
salt
freshly-ground pepper } to taste
tamari sauce

(a) Cut the tofu into dice-sized bits.
(b) Add all other ingredients, except the "to taste" ones. Mix gently.
(c) Add the mayonnaise (below). Now, season to taste, and mix once again. Chill, and serve in pita bread or on greens.

(II. THE MAYONNAISE:

1 cake (¼ lb) tofu
2 tsp. Chinese sesame oil
2 Tbs. cider vinegar
½ tsp. dry mustard
½ tsp. salt
½ cup refined peanut or vegetable oil

(a) Whip together the first 5 ingredients in a blender or food processor.
(b) Keep the machine going, and gradually drizzle in the oil. When all oil is in there, turn off the machine. You should have a nice, creamy, eggless mayonnaise, ready to add to your eggless egg salad.

Salad Dressings

Garlic & Herb Vinaigrette

2 medium cloves of garlic, crushed
5 Tbs. olive oil
5 Tbs. red wine vinegar
¼ tsp. salt (more, to taste)
black pepper
a pinch of celery seed

¼ tsp. each: dry mustard
                 dill weed
                 oregano
                 basil
2 small scallions, minced
1 Tbs. orange or lemon juice

Combine everything and mix well. Store in a tightly-covered jar. <u>Yield</u>: ¾ cup (easily doubled).

Creamy Mustard Dressing

2 Tbs. dark mustard (Dijon-style)
¼ cup dry white wine
½ cup olive oil
¼ cup half & half
salt
black pepper } to taste
cayenne

Whisk together until well-combined.
<u>Yield</u>: a little over a cup.

Orange & Sesame Dressing

1 cup orange juice
¼ cup red wine vinegar
½ cup vegetable oil
1 Tbs. tamari sauce
2 Tbs. Chinese sesame oil

½ tsp. salt
½ tsp. dry mustard
½ tsp dill weed
1 large clove of garlic, crushed

Combine everything; mix well.
<u>Yield</u>: 2 cups.

Apple Vinaigrette

3/4 cup apple juice
2/3 cup cider vinegar
1/2 cup oil

1/2 tsp. salt
fresh black pepper
1 tsp. prepared mustard
1/4 tsp. celery seed

Whisk everything together until well-combined.
<u>Yield</u>: approximately 2 cups.

Tofu Dressing

1 lb. (usually 4 cakes) soft tofu
1/2 cup cider vinegar
2 Tbs. tamari sauce
1 tsp. dill weed
1/4 cup oil

lots of black pepper
1/4 tsp. salt (more, to taste)
1/4 cup finely-minced green pepper
1/4 cup finely-minced fresh parsley
2 medium cloves of garlic, crushed

1) Purée the tofu with the vinegar and tamari in a blender or food processor fitted with the steel blade.
2) Mix in remaining ingredients. Chill in a tightly-covered container
Yield: approximately 2³/₄ cups.

Buttermilk & Cucumber Dressing

1 medium (7") cucumber, seeded & chopped
1 1/2 cups buttermilk
1 clove garlic, crushed
1/2 tsp. salt

1/4 cup red wine vinegar
2 tsp. prepared horseradish
1 tsp. dill weed
1 tsp. mild paprika

Purée everything together in a blender or a food processor fitted with the steel blade.
<u>Yield</u>: approximately 2³/₄ cups.

Mayonnaise
...and variations

Basic

2 Tbs. cider vinegar
2 Tbs. fresh lemon juice
1 large egg
¼ tsp. salt

1¼ cups oil (vegetable or olive,
        or a combination)

(1) Combine vinegar, lemon juice, egg, and salt in the jar of a blender, or in a food processor fitted with the steel blade. Turn on the machine to a steady whir.

(2) Gradually pour the oil, in a thin stream, into the whirling mixture (through the feed tube, if you are using a processor). Keep the machine going until all the oil is in, then turn it off. You now have real mayonnaise before you.

For each of these variations, add the ingredients to the vinegar-lemon-egg mixture, and proceed as described above.

Avocado

1 medium (4" long) avocado

Spicy

1 small clove crushed garlic
¼ tsp. cayenne pepper
1 tsp. dry mustard
2 tsp. prepared horseradish

Curried

½ tsp. dry mustard
¾ tsp. cumin
¾ tsp. turmeric
¼ tsp. cayenne pepper

What are these strange-looking objects, and furthermore, why do they appear on this page?

These 3 vegetables are unknown to many, but well-worth discovering, especially for salads.

← Pictured at left is a **KOHLRABI**. This drawing is slightly smaller than actual size. Kohlrabi is a pale green color and sometimes it has a purple blush. Perhaps you've seen it in produce markets — it's the only vegetable that looks like it was grown on Mars.

The edible part is the swollen stem of the plant. Remove the leaves, peel it, and blanch in boiling water 8-10 minutes. Cool, and slice thin for salads. Kohlrabi has a spunky taste — sort of like a cross between cabbage and radish.

Pictured here are leaves (actual-size drawing) of **ARUGULA**. This dark green leaf is common in Italian cuisine, but nowhere else. And that's too bad, because it has one of the most exciting flavors that can happen to your salad! It is hard to describe this euphoria-producing sensation: it is as though the leaves have somehow been deeply, aromatically <u>roasted</u>, and yet they still retain their crisp, refreshing texture. Unfortunately, arugula is hard to find. Look in Italian food markets. (Also, look for packages of seeds. It grows easily.)

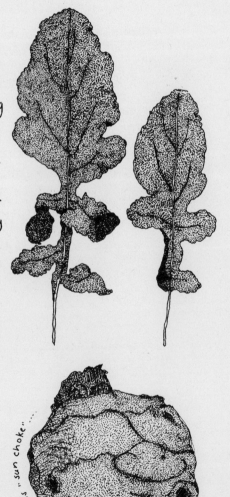

...also known as "sun choke"...

→ The JERUSALEM ARTICHOKE is neither from Jerusalem nor an artichoke. But please don't get the wrong impression; this vegetable is in every other way Upright and Honest. It is actually the sweet, crisp, and delicious tuber of a yellow sunflower. It is a hardy perennial, and if you plant it, you will have it on hand forever. Don't bother to peel — just scrub and slice. Put them, raw, in vegetable or fruit salads. Steam or sauté them. Marinate them in lemon juice and have them for snacks. (very low-caloried!)

A Pep-Talk for Wilted Saladmakers

WHY IS IT THAT SOME SALADS BRING FORTH "OOOHs" and "AHHHs", WHILE OTHERS CAN'T SEEM TO ELICIT MUCH MORE THAN A "ZZZZZ..." ???

Attention to certain little preparation details can really make the difference (s) between salad A. and salad B. Try to cultivate all or some of the following habits, and your salads will become increasingly wonderful:

(1) (a <u>Must</u>) - Always wash your greens thoroughly, leaf by leaf, in cold water. Dry them equally thoroughly. (The single most important gadget-for-salads you can own is a lettuce spinner.) After drying the leaves, chill them until use.

(2) Become a marinater of things. Keep a jar of vinaigrette dressing on hand (recipe on p.77), and house your leftover cooked beans (especially garbanzos) in there. Try marinating sliced raw mushrooms in salad dressing. If you have leftover steamed vegetables, and they are in reasonably good spirits, marinate these in vinaigrette (or in any dressing of your choice). Add marinated things to green salads just before tossing.

(3) Keep pots of fresh herbs on your windowsill (or keep them growing in a garden spot near your kitchen door, if possible). Especially: chives, parsley, basil, thyme. (More on fresh herb-growing, p.287.) Just snip fresh herbs into your salads, with scissors.

(4) Oil-rule-of-thumb: when in doubt, use olive oil. Of course, this presupposes that you have some on hand. Nine out of ten Earnest Saladmakers have olive oil on their shelves at all times (even when they have nothing else in the house). ← This, according to the latest poll of Earnest Saladmakers.

(5) Get a good knife with a straight-edged blade, and keep it sharp, thus enabling yourself to cut sublimely-thin slices of anything (see p.233).

(6) When using garlic: <u>FRESH</u> only!

(7) Greens should always be dressed only at the <u>very</u> <u>last</u> <u>minute</u>! (otherwise, sogginess.)

(8) Don't forget about the charms of: <u>toasted cashews</u>, <u>sunflower seeds</u>, <u>sesame seeds</u>, <u>thin slices of tart apple</u>, <u>grated parsnips</u> (a sweet surprise), <u>marinated tofu</u> (p.197), <u>grated cheese</u>, <u>finely-chopped hard-cooked egg</u> ......and whatever else you find charming.

some menus for
Salad Smorgasbords

On a hot evening, when no one within a 200-mile radius has any desire to cook or eat (or even think about) a hot meal, try serving a buffet of salads for dinner. All the preparations can be done well in advance (for instance, in the early morning, when it's cooler), and the only last-minute requirement is to take things out of the refrigerator and set them up.

Here are 5 suggested salad combinations, which complement one another in appearance as well as in taste. Choose a chilled soup (pp. 45-52) and some homemade bread to round out the meal.

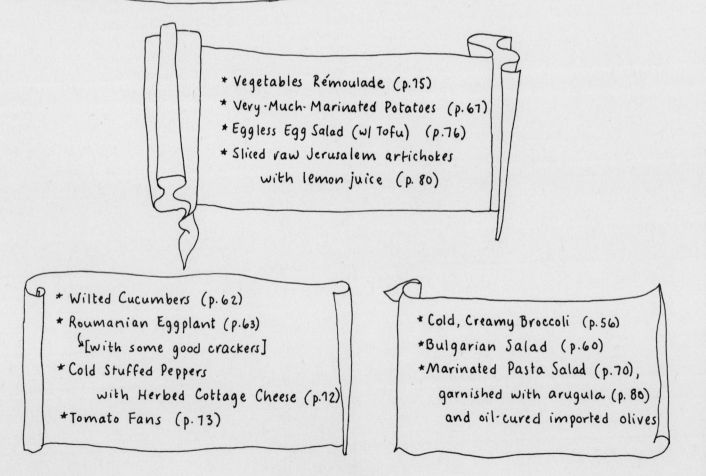

*Chilled, Marinated Cauliflower (p.57)
*Russian Beet Salad (p.58)
*Chilled Asparagus in
     Dilled Mustard Sauce (p.69)
*Zucchini Julienne (p.74)

* Swiss Green Beans (p.59)
* Dill Pickle Potatoes (p.66)
* Italian Eggplant (p.65)
* Stuffed Cantaloupe (p.73)

* Vegetables Rémoulade (p.75)
* Very-Much-Marinated Potatoes (p.67)
* Eggless Egg Salad (w/ Tofu) (p.76)
* Sliced raw Jerusalem artichokes
     with lemon juice (p.80)

* Wilted Cucumbers (p.62)
* Roumanian Eggplant (p.63)
     [with some good crackers]
* Cold Stuffed Peppers
     with Herbed Cottage Cheese (p.72)
*Tomato Fans (p.73)

* Cold, Creamy Broccoli (p.56)
*Bulgarian Salad (p.60)
*Marinated Pasta Salad (p.70),
     garnished with arugula (p.80)
     and oil-cured imported olives

Breads

BREADS:
Table of Contents

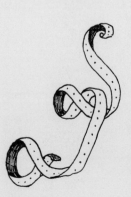

It is difficult to talk about bread-baking without lapsing into sentimentality. One is tempted to go on and on about how exhilarated and connected to the universe one feels, about how the kitchen atmosphere acquires sublime soulfulness, about how born-again bread-makers are magical, charismatic individuals ..... etc. However, it is not my place to promise you a transformed existence. What I do offer you is one with more bread recipes in it. The rest is what you make of it.

This chapter begins with an illustrated guide to yeasted bread-baking, which takes you step-by-step through that process from beginning to Bread. If you are new to this, and if yeast has been an intimidating unknown to you in the past, I hope this simplified presentation will encourage you to go ahead and try it. Following the illustrated guide is a Question & Answer article that gives more technical detail about the breadbaking process. (This article is an extra, rather than an essential. You could skip it, if you lack the patience or desire to read it, and you could still bake decent bread. On the other hand, you could read it, and enhance your understanding of (and sympathy for) such things as a day in the life of Yeast, or poetic analogies for the structure of Developed Gluten...)

After a batch of recipes for yeasted breads, you will find some for quick breads, muffins, and other treats. You may be surprised at how accessible and straightforward a process bread-baking can be. You might find yourself with a new hobby (not to mention a great-smelling kitchen).

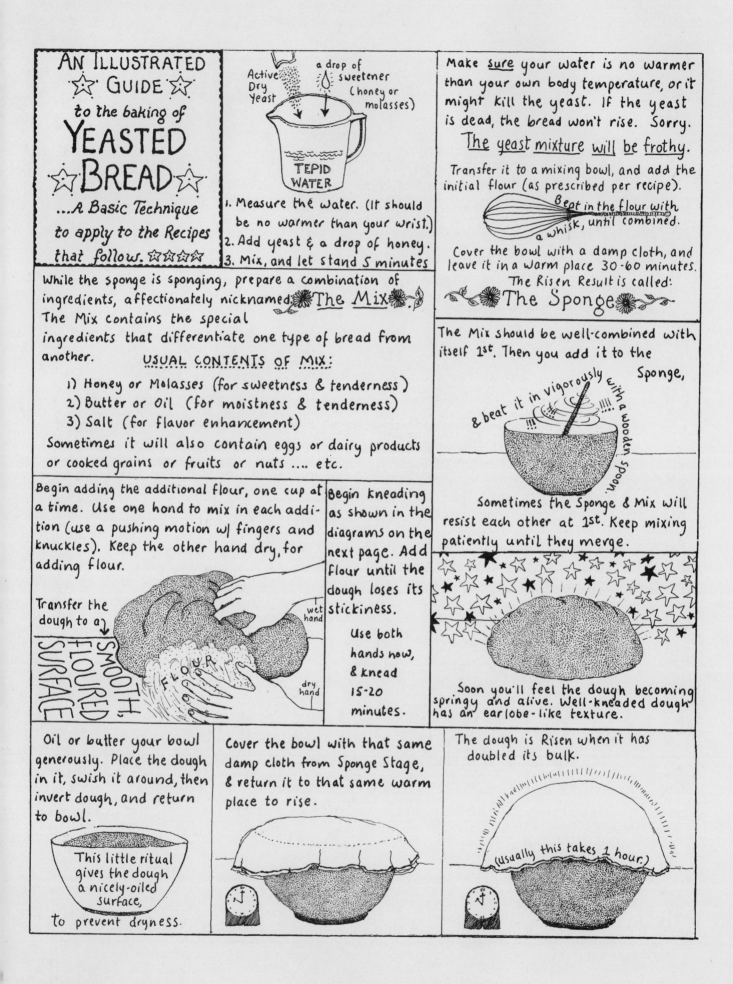

AN ILLUSTRATED ☆ GUIDE ☆
to the baking of
☆ YEASTED ☆
☆ BREAD ☆
...A Basic Technique to apply to the Recipes that follow. ☆☆☆☆

Active Dry Yeast

a drop of sweetener (honey or molasses)

TEPID WATER

1. Measure the water. (It should be no warmer than your wrist.)
2. Add yeast & a drop of honey.
3. Mix, and let stand 5 minutes

Make **sure** your water is no warmer than your own body temperature, or it might kill the yeast. If the yeast is dead, the bread won't rise. Sorry.

The **yeast** mixture **will** be **frothy**.

Transfer it to a mixing bowl, and add the initial flour (as prescribed per recipe).

Beat in the flour with a whisk, until combined.

Cover the bowl with a damp cloth, and leave it in a warm place 30-60 minutes. The Risen Result is called:
❀ The Sponge ❀

While the sponge is sponging, prepare a combination of ingredients, affectionately nicknamed ❀ **The Mix** ❀. The Mix contains the special ingredients that differentiate one type of bread from another.

USUAL CONTENTS OF MIX:

1) Honey or Molasses (for sweetness & tenderness)
2) Butter or Oil (for moistness & tenderness)
3) Salt (for flavor enhancement)

Sometimes it will also contain eggs or dairy products or cooked grains or fruits or nuts .... etc.

The Mix should be well-combined with itself 1st. Then you add it to the Sponge, & beat it in vigorously with a wooden spoon.

Sometimes the Sponge & Mix will resist each other at 1st. Keep mixing patiently until they merge.

Begin adding the additional flour, one cup at a time. Use one hand to mix in each addition (use a pushing motion w/ fingers and knuckles). Keep the other hand dry, for adding flour.

Transfer the dough to a SMOOTH, FLOURED SURFACE

wet hand

dry hand

Begin kneading as shown in the diagrams on the next page. Add flour until the dough loses its stickiness.

Use both hands now, & knead 15-20 minutes.

Soon you'll feel the dough becoming springy and alive. Well-kneaded dough has an earlobe-like texture.

Oil or butter your bowl generously. Place the dough in it, swish it around, then invert dough, and return to bowl.

This little ritual gives the dough a nicely-oiled surface, to prevent dryness.

Cover the bowl with that same damp cloth from Sponge Stage, & return it to that same warm place to rise.

The dough is Risen when it has doubled its bulk.

(usually this takes 1 hour.)

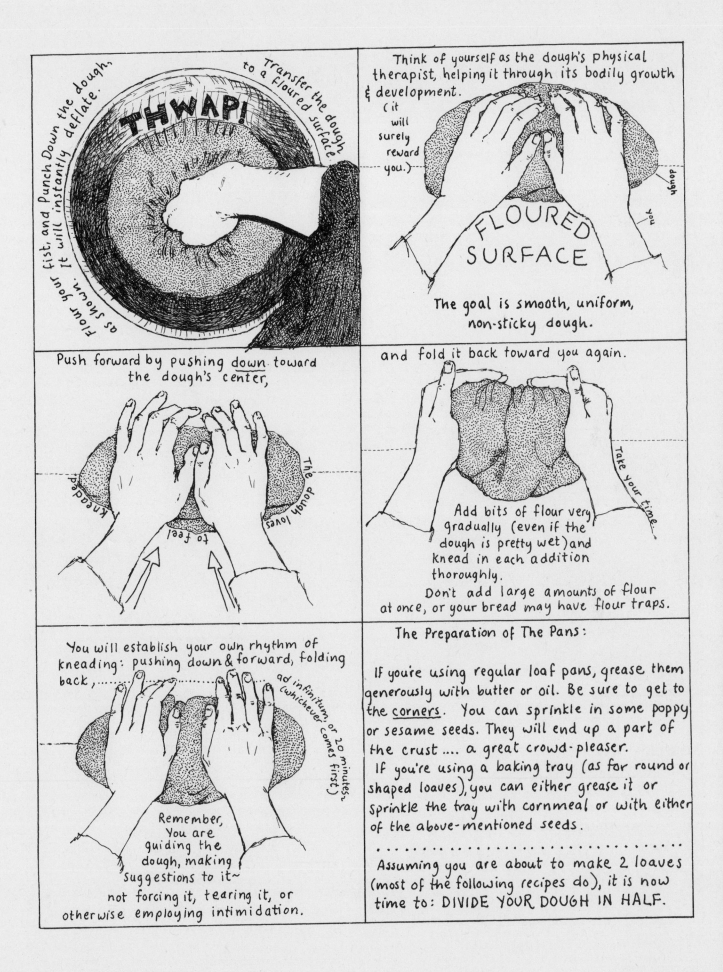

Flour your fist, and Punch Down the dough. It will instantly deflate.

Transfer the dough to a floured surface as shown.

THWAP!

Think of yourself as the dough's physical therapist, helping it through its bodily growth & development. (it will surely reward you.)

FLOURED SURFACE

dough

you

The goal is smooth, uniform, non-sticky dough.

Push forward by pushing down toward the dough's center,

The dough loves

to feel

kneaded

and fold it back toward you again.

Take your time

Add bits of flour very gradually (even if the dough is pretty wet) and knead in each addition thoroughly.

Don't add large amounts of flour at once, or your bread may have flour traps.

You will establish your own rhythm of kneading: pushing down & forward, folding back,........

ad infinitum, or 20 minutes (whichever comes first)

Remember, You are guiding the dough, making suggestions to it~ not forcing it, tearing it, or otherwise employing intimidation.

The Preparation of The Pans:

If you're using regular loaf pans, grease them generously with butter or oil. Be sure to get to the corners. You can sprinkle in some poppy or sesame seeds. They will end up a part of the crust .... a great crowd-pleaser.

If you're using a baking tray (as for round or shaped loaves), you can either grease it or sprinkle the tray with cornmeal or with either of the above-mentioned seeds.

Assuming you are about to make 2 loaves (most of the following recipes do), it is now time to: DIVIDE YOUR DOUGH IN HALF.

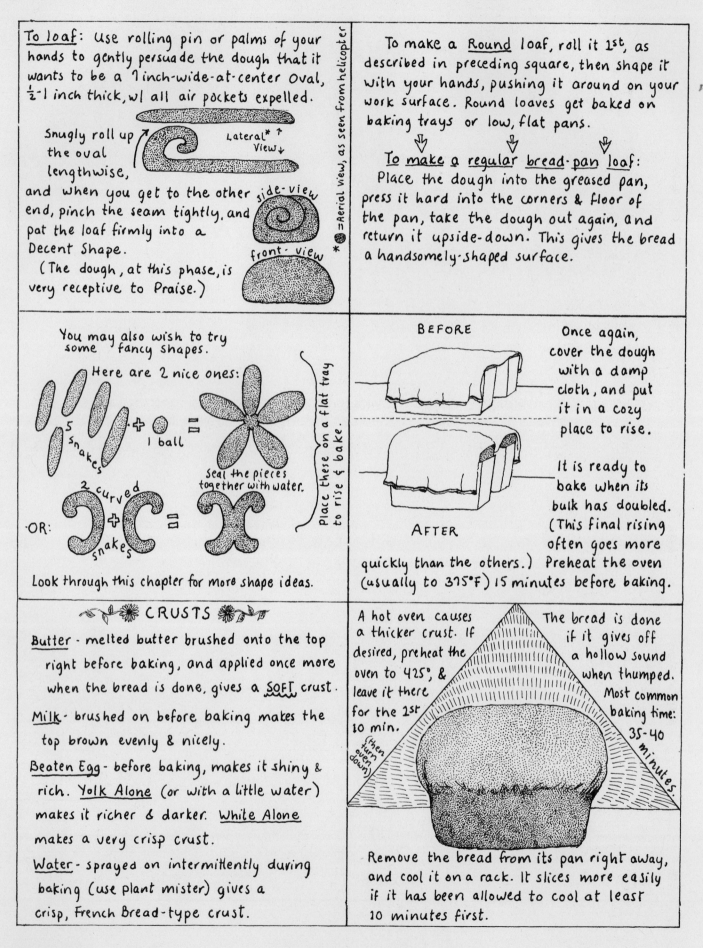

To loaf: Use rolling pin or palms of your hands to gently persuade the dough that it wants to be a 7 inch-wide-at-center Oval, ½-1 inch thick, w/ all air pockets expelled.

Snugly roll up the oval lengthwise,

and when you get to the other end, pinch the seam tightly, and pat the loaf firmly into a Decent Shape.

(The dough, at this phase, is very receptive to Praise.)

Lateral* View

side-view

front-view

* =Aerial view, as seen from helicopter

To make a <u>Round</u> loaf, roll it 1st, as described in preceding square, then shape it with your hands, pushing it around on your work surface. Round loaves get baked on baking trays or low, flat pans.

<u>To make a regular bread-pan loaf:</u>
Place the dough into the greased pan, press it hard into the corners & floor of the pan, take the dough out again, and return it upside-down. This gives the bread a handsomely-shaped surface.

You may also wish to try some fancy shapes. Here are 2 nice ones:

5 snakes + 1 ball =

Seal the pieces together with water.

·OR: 2 curved snakes + =

Place these on a flat tray to rise & bake.

Look through this chapter for more shape ideas.

BEFORE

AFTER

Once again, cover the dough with a damp cloth, and put it in a cozy place to rise.

It is ready to bake when its bulk has doubled. (This final rising often goes more quickly than the others.) Preheat the oven (usually to 375°F) 15 minutes before baking.

🌼 CRUSTS 🌸

<u>Butter</u> - melted butter brushed onto the top right before baking, and applied once more when the bread is done, gives a <u>SOFT</u> crust.

<u>Milk</u> - brushed on before baking makes the top brown evenly & nicely.

<u>Beaten Egg</u> - before baking, makes it shiny & rich. <u>Yolk Alone</u> (or with a little water) makes it richer & darker. <u>White Alone</u> makes a very crisp crust.

<u>Water</u> - sprayed on intermittently during baking (use plant mister) gives a crisp, French Bread-type crust.

A hot oven causes a thicker crust. If desired, preheat the oven to 425°, & leave it there for the 1st 10 min. (then turn oven down)

The bread is done if it gives off a hollow sound when thumped. Most common baking time: 35-40 minutes.

Remove the bread from its pan right away, and cool it on a rack. It slices more easily if it has been allowed to cool at least 10 minutes first.

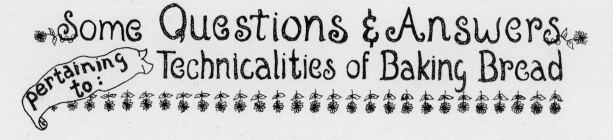

Some Questions & Answers
pertaining to: Technicalities of Baking Bread

What are the differences between yeasted and quick breads?

❀ *Technically~* Quick breads are leavened <u>chemically</u>, with either or both baking powder and soda. Yeasted breads are leavened <u>biologically</u> by yeast, a live substance. Yeasted rising depends on the activation and nurturing of the yeast; therefore, it takes more time than chemical rising, which occurs during baking only. In yeasted breads the major rising occurs <u>before</u> the dough bakes, and the oven heat mostly just finalizes the rising that has already taken place.

❀ *Texturally~* The texture of quick bread is cakey and crumbly. Yeasted bread is breadier, chewier, more durable. These differences are due to the greater development of gluten in the yeasted dough.

❀ *Nutritionally~* Since neither baking soda nor baking powder has any nutritional value, and active dry yeast (not to be confused with Brewer's or nutritional yeast!) has only a trace, the nutritional value of bread depends on other ingredients (grains, eggs, milk, etc.).

What is the yeast actually doing in there?

❀ It is coming to life from a dry, dormant state. This happens when it first contacts moisture (when you add the yeast to the lukewarm water).
As the yeast awakens, it feels a surge of Life Impulse. It wants to grow, and gets hungry for starches and sugar. This is your cue to add sweetener and flour. The yeast is not shy. It partakes greedily.

❀ As the yeast eats, it grows. It also gives off waste products, one of which is carbon dioxide, a gas which accumulates in the dough, causing it to expand. This is the <u>RISING</u>.

❀ Unfortunately, the yeast must be forced to cash in its chips at a certain point, otherwise the dough might continue to expand forever and take over the universe. Yeast prefers human body temperature and will survive refrigeration, but it can't survive baking temperature. After one final, noble gesture of expansion, it dies in the heat of the oven. The loaf retains its shape because the developed gluten holds it up.

What is gluten, anyway?

❀ Gluten is a group of proteins in the wheat kernel. It remains, in whole wheat and in white flours alike, after the wheat is ground into flour.

What is gluten "development", and what has it to do with kneading?

🌼 When the flour comes into contact with moisture and agitation, the gluten becomes activated, and its physical form alters. Think of the pre-activated gluten as wool, freshly-shorn from its sheep. It has a random form which gets converted into strands when it is spun, and greatly rearranged when it is finally woven or knitted. The formal structure is changed (it is now a sweater instead of a sheepsuit), but its substance is unchanged (it is still wool). Spinning and weaving are analogous to the mixing and kneading of yeasted dough. Kneading changes random gluten blobs into elongated, interlocking strands. This woven gluten serves as a basket to house the carbon dioxide as it escapes from the yeast. So the yeast _causes_ the rising, and the gluten _contains_ the risenness.

Why is a "sponge", and not the complete dough, put up for the first rise?

🌼 A sponge is advantageous for whole-grained breads and/or breads with dense ingredients. The major reasons for this are:

🌼   → It gives the yeast and gluten a head-start on their activity by allowing them a first rise free from obstruction by heavier materials. (The "sponge" is just yeast, water, a drop of sweetener, and about half the total flour.)

🌼   → Extra ingredients (the Mix and the additional flour), which are the densest part of the dough, are more easily incorporated into a risen sponge than they are combined with all the other ingredients at the outset.

🌼   → Sponge-method bread can be more tender, as the grain of the flour gets more softening time, with a greater proportion of available liquid (sponge stage). Also, the gluten has time for a more gradual development.

🌼 There does exist a straight-dough method, which combines all the ingredients before the first rising. It has one less rising period than the sponge method, so it takes less time. (This straight-dough method is fine for white breads without additional, rich ingredients.)

What does punching-down accomplish?

🌼 It interrupts the rising immediately. If the rising isn't stopped in time, the elastic bands of gluten will break (like a rubber band stretched to its limit), and broken gluten fibers can't be reunited. The result will be a coarse loaf.

Punching-down also expels waste products given off into the dough by the growing yeast. An accumulation of these could toxify the dough, giving it a sour flavor.

Can caked yeast be substituted for active dry yeast?

🌼 Yes. One commercially-packaged unit of one equals ditto of the other (= 1 Tablespoon).

Why do some yeasted doughs work with no kneading?

🌼 They simply end up with less gluten development, and the difference is textural. Bready breads are those which have been kneaded and slowly risen. Cakey breads result from less kneading and rising.

🌼 There is no difference in the protein value of more-or-less developed gluten.

How do the available wheat flours differ?

🌼 _Whole Wheat "Bread" Flour_ has a higher gluten percentage than other whole wheat flours; it is sometimes called "high protein" flour. The gluten content has to do with the type of wheat involved.

🌼 _Whole Wheat "Pastry" Flour_ is more finely-milled and lower in gluten than "bread" flour. The lower gluten content makes it a better choice for flaky, light results~ pie crusts, cookies, cakes, pancakes~ in short, most baked goods other than bread. (Those of you who shop in supermarkets, and not in natural foods stores, can ignore these fine points, and use commercially-milled "Whole Wheat Flour" across the board.)

🌼 _Bleached ≡vs≡ Unbleached White Flour_: The major complaint against bleached white flour is that it contains residues from bromine and chlorine (its chemical bleaching agents). Unbleached is less refined and has a much fresher taste.

Can flour get stale? What is a good storage method?

🌼 All flours can age, acquiring a stale flavor. Whole-grain flours have oil in them, so they can get rancid. You can tell by smelling it. Buy smaller quantities more frequently, for insurance. 🌼 Store whole-grain flours in a cool, dry place, such as the Refrigerator. The humble brown paper bag, believe it or not, is one of the best flour-storage containers. It is slightly porous, and keeps the flour fresh by allowing it to breathe. Wrap the paper bag loosely in a plastic bag, to keep it dry. 🌼 Or, store flour in glass jars whose tin lids have been ever-so-infinitesimally punctured here and there (again, for respiratory purposes).

What are the best bread pans made of?

🌼 ...Heavy, dark, tinned steel. Pyrex is also good, but glass holds heat more efficiently than other materials, so set your oven 25°F _lower_ for glass pans. Thin, lightweight metal pans (like aluminum) can cause scorched outsides and underbaked insides, so try to avoid them. Cast-iron cookware works well. (Use your frying pan for round loaves, for a homey effect.)

Where is the best place for dough to rise? What should be done if the dough gets too hot during rising?

❀ The best rising temperature is human body temperature. Remember, you are dealing with a living organism that needs comfort to grow. With a gas stove, pick a spot near the pilot light. With an electric stove, turn the oven to "warm" for a few minutes, turn it off, and leave the dough in there to rise. Retain heat by placing a kettleful of just-boiled water in the oven, near the dough. If a spot is too hot to touch, chances are it will disturb the dough and could possibly even kill the yeast. If there is any doubt, insulate the bowl of dough by first placing it in a pan of warm water. Put the whole pan-of-water-with-bowl-of-dough-in-it in the rising spot.

The symptoms of too much heat are: too quick a rise (say, if it doubles its bulk in 5 minutes) and/or a partially cooked or crusted bottom. Remedy: punch down the dough immediately, remove it from the bowl, cut away the crust, and knead for several minutes. Put it up to rise again in a cooler spot. It will probably recover (if the yeast hasn't died). It has a chipper and forgiving disposition.

Which ingredients help the dough rise? Which ones slow it down?

D O U G H · H E L P E R S

Eggs are agents to rising, especially when beaten first. They also make the bread richer and higher in protein. A large egg equals a scant quarter cup of liquid, and can be substituted in most recipes.

<u>The <u>correct</u> <u>amount</u> <u>of</u> <u>sweetening</u></u> is also an agent to rising, as it feeds the yeast. Too much sweetener, however, retards rising (the yeast overeats and gets lazy). This is why, in sweeter breads and coffeecakes, a larger proportion of yeast is used: it accommodates the extra sugar.

<u>Warmth</u> is an agent to rising, too. The warmer your kitchen, the faster your dough will rise. You also contribute your own warmth through your hands as you knead.

D O U G H · R E T A R D E R S

<u>Salt</u> is a retarder, because it interferes metabolically with the yeast.

<u>Oil</u> (or butter) is a retarder, because it lubricates the strands of gluten, making it more difficult for them to adhere together.

Although they are retarders, salt and oil (or butter) are necessary, respectively, for flavor and tenderness. To prevent their being a hindrance, exclude them from the sponge stage, and add them later, as part of the Mix. This gives the sponge an unencumbered head-start rise by itself, before other things get added.

<u>Cold</u> is a retarder. If your kitchen is chilly, the rise will take longer.

Can yeasted dough be refrigerated overnight?

❀ Yes. The rising will still occur, but it will take 2-3 times longer. If you refrigerate it all night, oil the dough's top surface thoroughly, and place it in a larger-than-itself bowl. Seal the bowl with plastic wrap. Dough can be refrigerated like this for up to 2 days, if it is periodically punched down and the surface re-oiled. Unbaked loaves can also be refrigerated while rising. Be sure they are in sealed plastic bags which leave them room to expand. (If you have a choice between refrigerating at the bowl-of-dough or the already-loaved stage, choose the latter. It works better.)

Is it possible to over- or under-knead?

❀ Old cookbooks used to recommend that each kneading session last 45 minutes to an hour, at least. So if you are kneading by hand, don't worry about over-kneading.

❀ However, if you use a mixer with a dough hook attachment, you _can_ overknead, causing overdeveloped gluten and a toughened loaf. With a dough hook, use a low speed and watch it carefully. The dough is amply kneaded when it acquires the consistency of your earlobe.

❀ It is definitely possible to under-knead. The resulting loaf could easily be mistaken for a brick. Average kneading time, if you are an average sort of person, is 15 to 20 minutes of vigorous activity. Try the earlobe test if you are unsure.

Why do bread recipes often have indefinite instructions (about final amounts of flour, rising time, baking time, etc.)?

❀ There are many variables in your kitchen environment: humidity, temperature, etc., _and_ in your ingredients (age of yeast, type of flour, etc.), which affect the dough's characteristics. For example, older yeast takes longer to grow, dryer weather decreases the amount of flour the dough can absorb, pans of different materials absorb heat at different rates...... and so forth. Altitude is also a factor (see below). Good bread bakers come to know by feel. This comes naturally with practice, it really does.

How should one accommodate altitude in yeasted baking?

❀ The rising goes more quickly the higher you are. A too-quick rise can deprive the yeast and gluten of their full maturation time. Remedies: Use less yeast and/or refrigerate it during some of the rising. Try to give it extra rising periods of shorter durations. Example: do two 1-hour rises instead of one 2-hour one (punch it down in between). These tricks will help your yeast and gluten get a chance to fully develop.

A BASIC BREAD RECIPE

...."Your regular, smooth loaf."

This is a sample recipe for a plain loaf of part-white, part-whole wheat bread. It's a good one to start with if bread-baking is new to you. Or, if you're already comfortable with the craft, but you'd like to experiment and improvise for the first time, this is a good one to use as a sturdy backbone for your increasingly daring and exotic Additions.

ONE MORE GENERAL COMMENT on the organization of this bread chapter: Since the Illustrated Guide (a few pages ago) goes into the techniques of yeasted bread-baking in great detail, all of the following yeasted bread recipes will rely on your having read the Guide – to the point of familiarity – beforehand. Okay? This will avoid repetition, thus avoiding repetition. ALSO: There will not be any "preparation time" notices posted at the tops of the yeasted bread recipes. It is assumed you have no deadline, and were planning, anyway, to spend a chunk of time puttering around at home, intermittently playing with dough.

. . . .

This yields 2 loaves.

The Sponge: 2 pkg. (2 Tbs.) active, dry yeast
                 1½ cups wrist-temperature water
                 a drop of honey or molasses
                 1 cup whole wheat flour
                 1 cup unbleached white flour

1) Sprinkle the yeast into the water. Add the sweetener, and let it stand 5 minutes.
2) Beat in the flour, cover with a towel, and let rise 30-60 minutes. While it rises, prepare:

The Mix: ¼ cup melted butter   ⎫ Beat together. Add to risen
              ⅓ cup honey or molasses   ⎬ sponge, and beat 100 strokes
              2 tsp. salt   ⎭ with a wooden spoon.

<u>Additional Flour</u>: approximately 2 more cups of whole wheat
PLUS approximately 2 more cups unbleached white

1) Add the flour, about ½ cup at a time, graduating from wooden spoon to hand-mixing, as the dough thickens. When all the flour is added, turn out the dough onto a floured surface, and...

2) Knead it a good 15-20 minutes. Add small amounts of extra flour if the dough persists in stickiness.

3) Return the kneaded dough to an oiled bowl, roll it around in the bowl so that it gets all nicely oiled, and let it rise, covered with a towel, until its bulk has doubled. (about an hour)

4) Punch down the risen dough, turn it out onto a floured surface, and knead it another 15-20 minutes (again, add bits of flour only if necessary).

5) Form your desired loaves, place them in or on pans or trays (if you use pans, butter them well!), cover with towel, and let rise until doubled in bulk one more time. Meanwhile, preheat the oven to 375°F.

6) Bake 30-40 minutes, or until the loaves sound hollow when tapped. If you're using bread pans, remove the loaves right away, so the crust can crispen (not necessary with trays). → If you can restrain yourself from pouncing upon the bread with eager knife and mouth for about 10 minutes, you will find that this cooling-off period will allow it to slice more easily.

↓ ↓ ↓ ↓ ↓ ↓ ↓ ↓ ↓ ↓ ↓ ↓ ↓ ↙

→ OPTIONAL ADDITIONS (and ↞
→ good ones to begin with if you are ↞
→ a neophyte Improviser): ↞

An Egg. . . . . Beaten in w/ Mix. Reduce water by ¼ cup
Wheat Germ . . . . Replace up to 1 cup of "additional flour"
Seeds . . . . Sesame ^{and}⁄_{or} Sunflower ^{and}⁄_{or} Poppy
Chopped Dried Fruits . . . . . . ⎫
Chopped Nuts . . . . ⎬ Add with Mix
Cooked Grains (up to 1 cup) . . ⎭

150%
Whole Wheat
Bread

2 Loaves

Review the Method:
pp. 86-88.

The Sponge:
2 pkg. (2 Tbs.) active dry yeast
1 cup lukewarm water
a drop of molasses
2 cups whole wheat flour

*Dissolve yeast in water. Add molasses; let stand 5 minutes.
*Beat in flour. Cover, and let rise 30-60 minutes.

The Mix:
1 cup (raw) bulghur or cracked wheat
1 cup boiling water
2 tsp. salt
$\frac{1}{4}$ cup sweet butter
$\frac{1}{4}$ cup molasses
$\frac{1}{2}$ cup golden, seedless raisins

*Combine all ingredients. Let stand 30 minutes covered, and 30 minutes uncovered.
*Beat mix into risen sponge.

Flour: About 3-4 additional cups of whole wheat, & continue with the usual procedure.

Recommended Crust: Melted butter, brushed on just before, and after, baking.

Baking Temperature & Timing: 375°F ≡ 30-40 minutes.

. . . .

200% Whole Wheat Bread
...nice & chewy...

Follow the above recipe, adding the below recipe to the Mix.

Cook: 1 cup (raw) wheat berries in 3 cups of water until tender. Sometimes they take 1-2 hours to cook fully, so do this in advance. Watch the water level as they cook (they absorb a lot, and might need extra), and drain them well when they're done.

CHALLAH

2 pkg. (2 Tbs.) active, dry yeast
1 cup lukewarm water

> Dissolve the yeast in the water. Let stand 5 minutes.

2 Tbs. honey
¼ cup soft butter
4 large eggs, beaten
1 Tbs. salt
6-8 cups unbleached white flour

> Set aside about 3 Tbs. of the beaten egg (to be used for the crust).
>
> Beat the honey, butter, remaining eggs, salt and about 2 cups of flour into the yeast mixture. Gradually mix in remaining flour.

Turn the dough out onto a floured surface, and knead 15-20 minutes, until smooth, uniform, and unsticky. Place the kneaded dough in a large, buttered bowl, cover with a damp towel, and let rise in a warm place until doubled in bulk. Punch down the risen dough, and return it to the floured surface. Knead 5 minutes, and divide into thirds.

Knead each third 5-10 minutes, gradually transforming it into a 1½-inch-diameter snake. Line the 3 snakes up, and let them rest 10 minutes.

Here is a braiding diagram. It's easiest to begin from the middle and work toward one end, then invert and braid toward the other end. Press the ends together very firmly; seal them with a little water.

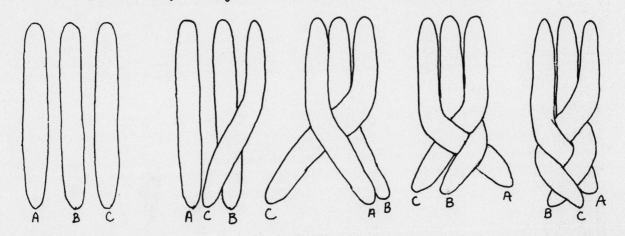

Place the braided challah on a large tray, which has been sprinkled with sesame seeds. Let it rise until doubled. Just before baking, brush it with the left over beaten egg, and sprinkle with sesames & poppies. Bake at 375°F, 30-40 minutes.

Sesame-Lemon Bread

2 LOAVES

SPONGE:

2 pkg. (2 Tbs.) dry yeast
1 cup lukewarm water
a drop of honey
2 cups unbleached white flour

MIX:

¼ cup tahini
¼ cup honey
½ cup hot water
¼ cup fresh lemon juice
2 tsp. salt

ADDITIONAL: ½ cup toasted sesame seeds
3 cups (approx.) more flour (half whole wheat)

After the Usual Fashion (method, pp. 86-88):

1) Make Sponge in usual fashion. Let rise.

2) Beat together mix members, and beat mix into sponge in usual fashion.

3) Knead in additional flour and sesame seeds. Proceed in usual fashion:
Rise → Punch → Knead → Loaf → Rise → Bake → Eat.

Bake in 375°F oven . . . . 30-40 minutes.

Cashew-Barley Bread

2 LOAVES

2 cups raw pearl barley

1½ cups ground cashews

SPONGE {
1 cup lukewarm water } dissolved together
2 pkg. (2 Tbs.) dry yeast
a drop of honey
2 cups unbleached white flour
}

MIX {
1 cup firm yogurt
3 Tbs. honey
1 Tbs. Chinese sesame oil
2 tsp. salt
}

Additional Flour: approximately 2 cups unbleached white flour

1) In a heavy skillet dry-roast the barley over low heat, stirring constantly, until the barley is evenly and lightly browned. Then grind it, in a blender or food processor fitted with steel blade, to a coarse flour.

2) Toast the cashews until lightly browned.

3) Combine the sponge ingredients. Cover; let rise 45-60 minutes.

4) Combine the mix ingredients. Add these to the risen sponge, along with the barley flour and ground cashews. Beat 100 strokes with a wooden spoon. Knead in additional flour. Let rise until doubled in bulk. Continue with usual procedure (pp. 86-88). Recommended: round loaves, baked on lightly-greased trays.

SUNFLOWER-MILLET BREAD

2 Loaves.
(Review the method:
pp. 86-88.)

I. The Sponge:

2 pkg. (2 Tbs.) dry yeast

1 cup lukewarm water

a drop of honey

2 cups unbleached white flour

II. The Mix:

$1\frac{1}{2}$ cups water

1 cup raw millet

$2\frac{1}{2}$ tsp. salt

$\frac{1}{4}$ cup butter

3 Tbs. honey

III. Furthermore:

1 cup sunflower seeds (increase, if desired)

1 cup unbleached white flour

Approximately 3 cups whole wheat flour

Recommended Crust: melted butter

1) Prepare sponge as per usual. Let rise 30-60 minutes.

2) Prepare mix: Bring the water to a boil in a medium-sized saucepan. Add the millet, cover, and turn heat to low. Cook 15 minutes, or until all water is absorbed. Uncover the millet, and fluff it with a fork (this lets extra steam escape, preventing overcookedness). Add remaining ingredients, and mix well. Let it cool to room temperature before adding it to the sponge.

3) Knead in sunflower seeds and additional flour. Carry on as usual with kneading, rising, punching, shaping, etc.
..... Bake the risen loaves at 375°F for 30-40 minutes.

Squash Bread

Golden & Sweet

You will need
2½ cups of mashed,
cooked acorn or
butternut squash.
Bake the squash

2 large loaves.

in advance: split them lengthwise, remove seeds, and place face-down on a buttered tray. Bake at 350°F until very soft. Then cool, and scoop out the insides. (I can't tell you exactly how much squash yields 2½ cups, because of enormous squash-size fluctuations~ and some have more seeds per pound, etc. Better to make a little extra, and to use it in casseroles or soups or whatever.)

THE SPONGE:
usual procedure (pp. 86-88)
- 2 pkg. (2 Tbs.) active dry yeast
- 1½ cups lukewarm water
- 2 cups unbleached white flour
- 1 cup whole wheat flour
- a drop of molasses

THE MIX:
Combine, as per usual (pp. 86-88)
- 2½ cups well-mashed squash
- 3 Tbs. molasses
- ¼ cup melted butter
- 2 tsp. salt
- 1 tsp. cinnamon
- ½ tsp. cloves

ADDITIONALLY:
knead, etc.
- approximately 3 more cups unbleached white flour
- and 5 more cups whole wheat flour

Potato Bread

...is similar to Squash Bread,
just adjust the Mix as follows:

- Mashed Potatoes, instead of squash
- ½ cup minced chives, instead of cinnamon & cloves
- Honey, instead of molasses.

(¼ cup firm yogurt : a purely optional addition)

Vegetable-Flecked Bread

Review
The Method
(pp. 86-88)

☆ ☆ ☆ ☆ ☆ ☆ ☆ ☆ ☆ ☆ ☆ ☆ ☆ ☆   2 Loaves

SPONGE: 2 pkg. (2 Tbs.) active dry yeast   drop of honey } Combine.
         1 cup lukewarm water   2 cups white flour } Let rise ½-1 hour.

MIX:

☆A 1 packed cup coarsely-grated zucchini } Salt lightly. Let stand in colander 15
     1 packed cup coarsely-grated carrot } minutes. Squeeze out excess moisture.

☆B ¾ cup minced red onion
     1 clove crushed garlic
     ½ cup sunflower seeds } Sauté together lightly about 5 minutes,
     ½ cup sesame seeds } or until onions are soft.
     4 Tbs. butter

☆C ¾ cup minced bell pepper   3 Tbs. honey } Combine all of these, to-
     2 tsp. salt   2 Tbs. lemon juice } gether with all of ☆A &
     ¼ cup minced parsley   1 cup bean sprouts } ☆B. Mix well, and beat into
     freshly-ground black pepper   risen sponge.

FLOUR: 5 cups whole wheat flour } knead in at Mix Stage. } THIS RECIPE TAKES
           1-2 cups white flour } knead in at Loaf Stage. } LOTS OF KNEADING.

→ This is a moist bread, which will want to bake about 40-50 minutes.

❋ ❋ ❋ ❋ ❋ # Carob Pumpernickel ❋ ❋ ❋ ❋ ❋

(Review the Method,
pp. 86-88)   2 Loaves

☽ ☽ ☽ ☽ ☽ ☽ ☽ ☽ ☽ ☽ ☽ ☽ ☽

I. SPONGE:

2 pkg. (2 Tbs.) active dry yeast
1 cup lukewarm water
a drop of Molasses } (as usual)
2 cups whole wheat flour

II. MIX:

½ cup carob powder
¼ cup Postum or Pero } Make a
1 cup hot water } uniform paste.
2 Tbs. molasses } (a blender does
3 Tbs. soft butter } this well.)
2 tsp. salt

III. FLOUR: 3 cups rye flour
            2 more cups whole wheat } This should be enough. But if you need extra,
                                     add more whole wheat, rather than rye.

IV. LOAVES: Round pumpernickels are nice ~ bake them on Corn Mealed trays.

V. CRUST: Egg Yolk, for authentic pumpernickelness, and sublime chewiness.

CAROB~SWIRL BREAD

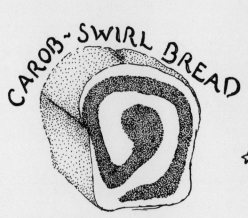

☆This bread requires 2 doughs: a dark one and a light one.

☆The sponges are identical, but the Mixes are different.

SPONGES: Take 2 separate bowls, and into <u>each</u> of them put:
- 1 pkg. (1 Tbs.) active dry yeast
- ½ cup lukewarm water
- a drop of honey
- 1½ cups unbleached white flour

~ and follow the usual Sponge routine (pp. 86-88)

MIX I:
Blend to a smooth paste
- ½ cup carob powder
- 1 cup hot water
- 1 Tbs. molasses
- 1 Tbs. butter
- 1 tsp. salt

MIX II:
- 1⅓ cups milk
- 1 Tbs. honey
- 2 Tbs. melted butter
- 1 tsp. salt

Beat together.

~ add Mixes to Sponges in the Usual Way (pp. 86-88)

ADDITIONAL FLOUR: about 4½ cups whole wheat to <u>each</u> dough.

Okay, so now you have 2 fully-kneaded doughs, one dark and one light. You are ready to Loaf.... so the 1st thing you do is divide each dough in half. Set aside one dark and one light half, and with the other set,

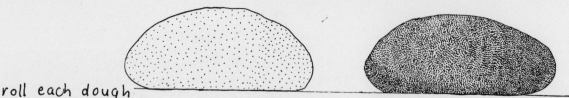

roll each dough with a rolling pin into a neat oval, about ½-inch thick. Try to get both dark and light ovals to the same dimensions, then brush the light one with water, and place the dark one on top. Roll them up together tightly, form a loaf, and arrange it in a buttered loaf pan. Repeat with the other half of the dough, for a 2nd loaf. Now, let the loaves rise.... etc. (Everything proceeds As Per Usual from here.)

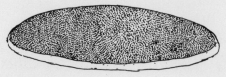

❖ Dark Swedish Rye ❖ .... 2 Loaves ❤ ❤

(METHOD·IN·DETAIL: PP. 86·88)

1) <u>Sponge</u>: 2 pkg. (2 Tbs.) active dry yeast   3/4 cup orange juice
            ¼ cup lukewarm water   1 cup whole wheat flour
            drop of molasses   1 cup rye flour

-Dissolve the yeast in the water, with the molasses droplet, first. Let stand 5 min.
-Beat in juice and flours.   Let rise 30·60 minutes.

2) <u>Mix</u>:   ½ cup orange juice   ¼ cup molasses
         2 tsp. salt   ½ cup buttermilk
         ¼ cup melted butter . . . . 2 tsp. anise or caraway seeds
                        Soak seeds in butter for
                     10 minutes first.
           Then mix everything, and beat into risen sponge.

3) <u>In Addition</u>:   2 cups each: Rye & whole wheat flour
4) <u>And Later</u>: An Egg Yolk Crust (save the white for a Soufflé....) on Round
     ▲ Loaves on Corn Meal-dusted trays. ▲

❖ Garbanzo-Cheese Bread ❖ .... <u>1</u> Loaf ❤ ❤

(METHOD·IN·DETAIL: PP. 86·88)

This recipe calls for 1½ cups cooked garbanzo beans (also known as Chick Peas). Soak
3/4 cup of them (raw) for 3-6 hours. Then cook them in water until tender.
Drain well, and proceed. (You might do well, as long as you're at it, to cook
extra garbanzos, to have them around for salads.)

1) <u>Sponge</u>: 1 pkg. (1 Tbs.) active dry yeast   2 cups unbleached white flour
          1 cup lukewarm water   1 cup whole wheat flour
          1 drop (or 2) of honey

2) <u>Mix</u>:   1½ cups cooked garbanzo beans   1¼ tsp. salt
   more, ⅓ cup grated sharp cheddar   1½ tsp. honey
  to taste 1 tsp. ground cumin   1 Tbs. olive oil

3) <u>Flour</u>: approximately 1½ cups more whole wheat flour

4) <u>Recommended</u> <u>Crust</u>: Olive Oil, brushed on before and after, baking.

🌸 Freshly-Fruited Bread 🌸

2 Loaves

Tart & Refreshing

SPONGE: 2 pkg. (2 Tbs.) active dry yeast   ²/₃ cup orange juice

⅓ cup luke warm water   2 cups unbleached white flour

a drop of honey

~Dissolve yeast and honey in water 1st. Then Add juice and flour. Beat, and let rise 30-60 minutes.

MIX: 1 cup finely-minced raw cranberries   2 tsp. salt

1 large, ripe banana, mashed   3 Tbs. soft butter

1 packed cup grated apple   4 Tbs. honey

½ tsp each: orange & lemon rind

Follow the procedure described on pp. 86-88.

FLOUR: 3 additional cups <u>each</u> - white and whole wheat flours

RECOMMENDED CRUST: Milk, brushed on before and during baking.

Date & Wheat Germ Bread

2 Loaves

SPONGE: 2 pkg. (2 Tbs.) active dry yeast   1 drop honey or molasses

1 cup lukewarm water   2 cups unbleached white flour

Follow the procedure described on pp. 86-88.

MIX: ½ lb. (approximately 1½ packed cups) chopped, pitted dates

2 cups boiling water   2 tsp. salt

3 Tbs. butter   1 cup raw wheat germ

~ Combine all mix ingredients. Let stand, uncovered, 30-45 minutes.

FLOUR: approximately 3½ cups <u>each</u>: white and whole wheat

RECOMMENDED CRUST: Melted butter, brushed on before and after baking.

Some Shapes for Rolls

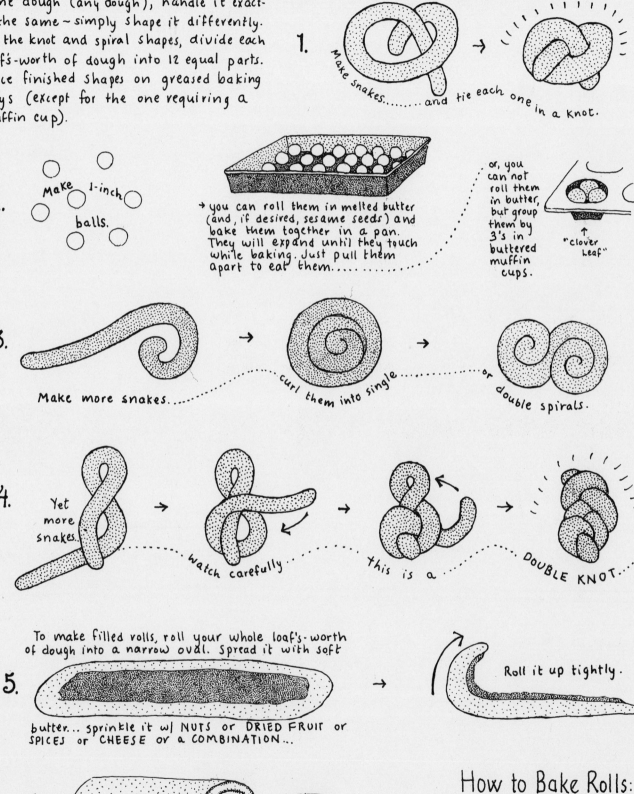

To make rolls instead of loaves: use the same dough (any dough), handle it exactly the same ~ simply shape it differently. For the knot and spiral shapes, divide each loaf's-worth of dough into 12 equal parts. Place finished shapes on greased baking trays (except for the one requiring a muffin cup).

1. Make snakes......... and tie each one in a knot.

2. Make 1-inch balls.

→ you can roll them in melted butter (and, if desired, sesame seeds) and bake them together in a pan. They will expand until they touch while baking. Just pull them apart to eat them.........

or, you can not roll them in butter, but group them by 3's in buttered muffin cups.

↑ "clover leaf"

3. Make more snakes......... curl them into single......... or double spirals.

4. Yet more snakes .... watch carefully .... this is a .... DOUBLE KNOT.........

5. To make filled rolls, roll your whole loaf's-worth of dough into a narrow oval. Spread it with soft butter... sprinkle it w/ NUTS or DRIED FRUIT or SPICES or CHEESE or a COMBINATION...

Roll it up tightly.

↳ Slice it, let it rise, and bake it.

How to Bake Rolls:
15-20 minutes

at 425°F

Quick Breads

also known as "Batter Breads"

Sweet Whole Wheat-Nut Bread

About 40 minutes to prepare.
About 50 minutes to bake.

Preheat oven to 350°F.
Butter a large loaf pan.

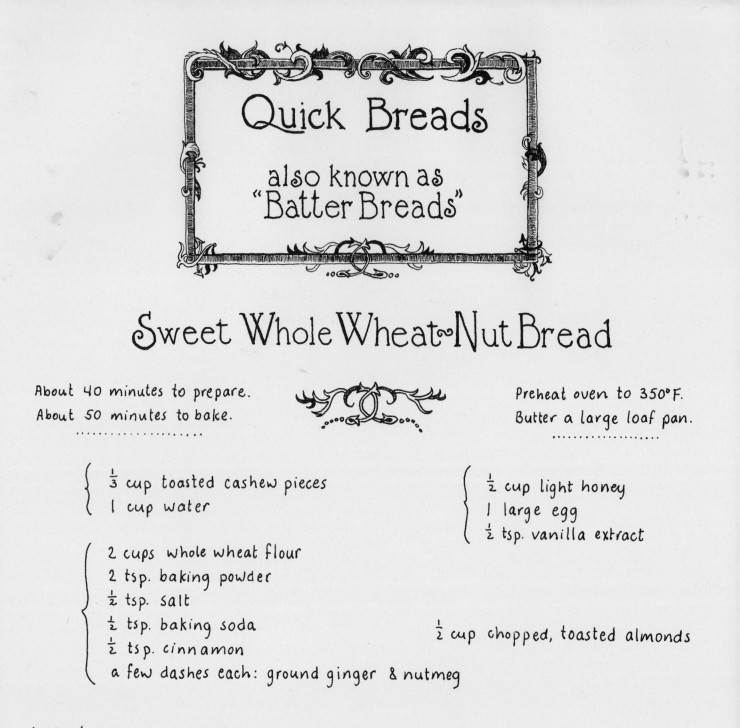

$\frac{1}{3}$ cup toasted cashew pieces
1 cup water

$\frac{1}{2}$ cup light honey
1 large egg
$\frac{1}{2}$ tsp. vanilla extract

2 cups whole wheat flour
2 tsp. baking powder
$\frac{1}{2}$ tsp. salt
$\frac{1}{2}$ tsp. baking soda
$\frac{1}{2}$ tsp. cinnamon
a few dashes each: ground ginger & nutmeg

$\frac{1}{2}$ cup chopped, toasted almonds

1) Purée together the cashews and water, until you have a smooth cashew milk.

2) Beat the honey at high speed for about 5 minutes (until opaque, fluffy and white).
Add the egg and vanilla, and beat well - a few minutes more.

3) Sift together the dry ingredients.

4) Add the sifted dry ingredients, alternately with the cashew milk, to the honey
mixture, stirring just enough to thoroughly blend after each addition. Add the
almonds with the last few stirs. Spread into a well-buttered, large loaf pan.
Bake 40-50 minutes.

Savory Nut Bread

40 minutes to prepare
45-55 minutes to bake

Preheat oven to 350°F.
Butter a large loaf pan.

1) Sauté onion in both olive oil & butter, with salt, for 5 minutes.
2) Add nuts; continue to stir & sauté another 8-10 minutes. Remove from heat; let cool.

- ½ cup finely-minced onion
- 2 Tbs. olive oil
- 3 Tbs. butter
- ½ tsp. salt
- ½ cup finely-minced walnuts
- ½ cup finely-minced almonds or pecans

Sift together into a large mixing bowl. Make a well in the center.

- 1½ cups unbleached white flour
- 1 cup whole wheat flour
- 2 tsp. baking powder
- 1 tsp. baking soda

Beat together buttermilk -or yogurt- with eggs. When frothy, add olives.

- 1½ cups buttermilk or yogurt
- 2 large, beaten eggs
- ½ cup chopped pitted black olives

1) Pour the buttermilk-egg mixture into the well in the center of the flour mixture.

2) Add the sautéed nuts & onions, scraping the pan well.

3) Stir with a wooden spoon until all is well-combined. The batter will be thick.

4) Spoon the batter into a well-greased loaf pan, and spread it into place.

5) Bake 45-55 minutes..(or until a knife inserted into the center comes out clean.)

6) Cool before slicing, or it will crumble greatly.

Yogurt & Herb Bread

30 minutes to prepare;
40-50 minutes to bake.

Preheat oven: 350°F.
Butter a loaf pan.

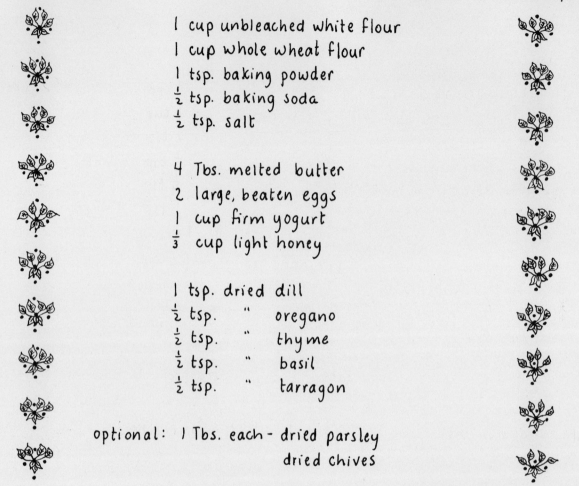

1 cup unbleached white flour
1 cup whole wheat flour
1 tsp. baking powder
½ tsp. baking soda
½ tsp. salt

4 Tbs. melted butter
2 large, beaten eggs
1 cup firm yogurt
⅓ cup light honey

1 tsp. dried dill
½ tsp.   "   oregano
½ tsp.   "   thyme
½ tsp.   "   basil
½ tsp.   "   tarragon

optional: 1 Tbs. each - dried parsley
                              dried chives

1) Sift together the 1st 5 ingredients. Make a well in the center of the bowl.

2) Beat together (high speed on an electric mixer) the next 4 ingredients for 3-5 minutes ~ until frothy. Add the herbs, and beat well.

3) Pour the liquid-herb mixture into the well in the center of the dry ingredients, and mix with a wooden spoon until thoroughly blended.

4) Pour into a well-buttered loaf pan, and bake 40-50 minutes (until knife inserted into center-of-bread comes out clean).

NOTE: The flavors of the herbs get stronger as the bread ages ~ you will have a chance to notice this if the bread sits around for several days before it is completely devoured.

Apple Bread

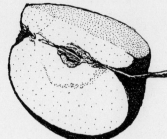

35 minutes to prepare;
40-50 minutes to bake.

Preheat oven to 350°F.
Butter a medium-sized
loaf pan.

2 packed cups coarsely-grated tart apple
3 Tbs. fresh lemon juice
(optional: ½ tsp. fresh lemon rind)

½ packed cup light brown sugar
4 Tbs. melted butter
1 large egg, beaten

1 cup unbleached white flour
1 cup whole wheat flour
2 tsp. baking powder
½ tsp. baking soda
¼ tsp. salt
1 tsp. cinnamon

optional { ¼ tsp. vanilla extract
{ ½ cup finely-chopped nuts

1. Combine grated apple, lemon juice & rind.
2. Beat together sugar, butter, and egg. Combine with apple.
3. Sift dry ingredients together into a mixing bowl. Make a well, and pour in the first mixture. (Add optional vanilla & nuts.) (Or not.) Stir until positively Combined.
4. Spread into buttered pan. Bake 40-50 minutes (until knife comes out clean).

Cottage Cheese ~ Dill Bread

20 minutes to prepare.
35-45 to bake.

Preheat oven to 350°F.
Butter an average loaf pan.

1 cup unbleached white flour
1 cup whole wheat flour
2 tsp. baking powder
½ tsp. baking soda
¼ tsp. salt

2 Tbs. fresh dill weed, (finely-minced)

1 cup cottage cheese
2 large, beaten eggs
6 Tbs. milk
1 Tbs. honey
4 Tbs. melted butter

1) Sift together dry ingredients.
2) Beat together the wet ingredients. Add the dill. Gradually sift the dry into the wet, stirring and scraping the sides as you go. Don't beat—just mix enough to thoroughly blend. The batter will be quite stiff.
3) Spread it into the pan (take your time) and bake it 35-45 minutes.

❁ GOOD W/ HOME-MADE MAYONNAISE & THIN CUCUMBER SLICES ❁

Sweet Zucchini ∞ Spice Bread

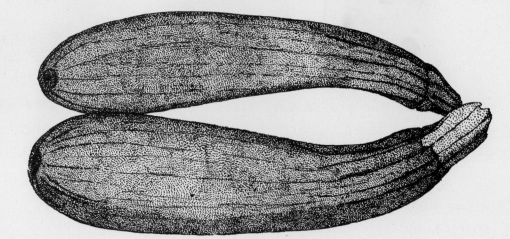

35 minutes to prepare
35-45 minutes to bake

Preheat oven to 350°F.
Butter a medium loaf pan.

<u>2 cups</u> coarsely-grated zucchini
(packed measure)

½ cup honey (light)
6 Tbs. melted butter
2 large eggs
½ tsp. vanilla extract

1 cup unbleached white flour
1 cup whole wheat flour
½ tsp. salt
2½ tsp. baking powder

¼ tsp. nutmeg
½ tsp. allspice
½ tsp. cinnamon
¼ tsp. ginger

Optional: ½ cup chopped nuts and/or ½ cup currants

(1) Place the grated zucchini in a colander over a bowl or sink. Let stand 10-20 minutes, then squeeze out all the excess moisture.

(2) With an electric mixer at high speed, beat the honey for about 5 minutes, or until white & opaque. Beat in the butter, eggs, and vanilla. Beat several minutes more.

(3) Sift together the dry ingredients.

(4) Add the sifted dry ingredients, alternately with the zucchini, to the honey mixture, beginning and ending with the dry (flour/zuke/flour/zuke/flour). Mix just enough to blend after each addition.

(5) Stir in optional nuts and currants last.

(6) Spread into a medium-sized, buttered loaf pan. Bake 35-45 minutes.

Green Chili & Cheese Corn Bread

~~~~~~

10 minutes to
combine;
30-35 minutes
to bake.

Butter an 8" square pan
- or its equivalent.
Preheat oven to 350°F.

½ cup whole wheat flour
2 tsp. baking powder
1 tsp. baking soda
¼ tsp. salt
1½ cups yellow corn meal
⅓ cup (packed) dark brown sugar
1 large egg
1 cup sour cream or yogurt
¼ cup (generous measure) diced canned green chilies
¼ cup (packed) grated jack cheese

(1) Sift together —into a bowl— the whole wheat flour, baking powder, baking soda and salt.

(2) Stir in the corn meal.

(3) Crumble in the brown sugar. Mix these dry ingredients together, with a fork, until they are well-blended. Make a well in the center.

(4) Beat together the egg and the sour cream or yogurt. Pour this mixture into the well in the center of the dry ingredients.

(5) Mix with a wooden spoon. The batter should readily blend with a few swift strokes.

(6) Add the green chilies and the cheese. Mix until uniform.

(7) Spread into a buttered 8" square pan (or its equivalent). Bake at 350° for 30-35 minutes, or until the center springs back when touched.

Cranberry Brown Bread

30 minutes to prepare;
45-50 minutes to bake.

Butter a medium-sized
loaf pan.
Preheat oven to 350°F.

1½ cups whole, raw cranberries
½ cup butter, melted
½ tsp. cinnamon
⅓ cup minced walnuts
1 cup whole wheat flour
1 cup unbleached white flour

2 tsp. baking powder
½ tsp. baking soda
½ tsp. salt
½ tsp. vanilla extract
¼ cup molasses
2 large eggs
⅓ cup brown sugar

(1) In a large skillet, cook the cranberries and walnuts with cinnamon in melted butter over medium heat, stirring, for 8-10 minutes. Remove from heat.

(2) Sift together flours, baking powder, baking soda, and salt.

(3) In a large bowl, beat together vanilla, molasses, eggs, and brown sugar — until well-blended and frothy.

(4) Add flour mixture and cooked cranberry mixture alternately to egg/molasses mixture, stirring after each addition. Be sure to scrape in all the butter from the cranberries.

(5) Spread into a buttered, medium-sized loaf pan. Bake 45-50 minutes at 350°F. Cool in pans 10 minutes before removing. (Rap pan sharply to remove.)

Oatmeal~Maple Bread

10 minutes to prepare
45-55 minutes to bake.

Butter a medium loaf pan.
Preheat oven to 350°F.

1 cup unbleached white flour
1 cup whole wheat flour
1½ tsp. baking soda
½ tsp. baking powder
¾ tsp. salt
1½ cups raw rolled oats

2 eggs
½ cup real maple syrup
1 cup buttermilk
½ tsp. vanilla extract
½ tsp. lemon rind
2 Tbs. fresh lemon juice
4 Tbs. melted butter

(1) Sift together into a large bowl: the flours, baking soda, baking powder, and salt. Stir in the oats. Make a well in the center.

(2) Beat well together all the remaining ingredients. Pour this into the well, and mix with a wooden spoon — a few swift strokes — until all is combined.

(3) Turn into a well-greased medium-sized loaf pan, and bake 45-55 minutes at 350°F. Let cool in pan 10 minutes, then remove by rapping pan sharply.

Muffins

Just-baked muffins have a way of instantly putting everyone in a good mood. As you linger in bed some morning when you don't have to be anywhere too early, consider this: Fresh muffins could be emerging from your very own oven in just 45 minutes.... what a mind-boggling realization! Assuming you have the ingredients, all you have to do is get up and make them.

Lemon~Yogurt Muffins

Preparation Time:
About 15 minutes, and then 25-30 more to bake.

Yield: about 12 2-inch muffins
Butter your muffin tins.
Preheat your oven to 375°F.

4-6 Tbs. light honey (6 Tbs. for Sweet-Tooths)
(Sweet-Teeth?)

4 Tbs. butter
1 cup yogurt
1 large egg
¼ cup freshly-squeezed lemon juice
½ tsp. freshly-grated lemon rind

1 cup unbleached white flour
1 cup wholewheat flour
a few dashes of nutmeg

1½ tsp. baking soda
¼ tsp. salt
(optional: ½ cup chopped nuts)

1- Melt the butter and honey together. Remove from heat.

2- Beat together yogurt, egg, lemon juice & rind. Add butter & honey. Beat well.

3- Sift together the dry ingredients. Make a well in the center, and add the wet. Stir briefly, in quick, decisive strokes. Fill cups ⅔ full. Bake about 25 minutes.

Pecan-Oat Muffins

About 20 minutes to prepare, and 25 to bake.

About 12 2-inch muffins. Preheat oven to 350°F.

$\frac{3}{4}$ cup minced pecans ⎤ Dry-roast in a cast-iron skillet,
1 cup raw rolled oats ⎦ stirring over low heat for about 10 minutes.

1 cup unbleached white flour
$\frac{1}{2}$ cup whole wheat flour
$\frac{1}{2}$ tsp. baking soda
$1\frac{1}{2}$ tsp. baking powder
$\frac{1}{4}$ tsp. salt (rounded measure)

1 cup buttermilk
1 large egg
3 Tbs. butter ⎤ melted together
3 Tbs. honey ⎦
$\frac{1}{4}$ tsp. vanilla extract

1- Sift together flours, soda, powder, and salt. Stir in dry-roasted pecans and oats. Make a well in the center.

2- Beat together the wet ingredients until thoroughly blended. Pour into the well. Mix just enough to blend. Fill greased cups $\frac{2}{3}$-full, and bake 20-25 minutes.

❀ ❀ ❀ Orange~Date Muffins ❀ ❀ ❀

About 20 minutes to prepare; 20-25 minutes to bake.

1 dozen 2-inch muffins. Preheat oven to 375°F.

1 navel (seedless) orange

1 cup unbleached white flour
$\frac{3}{4}$ cup whole wheat flour
1 tsp. baking soda
$\frac{1}{4}$ tsp. salt
$\frac{1}{2}$ cup unprocessed wheat germ

3 Tbs. butter ⎤ melted together
1 Tbs. honey ⎦
$1\frac{1}{2}$ cups buttermilk
1 large egg
$\frac{1}{2}$ cup chopped, pitted dates

1- Grate enough of the orange rind to make $\frac{1}{2}$ teaspoon. Set this aside, and proceed to remove and discard the remaining orange peel. Section the orange (do this over a bowl so you won't lose the juice), and cut the sections into small pieces.

2- Sift together flours, soda, and salt. Stir in the wheat germ, and make a well.

3- Beat together the buttermilk and egg. Add the melted butter and honey. Beat well. Stir in the orange pieces (plus juice), the rind, and the dates.

4- Add the wet mixture to the dry. Stir until thoroughly mixed. Spoon the batter into well-buttered muffin cups, and bake at 375°F for 20-25 minutes.

Grape Nut Muffins

15 minutes to prepare.
20-25 minutes to bake.

About 1 dozen 2-inch muffins.
Preheat oven to 400°F.

1¼ cups Grape Nuts cereal
3 Tbs. butter
3 Tbs. honey
1 cup milk
1 large egg

¾ cup whole wheat flour
¾ cup unbleached white flour
1½ tsp. baking powder
¼ tsp. salt
a few dashes of cinnamon

1- Sauté the Grape Nuts in the butter, over medium heat, stirring frequently. After about 5 minutes, remove from heat and add the honey. Mix well.

2- Beat together the milk and egg, until uniform. Add the Grape Nuts.

3- Sift together the dry ingredients. Make a well in their center, add the wet, and stir briefly, but emphatically. Fill your greased muffin cups ⅔-full and bake 20-25 min.

. . . .

Corn & Molasses Muffins

5-10 minutes to prepare.
25 minutes to bake.

About 1 dozen 2-inch muffins.
Preheat oven to 400°F.

1 cup yellow corn meal
1 cup unbleached white flour
½ cup whole wheat flour
½ tsp. baking soda
2 tsp. baking powder
¼ tsp. salt

1 large egg
1½ cups yogurt
4 Tbs. melted butter
4 Tbs. dark molasses
dash of cinnamon

1- Sift together flours, soda, powder and salt. Stir in the corn meal. Make a well in the center.

2- Beat together all the wet ingredients until very well-blended. Add the cinnamon. Pour into the well, and stir just enough to combine thoroughly. The batter will be stiff, so use spoons to drop it into your buttered tins (⅔ full.) Bake 25 min.

Blueberry Muffins

20 minutes to prepare.
30-35 minutes to bake.

Butter 12 muffin cups.
Preheat oven to 350°F.

1½ cups fresh blueberries (clean and set aside)

1½ cups unbleached white flour
½ tsp. baking soda
1 tsp. baking powder
½ tsp. salt
½ tsp. fresh lemon or lime rind

⅓ cup light honey } melted together.
¼ cup butter
⅓ cup milk
1 large egg
2 Tbs. fresh lemon or lime juice

(1) Sift together the 4 dry ingredients into a mixing bowl. Make a well in the center.
(2) Beat together the remaining ingredients (except the berries). Pour this into the well, and stir gently until just-blended, gradually adding the berries. Fill the muffin cups ⅔-full. (3) Bake 30-35 minutes. Cool in pans 5-10 minutes before removing and devouring.

Honey-Bran Muffins

15 minutes to prepare.
25-30 minutes to bake.

Butter 12 muffin cups.
Preheat oven to 350°F.

1 cup unbleached white flour
¼ tsp. salt
1 tsp. baking soda
1 cup raw, unprocessed bran

1 cup buttermilk
1 large egg
⅓ cup light honey } melted together.
3 Tbs. butter

⅓ cup raisins

(1) Sift together the flour, salt and baking soda into a large bowl.

(2) Stir in the bran. Make a well in the center.

(3) Beat together the liquid ingredients. Pour this into the well in the dry mixture. Add raisins, and stir everything just long enough to perfectly combine. Fill the cups ⅔-full. Bake 25-30 minutes.

Yeasted Coffeecakes

Some coffeecakes are true breakfast or brunch food (breadlike, as this one is), while others are more suited for dessert (cakelike, much sweeter and more crumbly, like Russian Coffeecake, p.267). In this recipe, which covers this and the next 2 pages, you will be presented with a basic yeast dough (a yogurt one, which has a nice tart flavor to complement a sweeter filling), 3 filling recipes, suggestions for inventing your own fillings, and instructions for shaping and baking.

❈x❈ Basic Dough ❈x❈

Total preparation time:
3½-4 hours.

Yield: 2 9-inch rings.

{
2 pkg. (2 Tbs.) active dry yeast
2 Tbs. wrist-temperature water
}

{
6 Tbs. melted butter (cool after melting)
1 tsp. salt
¼ cup honey
2 large eggs
1 cup firm yogurt
}

About 5 cups flour
  (recommended 1 cup whole wheat,
    the rest, unbleached white)

(1) Sprinkle the yeast into the water in a large bowl. Let it stand 5 minutes.

(2) Using a large wire whisk, beat in the next 5 ingredients until very well-blended.

(3) Add the flour, one cup at a time. Mix with a wooden spoon, then by hand. Knead it in the bowl for about 5 minutes, or until well-blended and smooth. (Add small amounts of extra flour if it is extremely sticky. It <u>will</u> be a little moister than a typical bread dough, though.)

(4) Cover with a damp towel, and let rise in a warm place until doubled in bulk. (1 hour.) ❈x❈x❈x❈x more→

(5) While the dough is rising, prepare the filling. Any one of the following recipes will make the right amount for 1 batch of dough:

✗✗✗1. Poppyseed & Prune Filling✗✗✗

2 cups sliced pitted prunes
⅔ cup fresh-squeezed orange juice
2 tsp. freshly-grated orange rind

2-3 Tbs. poppyseeds
⅓ cup (packed) brown sugar

(1) Place the prunes, orange juice, orange rind, and poppyseeds together in a saucepan. Bring to a boil, lower the heat to a simmer, and stew, uncovered, over low heat for 10 minutes.

(2) Remove from heat, stir in the brown sugar, and let cool to room temperature.

✗✗✗2. Ricotta~Nut Filling✗✗✗

1 cup chopped walnuts
2 Tbs. butter
½ tsp. cinnamon
a dash of salt

1 lb. (2 cups) ricotta cheese
1 egg
1 tsp. orange rind
1 tsp. lemon or lime rind

¼ cup lemon or lime juice
¼ cup honey
½ tsp. vanilla extract
¼ cup wheat germ

(1) In a heavy skillet, sauté the walnuts in butter with cinnamon for about 5 minutes. (Use low heat, and stir frequently.)

(2) Beat together all remaining ingredients. Stir in walnuts. Mix well.

✗✗✗3. Date~Meringue Filling✗✗✗

4 eggwhites (Save the yolks; they can be brushed on as a glaze before the cake goes into the oven.)
½ cup sifted confectioner's sugar
1 cup chopped pitted dates

1 cup chopped walnuts
1 tsp. orange rind

(1) Let the eggwhites come to room temperature.

(2) Beat them until stiff, gradually sprinkling in the confectioner's sugar.

(3) Separate the dates if they are all sticking together, and gently fold them, a few at a time, into the beaten whites.

(4) Gently stir in the walnuts and orange rind.

✗❀✗✗4. Improvised Fillings ✗❀✗
✗❀✗❀✗❀✗❀✗❀✗❀✗❀✗❀✗❀✗❀✗

This is a good place to begin if you have never improvised before, because the dough is a known quantity ——it will not pull any surprises on you. As long as the filling is not too wet, and as long as you don't use too much of it, just follow your instincts, and you may invent a new kind of coffeecake, which may make you famous for miles.

<u>Some suggestions</u>: raisins, soaked in rum
fruit preserves
grated semisweet chocolate
sweet spices mixed with softened butter
toasted nuts <u>and/or</u> coconut - with honey
sautéed fresh fruit (apples, peaches, pears...)
... COMBINATIONS OF THE ABOVE...

✗❀✗❀✗ Assembling & Baking ✗❀✗❀✗
✗❀✗❀✗❀✗❀✗❀✗❀✗❀✗❀✗❀✗❀✗❀✗

After the dough has doubled, punch it down (see p. 87). Transfer it to a floured surface, and divide it into 2 equal parts. Roll or pat each half into an oval shape, about ½-inch thick. (Try to make it a <u>long</u>, <u>narrow</u> oval.)

Spread the dough with soft butter (approximately ¼ cup per half), then with ½ the filling, spreading it to within 1 inch of the edge all around. Roll up the dough widthwise:

Roll it tightly, and seal the seam with a little water, and a few strong pinches. Curve the roll into a donut shape, and pinch the ends together: 1.   2.   3.   ← pinch here.

(Repeat with the 2ⁿᵈ half of the dough and the remaining filling.)

Place the completed forms on well-buttered trays (or pie pans). Let rise again, until doubled in bulk. → <u>Preheat</u> <u>oven</u> <u>to</u> <u>375°F.</u>

Brush the top surface with egg yolk, milk, or melted butter. (Optional: Sprinkle with cinnamon-sugar.) Bake 25-30 minutes.

Homemade Graham Crackers

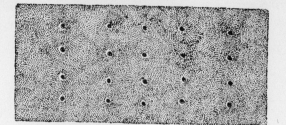

3 cups whole wheat flour
½ tsp. salt
½ tsp. baking powder
¼ tsp. cinnamon

6 Tbs. butter
½ cup honey

(1) Sift together flour, salt, baking powder, and cinnamon ~ into a bowl.

(2) Melt together the butter and honey. Pour this into the dry ingredients.

(3) Mix with a fork, then push the dough together with your hands. Don't knead or overmix. Place the dough on a well-floured surface, and roll it with a well-floured rolling pin to ⅛" thick. Cut rectangles (approximately 1¼" x 3") with a knife, and prick them with a fork. Place on a lightly-greased baking tray, and bake for just 10 minutes in a 375°F. oven. Cool on a rack.

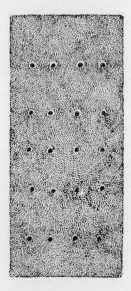
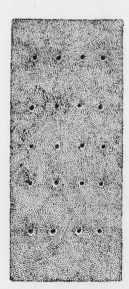
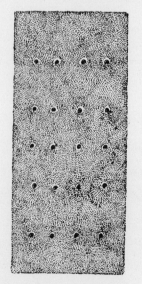
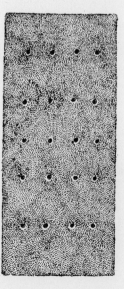

chappatis

This soft Indian flatbread is the simplest bread recipe in this book. It is basically the same idea as the Chinese MuShu pancake and the flour tortilla, except that these two are made entirely with white flour, instead of part-whole wheat.

In India, experienced chappati-makers can slap the dough into thin, supple pancakes with their bare hands. For most of us Westerners, however, a rolling pin is necessary.

Traditional Indian meals consist of many courses served all at the same time. Chappatis are a standard bread, appropriately served with any combination of Indian dishes (see menus on p. 222 and 223). You can make the dough and roll the pancakes in advance, and cook them shortly before serving, so they'll be a fresh, hot, and tender addition to the meal.

1 cup unbleached white flour
1 cup whole wheat flour
½ tsp. salt
1 Tbs. poppyseeds
½ cup water

¼ cup melted butter

(1) Set ¼ cup of the unbleached white flour aside. Combine the remaining flours with salt and poppyseeds in a bowl, and stir to mix well.

(2) Add water and stir until the moisture is absorbed, then turn out and knead about 5 minutes, using the reserved ¼ cup flour to flour the kneading surface.

(3) Divide the dough into 10 equal sections (8, if you want Really Big Ones), and form each into as round a ball as you can. Roll each ball into a very thin circle. (At this point, the chappatis can be stacked and refrigerated until cooking time.)

(4) Cook each chappati on each side on a hot, ungreased griddle or cast-iron skillet. A minute or 2 on each side is usually enough. The cooking is complete when each side begins to show brown spots. Brush each cooked surface with melted butter. Wrap the cooked chappatis in a tea towel, and if necessary, keep them warm in a low oven until serving time.

Whole Wheat-Buttermilk
Biscuits

Yield: 3 dozen.

Preheat oven to 450°F.

1 cup unbleached white flour

1 cup wholewheat flour

2 tsp. baking powder

½ tsp. baking soda

½ tsp. salt

1 large beaten egg

plus

enough buttermilk to make ⅔ cup

⅓ cup melted butter

[For cheese biscuits, add ½ cup (packed) grated cheddar]

(1) Sift together the dry ingredients —into a bowl. Make a well in the center.

(2) Pour the combined beaten egg and buttermilk into the well, along with the melted butter (and optional cheese). Stir until minimally-combined, then turn out onto a floured surface, and knead the dough briefly until it is uniform and smooth.

(3) Re-flour the work surface, and roll or pat the dough into a large oval, about ¼-inch thick. Cut it, with knife or cookie cutters, into your favorite shapes.

(4) Bake on a lightly-greased tray, 10-12 minutes at 450°F. Serve immediately.

Entrées

ENTRÉES:

Table of Contents

This is a broad unit, therefore it has been divided into 7 sections, in an attempt to make things easier to find. The boundaries overlap to some degree (i.e., there is a section on "Casseroles, Mélanges...etc.", but there are also bean and grain casseroles under "Beans & Grains"). However, each section has its own individual table of contents, so you should be able to find what you want. If you need further directory assistance, every recipe is listed by name in the index. The following page numbers refer you to the tables of contents for all 7 "Entrées" sections:

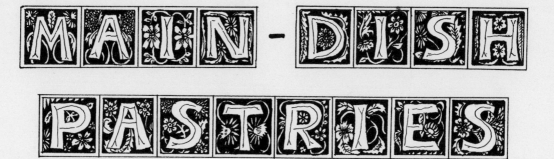

MAIN-DISH PASTRIES

.... a substantial filling sitting upon, wrapped in, or in some way surrounded by dough, crust, tortilla, or pancake......

AND

In the humble provincial kitchens of its native France, a quiche is considered a staple. However, as its fame and popularity have increased in North America, it has come to be revered as a Gourmet Item. Thus, many people assume that quiche-making is a difficult project, for experts only. I hereby endeavor to dispel this mystique. A quiche is really a simple, straightforward concoction: a pie crust filled with a few cooked vegetables, some cheese, and an egg custard. It is then baked until firm, and served hot, at room temperature, or cold—for breakfast, brunch, lunch, hors d'oeuvre, casual supper or elegant dinner.

If you can make a pie crust, you can make a quiche. In the following pages you will find recipes for numerous pie crusts (one basic, and the rest unusual), plus a list of fillings and custard instructions, which can be used as a guide for your own improvisations. In other words, here is a quiche formula, instead of quiche recipes.

What is the difference between a quiche and a vegetable pie? A quiche emphasizes a cheese-and-egg custard, while a vegetable pie can emphasize just about anything, from vegetables (sautéed and in a sauce) to purée (as in Sweet Potato Pie) to hard-boiled eggs (as in Devilled Egg Pie).

Following the quiche formula are some vegetable pie recipes. Try some of them, and then experiment with some inventions of your own.

Numerous Pie Crusts

Here are recipes for basic pie crust, plus several unusual ones, made from vegetables, or with nuts and cheese. Several of these crusts do not require the traditional Rolling Procedure — you simply pat them into the pie pan with spoon or fork or fingers (which many people prefer to rolling).

Basic (Regular) Pie Crust
~plenty of dough for a single-crusted 9" pie~

¼ cup (half a stick) cold butter, cut into small pieces
1 cup flour (can be part whole wheat)
dash of salt
up to 3 Tbs. cold water, milk, or buttermilk

(1) Use a pastry cutter, 2 forks or a food processor fitted with the steel blade, to cut together the butter pieces and the flour until they are a uniform substance resembling coarse corn meal. Add salt.

(2) As you stir with a fork (or as the food processor runs) add the liquid, 1 tablespoon at a time, until the dough sticks to itself readily. (Push the dough into itself in the center of the bowl as you stir. Stop adding liquid as soon as the dough holds together. The varying humidity will affect the amount of liquid needed.)

(3) You can chill the dough (wrap it well) to roll it out later, or you can roll it immediately (use extra flour to prevent sticking), and then chill the formed crust.

Mashed Potato Crust

(prebaked)

Butter a 9-inch pie pan.

-30 minutes to prepare; 45 minutes to bake
- Preheat oven to 375°F.

2 large (the size of a healthy fist) potatoes

2 Tbs. butter

¼ tsp. salt

freshly-ground black pepper

½ cup finely-minced raw onion

(~ a little extra oil ~ for
brushing on mid-way during baking)

(1) Scrub the potatoes, cut them into chunks, and boil them until soft. Drain and mash.

(2) Combine mashed potatoes with butter, salt, pepper, and onion. Mix well. Using a spoon and/or rubber spatula, sculpt a handsome crust with an even handsomer edge in your pre-buttered 9-inch pie pan.

(3) Bake 45 minutes. Halfway through the baking, lightly brush the entire top surface with oil. →It is not necessary to cool the crust before filling and re-baking.

Nut Crust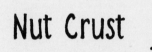

(not prebaked)

1 9-inch crust.

30 minutes to prepare.

½ cup finely, finely minced Nuts-of-your-choice (finely-minced = Just This Side of Ground. If you use a blender or food processor, go lightly, or you could end up with mushy nut butter.)

a dash of salt

4 Tbs. cold butter, cut into small pieces.

1¼ cups flour (use mostly white, with a little whole wheat)

approximately 3-5 Tbs. cold water

(1) Place nuts, butter, salt and flour together in a bowl. Use a pastry cutter to work the mixture until it is uniform and resembles coarse corn meal.

(2) Gradually drizzle in the cold water, and graduate from pastry cutter to fork. Mix by pushing the dough into itself in the center of the bowl. When the dough adheres to itself, you've added enough water.

(3) Roll out the dough and form your crust. Chill until time to fill.

Savory Crumb Crust

...just a few minutes to prepare;
10 minutes to prebake.

Butter a 9" pie pan.
Preheat oven to 350°F.

1 cup fine whole wheat bread crumbs
¼ cup whole wheat flour
½ cup raw wheat germ
½ cup raw rolled oats
¼ tsp. salt
a few dashes of basil and/or marjoram
½ cup melted butter

(1) Mix together all the dry ingredients, combining thoroughly.

(2) Drizzle in the melted butter, and toss with a fork, until the mixture is uniformly moistened.

(3) Press into a buttered 9" pie pan (you have permission to use your fingers), and prebake at 350°F. for 10 minutes.

Spinach Crust

 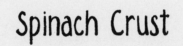 

15 minutes to prepare;
15 minutes to prebake.

Butter a 9" pie pan.
Preheat oven to 375°F.

¾ lb. spinach - chopped very fine
3 Tbs. butter
¾ cup unbleached white flour
¾ cup wheat germ
¼ tsp. salt
a dash of nutmeg

(1) Melt the butter in a cast-iron skillet, add the spinach, and cook it quickly over fairly high heat — stirring — until it is just limp.

(2) Remove from heat; add remaining ingredients, and mix well.

(3) Pat into a buttered 9" pie pan. Use a fork first, and then your fingers, to mold the crust.   Pre-bake for 15 minutes at 375°F.

Golden Vegetable Crust

≈ 15 minutes
to prepare;
≈ 40 minutes
to bake.

≈ Butter a 9" pie pan.

≈ Preheat oven to 375°F.

This recipe features a Special Guest Star: PARSNIP! This surprisingly sweet and mild vegetable is often underrated, if not overlooked entirely. Discover it here, and you might find yourself grating it into your salads as well...

> 2 packed cups coarsely-grated yellow summer squash
> ½ packed cup coarsely-grated carrot
> ½ packed cup coarsely-grated parsnip (peel it first)
> ½ tsp. salt
> 2 Tbs. melted butter
> ⅓ cup whole wheat flour
> (extra melted butter to brush on top)

(1) Place the grated squash in a colander. Salt it lightly, and let it stand for 10 minutes over a bowl or sink. Squeeze out all excess moisture.

(2) Combine all ingredients and mix well. Transfer the mixture to a buttered 9-inch pie pan, and form a crust with fork and/or fingers.

(3) Bake for 40 minutes at 375°F. Midway through baking, brush the top surface with extra melted butter.

Cheese Crust

Make the Basic Pie Crust (p. 127), and add ½ packed cup grated cheddar cheese to the flour. Toss together well, then proceed as usual.

Poppyseed~Cheddar Crust

Make the Cheese Crust (above), and include 2-3 Tbs. poppyseeds with the cheese & flour.

Other Additions along these lines:
~ Other kinds of cheese
~ Sesame seeds instead of poppyseeds
~ Caraway seeds "   "

A Quiche Formula

After you have prepared the Chosen Crust for your quiche, there are 3 more steps before you ultimately bake it. These are: ① The Cheese, ② The Filling and ③ The Custard. By the way, these are all easy. With your finished crust in front of you, the most difficult part is behind you.

1. The Cheese

This is the first layer, deposited -in either grated or cubed form- directly upon the crust. There is a reason why the cheese goes in first: it has a lot of fat in it, and when it melts it forms a moisture-resistant barrier between the filling and the crust, thus helping to keep the crust from getting soggy. Recommended types of cheese: _Swiss_ types (especially gruyère) and _medium or sharp cheddar_. Recommended amount: ¼-⅓ lb., depending on a) whether it is cubed or grated (grated takes up less space), b) how much filling you're using, c) whether you're using a Quiche pan (straight-sided) or a pie pan.

2. The Filling

a) _Spinach_ (½ lb.-chopped and steamed)-with sautéed _onions_, dry mustard, and nutmeg.

b) _Mushrooms_ (½ lb.-sliced)- sautéed with scallions, oregano, and thyme.

c) Chopped, steamed _asparagus_, with tarragon and dill. (8-10 thin stalks)

d) Chopped, steamed _broccoli_ (1 large stalk), with lemon juice and garlic.

e) Tomato _slices_ (1-2 medium tomatoes) sautéed gently in olive oil and/or butter, with basil and dill.

f) Snippets of _fresh herbs_ (marjoram, thyme, basil, dill, chives, parsley....) with sautéed _onions_. and _peppers_

g) _Marinated artichoke hearts_ (drained and chopped).

h) Take it from here......

3. The Custard

After you apply the filling over the cheese beat together 3 eggs and 1 cup milk (4 eggs and 1½ cups milk for a straight-sided quiche pan). Pour it over the top. (Variations = sour cream or buttermilk instead of milk.) Dust the top with paprika. _BAKE_: 35-40 minutes at 375°F.

SWEET POTATO PIE

4·5 servings.

Note: eggless.

Preheat oven to 375°F.

WITH POPPYSEED~CHEDDAR CRUST

Traditionally a sweet potato pie is a dessert. This one is a supper dish— it isn't quite sweet, nor could it be considered savory. It is just pleasant and subtle. Serve it with a tossed green salad and some freshly-baked lemon-yogurt muffins (p. 113).

A poppyseed-cheddar crust (p. 130), unbaked

2 lbs. sweet potatoes
1 Tbs. butter
½ tsp. cinnamon
3 seedless oranges, peeled & sectioned
¾ cup chopped, toasted nuts (cashews and/or pecans)
¾ tsp. salt
1 Tbs. honey
(optional: ½ cup firm yogurt)

⅓ cup wheat germ }
½ cup grated cheddar } TOPPING
Dots of Butter }

(1) Peel the sweet potatoes, cut them into chunks, and boil them until soft.

(2) Drain the sweet potatoes, transfer them to a bowl, and mash them well. Add all the other ingredients (except those for the topping), and mix well.

(3) Spread into your unbaked crust. Sprinkle with wheat germ and cheese, and apply a few dots of butter here, there, and the other place. Bake at 375°F, uncovered, 40-50 minutes.

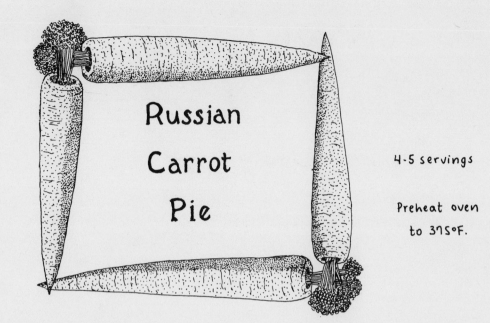

Russian Carrot Pie

Preparation time:

CRUST: 35 minutes

FILLING: 40 minutes

BAKING: 45 minutes

TOTAL: 2 hours

4-5 servings

Preheat oven to 375°F.

1 nut crust (p. 128) (Recommended nuts for this pie = almonds & pecans.)

3 Tbs. butter
1 cup onions, finely-minced
½ tsp. salt
1 lb. carrots, very thinly-sliced
1 Tbs. unbleached white flour
1½ cups firm cottage (or pot) cheese

½ cup grated mild white cheese
1 beaten egg
lots of freshly-ground black pepper
1 tsp. dill weed
3 Tbs. wheat germ
paprika

(1) Melt the butter in a large, heavy skillet. Add onions and salt. Cook over medium heat, stirring frequently, until the onions are soft (5-8 minutes).

(2) Add carrots, stir, and sprinkle in the flour. Cook and stir until the carrots are tender but not mushy (use your own judgment). If the mixture seems to be sticking to the pan, add up to 3 Tbs. of water, a little at a time. Remove from heat.

(3) In a large bowl, beat together the cheeses and the egg. Add the cooked carrot mixture (ok if it's still hot), and beat well. Stir in black pepper and dill. Spread into your eagerly awaiting Nut Crust.

(4) Sprinkle the top of the pie with wheat germ and paprika. Bake for 15 minutes at 375°F, then turn the oven down to 350°F, and bake it another 30 minutes. Let it cool for 5 minutes or so before cutting it.

Sour Cream & Onion Pie

with **Walnut Crust**

Preparation Time:

CRUST: 30 minutes

FILLING: 50 minutes

BAKING: 45 minutes

TOTAL = 2¼ hours

4-6 servings

Preheat oven to 375°F.

I. A Nut Crust (p. 128)... using walnuts as "Nuts"

II.
- 3 Tbs. butter
- 4 cups onions, thinly sliced
- ¾ tsp. salt
- ½ tsp. dry mustard
- 3 Tbs. fresh lemon juice
- 3 Tbs. unbleached white flour
- 3-4 Tbs. water

1) Melt butter in a large, heavy skillet.
2) Add onions, salt, mustard, and lemon juice. Cook, stirring, over medium heat until the onions are soft (5-8 minutes).
3) Sprinkle in flour. Stir constantly, and cook another 8-10 minutes over low heat.
4) Add water, as needed, to prevent sticking.

III.
- ¾ cup sour cream
- ¾ cup firm yogurt
- 1 whole egg
- 1 egg yolk (save the white!)
- 2 tsp. prepared horseradish
- lots of fresh black pepper
- ⅓ cup (packed) grated Swiss or cheddar cheese
- 2 Tbs. freshly-minced parsley

Beat together all of these ingredients, except the Saved Eggwhite, until very well-blended.

IV.
- ½ tsp. caraway seeds
- paprika

TO ASSEMBLE:

1) Brush that Saved Eggwhite onto the unbaked, prepared pie shell (this keeps the crust extra crisp).

2) Combine mixtures "II" and "III". Mix very well.

3) Pour the filling into the crust; sprinkle the top with caraway seeds and paprika. Bake at 375°F. for 45 minutes.

Devilled Egg Pie

with mashed potato crust

Preparation Time:
1¼ hours for crust;
1 hour for filling.
(includes baking.)

1 9-inch pie.
(serves about 4.)

Preheat oven to 375°F.

1 mashed potato crust (p.128)
4 not-so-hard-cooked eggs*
* 4½ minutes in boiling water
3 Tbs. butter
4 Tbs. unbleached white flour
1 cup scalded (heat just to boiling) milk

½ tsp. prepared horseradish (to taste)
1 tsp. dry mustard
½ tsp. dill weed
½ tsp. salt
freshly-ground black pepper
a good, mild paprika

(1) Prepare crust (p. 128). Set aside.

(2) Prepare eggs (the yolks should not be dry). Peel them, and cut them in half lengthwise. Set aside.

(3) In a medium-sized saucepan, melt the butter. Sprinkle in the flour, and cook, whisking, over low heat, about 2 minutes.

(4) Gradually drizzle in the hot milk, whisking continuously. Add horseradish, mustard, dill, salt and pepper. Whisk steadily, and continue cooking over medium heat until it thickens (5-8 minutes). Scrape the bottom and sides intermittently with a rubber spatula. Remove the thickened sauce from the heat.

(5) Arrange the 8 egg halves symmetrically, yolks-up, in the prebaked crust,
Like so:

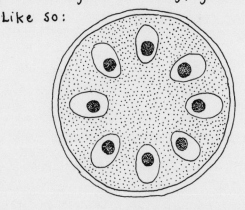

(6) Carefully spoon the sauce over the eggs, filling the crust, and moistening each yolk. Sprinkle gracefully with paprika. Bake uncovered at 375°F. for 25 minutes, or until bubbly. Let it sit about 10 minutes before serving.

Mushroom ∾ Yogurt Pie

with Spinach Crust

Preparation Time
(including crust
& baking)
= 2 hours

4 servings

Preheat oven to 350°F.

1 spinach crust (p.129)	1 egg $\}$ at room temperature.
1 Tbs. butter	1 cup firm yogurt
1 cup minced onion	lots of fresh black pepper
½ tsp. salt	½ cup grated cheddar
12 oz. mushrooms, sliced	¼ cup freshly-minced parsley
2 Tbs. fresh lemon juice	extra cheddar $\}$ for the top
3 Tbs. flour (white or w.wheat)	paprika

(1) In a large, heavy skillet, cook the onions in butter with salt, until the onions are soft (5-8 minutes).

(2) Add the mushrooms and the lemon juice. Cook, stirring, over medium heat about 5-8 more minutes.

(3) Gradually, as you stir, sprinkle in the flour. Keep cooking and stirring over medium-low heat another 8-10 minutes. Remove from heat.

(4) Beat together the egg, yogurt, pepper, cheddar, and parsley. Stir the mushroom sauté into this mixture, then beat it well.

(5) Turn the filling into the pre-baked crust (you don't need to cool the crust first). Top with extra cheese and paprika.

Bake for 30 minutes at 350°F.

⌁⌁ Working with Strudel-Leaf Pastry ⌁⌁

Strudel-leaf pastry, also called **FILO** or **PHYLLO** dough, is available commercially in many food stores, especially those of Greek extraction. Strudel leaves come frozen, in long, rectangular one-pound packages. You must defrost the pastry thoroughly <u>before</u> you unwrap it, and this usually takes several hours. Once thawed, unwrapped, and unrolled, the package of pastry becomes a neat stack of soft, dry, white rectangular sheets, each one very delicate and thin. There will be about 24 sheets of pastry in this stack.

One's initial contact with filo dough can be intimidating ~ like picking up a newborn infant for the first time, or trying to weed a garden full of flower seedlings ~ because of the Delicacy of the Event. The dough is sturdier than it seems, though, and here are some handy hints to help familiarize you with its traits:

ALWAYS MAKE SURE YOUR FILO DOUGH IS THOROUGHLY DEFROSTED BEFORE YOU EVEN OPEN THE PACKAGE! If you try to unwrap and unroll it too soon, the leaves will break into a thousand itty-bitty pieces, and you will have to throw them angrily into the garbage. (This kind of dough can't be stuck together again.) BUT, THE GOOD NEWS IS: defrosted, unused filo leaves, if they have not been allowed to dry out too much, can be re-wrapped (air-tight!) and refrozen, or stored in the refrigerator for a week or two.

RECOMMENDED UNWRAPPING/REWRAPPING PROCEDURE:

(a) Defrost the whole package, still wrapped.

(b) Unwrap just before using; unroll, and take off the amount you need. Half a package usually makes about 6 servings.

(c) Immediately re-wrap the unused half by rolling it in waxed paper first, and then sealing the roll in a plastic bag, air-tight. Refrigerate — or freeze — until your next strudel caper.

(d) Another VERY CONVENIENT ALTERNATIVE is to make a double batch of filling (or single batches of 2 different fillings), and use the entire pound of pastry leaves, even if you only immediately plan to serve half. Bake all of it, then freeze some of it (wrap it in foil) — either in individual pieces, or all together.

⌁⌁ BAKED STRUDEL FREEZES, DEFROSTS, AND RE-HEATS VERY WELL! ⌁⌁

Then, if you come home tired and grumpy some bleak night, you can pull a ready-made pastry out of the freezer, heat it in a 350°F. oven for 35 or 40 minutes, and you will be instantly transformed into Contentment Itself.

The Actual Handling of Strudel-Leaf Pastry

Filo dough dries out very quickly, once unwrapped. Keep the dough all piled up as you use it; always take a sheet from the top of the pile. Cover the pile with a clean towel between sheet-takings.

No matter what shape your strudel or tyropita or borek or pizza or pie will become, the initial treatment of the pastry leaves will always be the same – i.e., the dough will be layered, and each leaf will be brushed generously with with melted butter and/or oil before the next one is placed on top of it. This procedure strengthens the dough, seals it against the moisture of the filling, and gives the finished product that characteristic brown color and exquisite crispness.

ALWAYS HAVE THE FILLING FULLY-PREPARED BEFORE ASSEMBLY TIME.

AND, HAVE THE MELTED BUTTER READY AS WELL, WITH YOUR PASTRY BRUSH AT HAND. In other words, set up a production line, with all items present and reachable, so that once you begin stacking the leaves, you can work steadily to prevent the dough from drying out.

A plain wooden or formica surface is easiest to work on. Or, you may wish to use a large tray as the surface for layering your filo. If you do use a tray, make sure you brush it with melted butter first.

The actual lifting of each filo leaf from its pile, and the placing of it as precisely as possible upon the preceding, buttered leaf, is a little tricky, but it gets easier with practice. If a leaf tears or puckers or breaks, you can still use it (unless it is mutilated), as the other layers will compensate. If several leaves tear or break, use a few extra in the total layering, for more reinforcement.

Once assembled, the pastry can be refrigerated for several hours before baking. Bake it right before serving.

Cheese Tyropitas

1½ hours to prepare; 35 minutes to bake.
About 6 servings (2 per person)
Preheat oven to 375°F.

2 lb. (4 cups) firm cottage or pot cheese
1 cup finely-minced raw onion
½ tsp. salt
lots of freshly-ground black pepper
1 tsp. crushed, dried mint

½ cup sunflower seeds
1 medium-large clove of garlic, crushed
juice from 1 medium-sized lemon
{ 1 lb. filo pastry leaves, defrosted
{ 1 cup (2 sticks) melted butter

(1) To make the filling, simply mix together all ingredients except the filo and the butter.

(2) For each individual tyropita, layer 2 sheets of filo, with plenty of melted butter brushed between them. Butter the top surface of the second sheet.

(3) Fold the now-double sheet into thirds lengthwise, one side over, then the other:

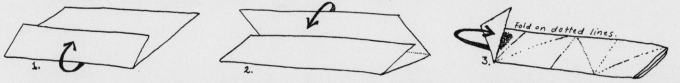

fold on dotted lines.

1.   2.   3.

Place about ¼ cup of filling a few inches from one end. Fold the nearest corner over it triangularly (as shown). Keep folding the triangle of filling over until you reach the end. Brush the top of the Tyropita with butter; place it on a buttered baking tray. Repeat, until you've used up the filling.
Bake at 375° – 35 minutes.

Spinach Borek

1½ hours to prepare; 35 minutes to bake.
About 6 servings (2 per person)
Preheat oven to 375°F.

2 lbs. fresh spinach – cleaned and chopped
2 Tbs. butter
1 medium clove garlic, crushed
1½ cups minced onion
½ tsp. salt
lots of freshly-ground black pepper
½ tsp. dill weed

1 cup finely-chopped walnuts
½ tsp. freshly-grated orange rind
½ cup dark raisins
a few dashes of nutmeg
1 packed cup grated mild cheddar
{ 1 lb. filo leaves, defrosted
{ 1 cup (2 sticks) melted butter

(1) Wash the spinach, chop it fine, and put it in a colander over the sink to drain.

(2) In a large, heavy skillet, sauté the onion and garlic in 2 Tbs. butter for about 5 minutes or until the onions are soft. Add the salt, spinach, dill, pepper, and walnuts. Cook, stirring, over high heat, until the spinach is slightly wilted.

(3) Remove from heat. Add all remaining ingredients except the last 2. Mix well.

(4) Assemble the filo exactly as in the above recipe, but fold the filling in squares instead of in triangles.

← Fold side edges over first
(dotted lines lengthwise)

VEGETABLE STRUDEL

*About 1¼ hours to prepare; 35-40 minutes to bake.

*Preheat oven to 375°F.

*Butter a 9x13" baking pan.

*4-6 servings.

½ lb. filo pastry leaves
¾ cup melted butter

2 Tbs. butter
1 cup minced onion
½ tsp. salt
1 large carrot, diced
1 cup chopped broccoli
½ lb. chopped mushrooms
½ tsp. dill weed
lots of freshly-ground black pepper

2 Tbs. flour
2 Tbs. dry sherry
6 Tbs. yogurt or sour cream
1 large egg
¼ cup (packed) minced parsley
1 cup wheat germ
optional: extra dill weed

(1) In a large, heavy skillet, cook the onions in 2 Tbs. of butter with salt, until the onions are soft.

(2) Add the carrot, broccoli, mushrooms, and dill, and continue to cook, mixing intermittently, over medium heat.

(3) When the vegetables are brightly-colored and just tender (about 8-10 minutes later), gradually sprinkle in the flour and the sherry. Continue mixing and cooking over medium-low heat another 5-8 minutes. Remove from heat; let it cool to room temperature.

(4) Beat together the egg and yogurt (or sour cream). Add this to the cooled vegetables, along with the parsley and wheat germ. Mix well.

(5) Begin layering sheets of filo (see pp. 137-38) in your buttered 9x13-inch pan, brushing lavishly with melted butter between the layers. The filo sheets will slightly out-dimension your pan; it's fine to let the excess dough hug the inside edges of the pan ~ this will make a crispy border.

(6) When you've layered about 8 sheets of dough, spread on the filling, distributing it to within ½ inch of the edges. Continue to layer filo on top of the filling; there should be about 4 of them remaining in your ½ pound. Don't forget to keep brushing melted butter between all the layers, and finally, on the very top. OPTIONAL: Sprinkle some extra dill weed on top.

(7) Bake uncovered for 35-40 minutes. Let it cool for 5-10 minutes before gently cutting it, with a serrated knife, into delicious squares.

ᏎREEK PIZZA

About 1 hour
to prepare;

30 minutes
to bake.

4-6 servings.

Preheat oven to 400°F.

Butter a large baking tray.

½ lb. filo pastry leaves
½ cup melted butter } combined
¼ cup olive oil

2 Tbs. olive oil
1 cup chopped onion
¼ tsp. salt
3 large cloves crushed garlic
½ tsp. crushed basil
½ tsp. oregano
juice from ½ large lemon

1 lb. fresh spinach ~ cleaned, stemmed & chopped
↳ (OR: 1 10-oz. package frozen, chopped spinach)
lots of freshly-ground black pepper
1 lb. grated mozzarella cheese
1½ cups crumbled feta or farmer's cheese
2 medium tomatoes, in thin slices
½ cup fine bread crumbs

(1) Please read pp. 137-38 to familiarize yourself with the handling of filo pastry.

(2) In a large skillet, cook the onions and garlic with salt in 2 Tbs. olive oil, until the onions are clear and soft. Add herbs, lemon juice and spinach, and cook over fairly high heat, stirring, until the spinach is limp and the liquid is evaporated.

(3) On a large, buttered baking tray begin layering the sheets of filo dough, brushing each surface with a generous amount of combined butter and olive oil. Continue layering the pastry leaves until you've used them all. Brush the top surface of the stack with the remaining butter/olive oil mixture.

(4) Use a slotted spoon to transfer the spinach mixture from its skillet to the pastry stack, leaving behind whatever liquid failed to evaporate. Spread the spinach mixture evenly in place, leaving a ½-inch border of pastry.

(5) Sprinkle on the crumbled feta or farmer's cheese, plus half the mozzarella.

(6) Dredge the tomato slices in bread crumbs, arrange these on top of the pizza, and toss the remaining mozzarella over the tomatoes. Bake uncovered for 25-30 minutes.

Bstilla

1½ hours to prepare;
40-45 minutes to bake.

4-6 servings.
Preheat oven to 375°F.

Serve this for Brunch
or a summer supper,
with Schav (p. 48)
and
a big bowlful of cut
fresh fruit, with nuts,
raisins, & coconut.

....a sweet and savory custard strudel.

½ lb. filo pastry leaves
½ cup melted butter
2 cups sliced, toasted almonds

2 cups buttermilk (at room temperature)
7 eggs (also at room temperature)
1 cup finely-minced onions
1 Tbs. butter
1 tsp. salt
black pepper (a small dosage)

½ tsp. each: ground ginger
allspice
cinnamon
¼ cup (packed) minced parsley

extra cinnamon (& optional sugar)

(1) Begin heating the buttermilk very, very gently in the top of a double boiler.

(2) Beat 6 eggs together well (put the 7ᵗʰ egg aside for later). When the buttermilk is warm to the touch (warmer than body temperature, but NOT boiling!) gradually drizzle in the beaten eggs, whisking constantly. Cook for 10-15 minutes, whisking frequently, until it begins to thicken. Remove from heat.

(3) In a small skillet, sauté the onions in butter with salt, until the onions are soft.

(4) Stir the onions, spices, and parsley into the custard. Let it stand, uncovered, for about 15 minutes. Stir it intermittently with a wooden spoon.

(5) ASSEMBLY: a. Generously butter a 9x13" baking pan
b. Layer 6 leaves of filo pastry in the pan (let the pastry edges climb up the sides of the pan, if necessary), brushing plenty of butter onto each (see pp. 137-38). Sprinkle half the almonds onto the 6th layer.
c. Add another 3 layers of pastry (butter between). Add the filling.
d. Pile the remaining pastry leaves on top of the filling. Beat the extra egg and brush this on top of the top layer. Sprinkle with the remaining almonds, and a generous amount of cinnamon (or, cinnamon-sugar.) Bake 40-45 minutes uncovered.

ENCHILADAS

An enchilada is a soft corn tortilla wrapped around a filling and baked in a sauce. Usually the filling is plain (cheese, chicken, or beef) and bland, while the sauce is traditionally the spicier element.

Enchiladas are easy to assemble, once the filling and sauce are prepared and the tortillas are pre-moistened. The recommended procedure for putting together an enchilada dinner is as follows:

(1) If you are using frozen tortillas (and most corn tortillas do come in frozen form), take them out of the freezer ahead of time to give them plenty of time to defrost. Defrost them <u>fully wrapped</u>, to prevent their drying out.

(2) Prepare the filling(s).

(3) Prepare the sauce.

(4) Pre-moisten the tortillas.

(5) Assemble the enchiladas by placing approximately ½ cup of filling on one side of each tortilla and rolling it up. Pour a small amount of sauce into a shallow baking dish, place the enchiladas on top, and pour the remaining sauce over. Cover with foil, and bake for 30 minutes in a 325°F oven.

Here are several ways to pre-moisten tortillas (necessary to encourage greater flexibility):

(1) Sauté them very briefly on each side in hot oil. ("very briefly" means approximately 10 seconds on each side.) <u>OR</u>:

(2) Dip them briefly in the sauce. ("briefly" means one dunking, not a bath.) <u>OR</u>:

(3) Dip them just as briefly in water (least desirable, however easiest).

The following 3 pages contain recipes for some unusual enchilada fillings (not so plain...) and for 2 sauces . . . . →

Enchilada Fillings

✳✳✳✳✳✳✳✳✳✳✳✳✳✳✳

Each of these recipes makes enough for 8 enchiladas (4 servings).

I. Cream Cheese with Surprises: Preparation time: 10 minutes

8 oz. (1 cup) softened neufchatel or cream cheese
½ cup chopped green, pimiento-stuffed olives
½ cup chopped black olives
1½ cups mixed minced green and red bell peppers
¼ cup (packed measure) black raisins
4 finely-minced scallions (greens and whites)
cayenne pepper, to taste

(1) Beat the cheese until it is light and creamy.
(2) Gradually add all other ingredients, mixing
    well after each addition, until all items
    are harmonious.

✳✳✳✳✳✳✳✳✳✳✳✳✳✳✳✳✳✳✳✳✳✳

II. Avocado and Cashew: Preparation time: 10 minutes

2 medium-sized avocados (perfectly ripe)
juice from 1 moderately-proportioned lemon
4 finely-minced scallions (greens and whites)
½ cup finely-minced fresh parsley
1 cup finely-chopped cashews, toasted
⅓ cup sour cream or firm yogurt
(optional: 1 medium clove of garlic, crushed)

(1) Mash the avocados until they are a smooth unit. Add
    the lemon juice immediately, thus preventing the smooth
    unit from turning brown.
(2) Add remaining ingredients, and mix well.

III. Egg & Olive with Cheese

4 hard-boiled eggs, chopped fine
1 cup chopped black olives
1 cup finely-minced raw onion
1 lb. Monterey Jack cheese, grated
salt and black pepper, to taste

Combine everything & mix well.

❋ ❋ ❋ ❋ ❋ ❋ ❋ ❋ ❋ ❋ ❋ ❋ ❋ ❋ ❋ ❋ ❋ ❋ ❋ ❋

IV. Zucchini and Pepper

2 Tbs. olive oil
2 medium-sized cloves of garlic, crushed
1 cup minced onion
½ tsp. salt
1 cup minced green bell peppers
2½ cups diced zucchini (about 2 smallish zukes)
½ tsp. each: cumin, oregano, basil
cayenne and black pepper, to taste

1 cup (packed) grated sharp cheddar cheese

(1) In a large, heavy skillet, sauté the garlic and onion in olive oil, with salt.

(2) When the onions are soft (after 5 or so minutes), add the peppers, zucchini, and herbs. Stir, and continue to cook over medium heat another 5-8 minutes, or until the zucchini is just barely tender.

(3) Remove from heat, and stir in the cheese. Allow to cool at least to room temperature before filling enchiladas.

Enchilada Sauces
(4 servings apiece)

1. Salsa Verde :

Preparation time: 1 hour.

5 large green tomatoes, diced

1 cup chopped onion

3 large cloves garlic, crushed

1 tsp. salt

[optional: 2-4 Tbs. dry sherry]

½ cup diced green chilies (canned)

¼ -½ tsp. cayenne pepper

small amounts { freshly-snipped parsley

" " basil

" " chives or scallion tops

1) Combine tomatoes, onion, garlic, salt, sherry, chilies, and cayenne in a sauce-pan. Bring to a boil, lower the heat, and cover. Let it simmer, covered, about 40-50 minutes.

2) Cool the sauce at least to room temperature before adding fresh snippets (to taste) of parsley, basil and chives or scallion tops.

2. Red Sauce: (uncooked)

Preparation time: 15 minutes

1 lb. fresh ripe red tomatoes

2 large, sweet red bell peppers

2 medium red onions

2 large cloves garlic

½ tsp. salt

½ tsp. crushed red hot pepper

¼ tsp. black pepper

¼ tsp. cumin

1) Cut the tomatoes, peppers and onion into smallish chunks. Combine everything in a blender or food processor, and purée.

2) That's all.

AND

Every culture seems to have some version of a savory filled pastry in its cuisine. In many cases, the dough is identical, the method of preparing and cooking very similar, and the distinguishing factor is the filling. One example of a ubiquitous pastry is that which is known as ravioli (if you're Italian), kreplach (if you're Jewish) and wonton (if you're Chinese). They all use the same noodle-type dough and are shaped in a similar fashion, but their fillings are all different, and their origins are worlds apart. (Realizations of this sort can lead us to philosophical reveries about the Connectedness of Us All. Or, they can simply lead us to conclude that a resounding majority of human beings just happen to love eating pastry.)

Another example of a ubiquitous pastry is one that is known to Russians as piroshki, and to Italians as calzone. Whereas the example of ravioli, kreplach, and wonton is one of a noodle dough, piroshki and calzone use a _yeasted_ dough. Essentially, they are filled breads: a soft, hot, savory inside and a crisp, chewy encasement. What separates piroshki and calzone is the type of filling used.

On the following page is a recipe for the dough that can be used for either piroshki or calzone. After the dough recipe and basic method are recipes for 3 different fillings for each.

❊Dough ❧ Method❊
...for Piroshki and Calzone❊❊❊

This is a yeasted dough, requiring only 1 rising period. The total preparation time, including rising (but not including baking) is about 2-2½ hours. The baking takes 20 minutes.

This will make enough dough for 6 calzone or 8 piroshki (piroshki are a little smaller) — altogther, about 4-6 servings.

1½ tsp. (half an envelope) active dry yeast
1 cup lukewarm (body temperature) water
2 tsp. honey

1½ tsp. salt
1½ cups unbleached white flour
1½ cups whole wheat flour
3 Tbs. olive oil or melted butter

(1) Combine the yeast, water, and honey in a large bowl. Stir, and then let it sit for 5 minutes.

(2) Beat in salt and flours. Use a wooden spoon until it is too thick to mix, then turn it out onto a floured surface, and knead until smooth (8-10 minutes). (Kneading diagram, p.87.)

(3) Use olive oil for calzone, and melted butter for piroshki, and grease the mixing bowl. Return the dough to the bowl, brush its top surface with oil or butter, and let it rise in a warm place until doubled in bulk (approximately 1 hour). PREPARE THE FILLING WHILE THE DOUGH RISES.

~ PREHEAT OVEN TO 450°F. ~

(4) Punch the dough to deflate it, and turn it out onto a floured surface. Divide it into 6 or 8 equal parts, and knead each part into a ball. Roll each ball into a circle about ⅛" thick. Place ⅙ or ⅛ of the filling onto one side of the circle. Bring the other side of the dough over the top of the filling, and seal the edges with water and the flat edge of a fork. The resulting shape will bear some resemblance to a U.F.O. Prick it with a fork in a few choice spots, and deposit it on a greased baking tray.

Bake for 20 minutes at 450°F, and serve immediately.

PIROSHKI

Each of the following 3 piroshki fillings is designed to fill 8 pastries. Figure on 2 per person for the main course of a meal. (For variety, try making half-amounts of 2 different fillings, so that each guest can have one of each.)

DILLED CHEESE

15-20 minutes to prepare.

2 lbs. firm cottage cheese (or pot cheese)
8 oz. (1 cup) crumbled farmer's or feta cheese
3 Tbs. fresh lemon juice
1 packed cup finely-minced scallions (whites and greens)
½ packed cup finely-minced parsley
1 tsp. dried dill weed (or 1 Tbs. freshly-chopped dill)
¾ packed cup grated mild white cheese
salt and pepper, to taste

Make the dough first (preceding page). As it rises, combine all above ingredients, and mix well. Proceed as described on opposite page.

CABBAGE·EGG

35-40 minutes to prepare.

2 Tbs. butter
1½ cups chopped onion
¾ tsp. salt
3 packed cups finely-shredded green cabbage
1 tsp. caraway seeds
½ tsp. dill weed
lots of freshly-ground black pepper
1 large carrot, coarsely-grated
1 tsp. prepared horseradish

6 hard-cooked eggs, finely chopped

1) In a large, heavy skillet, cook the onions with salt in the butter until clear & soft.

2) Add cabbage, caraway, dill, & pepper. Cook over medium heat, stirring, until the cabbage is tender (8-10 minutes).

3) Add carrots & horseradish. Cook several minutes more.

4) Remove from heat; stir in the chopped eggs. Proceed to fill the dough and bake as described on opposite page.

MUSHROOM

30 minutes to prepare.

2 Tbs. butter
1½ cups minced onions
¾ tsp. salt
fresh black pepper (lots)
1 Tbs. fresh lemon juice
1½ lbs. chopped mushrooms
¼ cup toasted sunflower seeds
½ cup wheat germ or fine crumbs
¼ cup (packed) freshly-minced parsley
1½ lbs. (3 cups) pot cheese (or very firm cottage cheese)

Dough recipe & method on p. 148.

(1) Melt the butter in a large, heavy skillet. Add onions, salt, and pepper. Sauté over medium-low heat until the onions are very soft (5-8 minutes).

(2) Add lemon juice and mushrooms. Stir and sauté over medium-high heat for 10-12 minutes, or until much of the liquid evaporates. Remove from heat. Transfer to a bowl.

(3) Add all remaining ingredients, and mix thoroughly. Fills 8 piroshki.

CALZONE
~~~~~~~~~~
(See method, p. 148.)

Pesto

Method A: 5 minutes to prepare.
Method B: 40 minutes to prepare.

A.   If you already have some pesto made (p.161), this filling is extremely simple. All you need to do is mix:

> 1 cup pesto
>
> with
>
> 2 cups ricotta cheese

B.   If you don't already have some pesto on hand, and you don't have the time or inclination to make real, bona fide pesto with real, bona fide fresh basil (and it is the dead of winter, and you can't find any fresh basil anywhere anyway) but you are CRAVING the flavor of pesto, and you <u>must</u> have it, here is a way to simulate it:

I call
this:
"winter pesto"

> 6 Tbs. dried basil (the freshest dried you can find)
> ½ cup olive oil
> ¾ cup ground (or very finely-minced) walnuts
> 5-6 medium cloves garlic, crushed
> ¾ cup grated parmesan cheese

(1) Place the basil and the olive oil in a heavy skillet. Let them sit there, so the basil can soak, for 15 minutes. Then add the walnuts, place over low heat, and sauté, stirring, for 8-10 minutes. Remove from heat.

(2) Combine with garlic and parmesan cheese. Mix well. Return to part A above, use this mixture in place of pesto, and combine with 2 cups ricotta cheese.   This fills 6 calzone, as per instructions (p.148).

Provolone

10 minutes to prepare.

combined {
4 Tbs. olive oil   1½ lbs. provolone cheese, grated
5-6 cloves garlic, crushed   1 large tomato, in 6 slices

Brush each circle of dough (see method, p.148) generously with the olive oil-garlic mixture. Divide the cheese into 6 parts; place ⅙ onto one side of each open calzone, top it with a tomato slice, fold over the other half, and crimp with a fork.

... Calzone Fillings, continued...
(method, page 148.)

Zucchini ♫ ♫ ♫

40 minutes to prepare;
Fills 6 calzone.

¼ cup olive oil

2 cups minced onion

4 medium cloves garlic, crushed

1 tsp. salt

1 tsp. each: oregano
                    basil

1½ lbs. zucchini, diced small

freshly-ground black pepper } to taste
crushed red hot pepper

½ lb. mozzarella cheese, grated

½ lb. (1 cup) ricotta cheese

(1) In a large, heavy cast-iron skillet, sauté the onion and garlic in olive oil, with salt, oregano, and basil – for 5-8 minutes.

(2) Add the diced zucchini. Stir and cook over medium heat, uncovered, for about 10 minutes, or until the zucchini is just tender. Add black and red pepper.

(3) Remove from heat, and immediately stir in the cheeses. Mix until very well-blended. Refrigerate until use.

NOTE: If liquid accumulates while the filling stands, drain it off before using.

A summer dinner:
*Chilled Cherry-Plum Soup (p.49)
Zucchini Calzone
*Chilled, Marinated Cauliflower (p.57)
and
*Chocolate Honeycake (p.274)

BLINTZES

There seems to be a special quality to the blintzes one makes at home in one's own kitchen. Somehow, those served in restaurants never quite measure up – they just don't compare, and I don't know why. It's possible that this is merely an illusion– the subjectivity of a person for whom the presence of a homemade blintz instantly summons memories of a loving mother or grand-mother frying something delicious in the next room. But I believe there is some truth to the theory that, in order for blintzes to come out Really Good (really, really good), the person making them must have great fondness for the persons eating them. This is known as the Fondness Theory of Successful Blintz-making.

A blintz pancake is practically identical to a crêpe, except that the blintz pancake, for some reason, is cooked on one side only. (The pancake recipe appears on the following page.)

Once filled, a blintz is usually fried in butter right before serving, whereas a crêpe is usually baked. (Instructions for blintz-frying are also on the next page.)

Blintz fillings are usually sweet. The most common filling is made from cottage cheese. Fruit (frequently cherries or blue-berries; sometimes peaches) is the next-most-common filling. (Filling recipes are on the page after next.)

Filled, fried blintzes can be frozen, then thawed, and reheated, covered, in a 325°F oven – for about 30 minutes. (But they do taste better when absolutely freshly-made.)

On page 156 is a wonderful recipe for leftover cheese blintzes: BLINTZ SOUFFLÉ. It is wonderful enough that you might not want to wait until you have leftover blintzes to try it. (It is a rare event to have leftover blintzes, anyway.)

THE BLINTZ PANCAKE

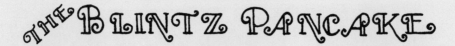

This recipe makes approximately 18 pancakes, enough to feed 6 people 3 apiece, or 3 people 6 apiece or any permutation in between. The batter can be made in advance, and stored in a covered container in the refrigerator for several hours. The cooked pancakes will not stack well, so they can't be stored easily. If you are making blintzes ahead of time, fill them, and store the filled pancakes in the refrigerator. Fry them just before serving.

- 3 large eggs
- ½ tsp. salt
- ¾ cup unbleached white flour
- 1⅓ cups milk
- 2 Tbs. oil or melted butter

Butter for frying.   /   Sour cream, for topping.

(1) Combine everything, and beat well. (You can do this in a blender. It works perfectly.)

(2) Heat a 6" omelette or crêpe pan over medium heat. Brush it lightly with melted butter. Pour in a small amount of batter – just enough to cover the bottom surface of the pan – and tilt the pan until the bottom is coated. Cook over medium heat until the edges of the pancake begin to pull away from the sides of the pan. Turn the pancake out – cooked side up – onto a clean, dry towel. Repeat until you've run out of batter. (NOTE: If you work quickly and keep the heat constant under the pan, you will only need to use butter for the first few pancakes. After that, the pan will season itself.

(3) **TO FILL:** Use 1 heaping tablespoon of filling (recipes opposite) for each blintz. Place the filling on one side, fold over once, fold in sides, and roll it up. Store on a platter until frying time.

(4) **TO FRY:** Use about 1 Tbs. butter for every 3 blintzes. Fry on both sides, in a heavy skillet, until quite brown and crisp. Serve right away, topped with sour cream.

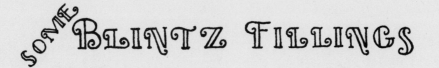

SOME BLINTZ FILLINGS

CHEESE:

...just a few minutes to prepare.

1 lb. cottage cheese

2 beaten eggs

2 Tbs. sugar

1 Tbs. flour

¼ tsp. salt

a dash or 2 of white pepper

(1) Press the cottage cheese through a sieve.

(2) Add remaining ingredients; beat well.

FRUIT:

about 30 minutes to prepare.

3 cups fruit (whole blueberries or whole pitted cherries or sliced peaches)

1 Tbs. lemon juice

3 Tbs. flour

3 Tbs. sugar (white or brown)

OPTIONAL: a few dashes of cinnamon and/or a few drops of almond extract

(1) Place the fruit in a saucepan all by itself. Cook it alone, partially-covered, over medium heat for 5 minutes.

(2) Add lemon juice. Gradually sprinkle in flour, as you stir. Continue to cook it, stirring, another 10 minutes over medium heat. Midway into the cooking, add sugar (and optional seasonings). Remove from heat; cool before filling blintzes.

BLINTZ SOUFFLÉ

This recipe is the creation of Louis Bardenstein, who is renowned in Rochester, New York as Bardy, the Kosher Caterer. I have personally witnessed people swooning with pleasure while eating this rich, yet ethereal delicacy at parties catered by Bardy. So be forewarned, hold on to your chair while consuming Blintz Soufflé, or you may find yourself transported out of this realm and into Blintz Heaven.

Two Notes:

1. This dish is called a soufflé, but technically, it is a custard, as the eggs aren't beaten separately, and there is no sauce. I'm qualifying this, so you won't get confused when you read the soufflé method on pages 170 and 171, and wonder why it doesn't apply here.

2. If this recipe seems just too rich for you, you can substitute yogurt for half the sour cream. You can also cut the sugar back to ⅓ cup (or even ¼ cup), and it will still come out just fine.

Once the blintzes are made, preparation time= 20 minutes. baking time= 1 hour.

6-8 servings. Preheat oven to 350°F.

¼ cup melted butter
18 cheese-filled blintzes (unfried) (pp. 154-55)
2 cups sour cream
6 eggs
½ cup sugar
1 tsp. vanilla extract
1 tsp. cornstarch
¼ tsp. salt

(1) Coat the bottom of a 9×13" oblong pan with melted butter.

(2) Arrange the blintzes side-by-side in the pan (in 2 rows).

(3) Beat together the sour cream and eggs until very light and fluffy. Add the remaining ingredients. Beat well. Pour this custard over the blintzes, and bake at 350°F. for 1 hour, uncovered. Serve hot, with fresh fruit.

Pasta

Homemade Pasta

If you wonder why some people go to the trouble of making fresh pasta instead of buying it dried in a store, the answer is: there really is a difference. Homemade pasta almost belongs to a separate category of food; its texture, flavor, satisfaction-inducing properties, and just general depth of character make fresh pasta a worthwhile and substantial main-dish. (The first time I tasted homemade pasta I was struck by how readily I could taste the egg in it! It's been difficult to go backwards to commercially pre-packaged pasta since this awakening.)

Fresh pasta has enough of its own quality to recommend it, so it is best to enhance it minimally, rather than to overwhelm it with oceans of sauce. Pasta Primavera (p. 162) is a good way to do justice to homemade pasta, and so is pesto (p. 161). You can go one step simpler, and just coat freshly-cooked drained noodles with some olive oil, a few sautéed mushrooms, and a small amount of grated cheese. Or simplest of all: try it with just butter and parmesan.

Those of you who have already discovered the pleasures of home-made pasta, and are convinced of its importance in your lives, have likely purchased your own pasta machines by now. (For those of you who are unfamiliar with this gadget: a pasta machine rolls very thin pasta with a hand crank, and cuts precise pasta shapes with uniform cutters. It is indispensible for serious pasta-makers who make pasta frequently and for more than 2 or 3 people.)

These few pages of introduction to pasta-making are not aimed at the experienced machine owners (who probably know everything I am about to say, plus a good deal more), but, rather, at the neophytes, who have never made pasta before. The yields of the following recipes are modest (2-3 servings at a time), as a lot of rolling and cutting are needed to turn out pasta by hand. If you find yourself loving the results, and you are seized with a passionate desire to make more pasta, you might consider saving up for a pasta machine of your very own (or, go in on one with a friend or two).

⭕ EGG PASTA DOUGH ⭕

The dough takes
about 15 minutes
to assemble, then
it needs 1 hour
to rest.

Rolling and cutting
take 45 minutes
to 1 hour. Cooking,
once the water is
boiling, takes
minutes.

Yield: enough pasta
for 2-3 servings.
(Double amounts
for lasagna.)

1½ cups unbleached white flour
or white bread flour
2 large eggs, at room temperature

NOTE: Unbleached white flour or white bread flour seem to be the best
choices when you are making pasta by hand, as they are glutinous
enough to become elastic and flexible when rolling the dough.

(1) Place the flour in a bowl, and make a well in the center.

(2) Beat the eggs well, and pour them into the well in the center of the
flour.

(3) Mix with a fork at first, then flour one of your hands, and knead the
dough until it is uniform and smooth. Add a little more flour if the
dough seems unreasonably sticky.

(4) Cover the dough with a clean tea towel, and let it rest at room temperature
for 1 hour.

(5) Roll and cut the dough, as described on the following page.

🍃 SPINACH PASTA DOUGH 🍃

This dough's
initial assembly
takes 20 minutes
longer than above.

Yield: enough pasta
for 3-4 servings.
(Double amounts
for lasagna.)

1 1-lb. bunch fresh spinach
2¼ cups unbleached white flour
or white bread flour
1 large egg, at room temperature

(1) Stem and wash the spinach. Chop it coarsely, and cook it in a heavy skillet
quickly, over high heat, with no additional water — until it is just limp,
but still brightly-colored. Purée in a blender, food mill, or food processor.

(2) Place the flour in a bowl. Make a well in the center, and add the purée
and the egg, beaten. Proceed as with the egg pasta, above.

After the pasta dough has rested for an hour, turn it out onto a lightly-floured surface, and knead it for 5 minutes. Divide it into 2 equal parts, and form each half into a ball. Roll them out, one at a time, slowly and patiently, with a rolling pin. Turn the dough over from time to time, and keep both rolling pin and work surface lightly-floured. Continue rolling until the dough is very thin. (As the dough gets thinner, it becomes increasingly important to keep the surface under it floured, so the pasta will not become permanently affixed to your kitchen counter...) The thinner, the better, as the egg and the flour will both expand as the pasta cooks, causing it to puff a little.

Now it is time to cut the pasta. (This is more fun than the rolling was.) Use a small or medium-sized sharp knife, and cut strips of whatever width you desire. The most common widths are:

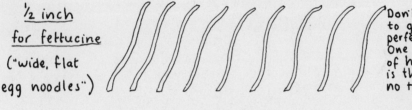

½ inch
for fettucine
("wide, flat
egg noodles")

Don't struggle too hard to get them all perfectly uniform. One of the charms of hand-cut noodles is that there are no two alike.

AND
2 inches
for lasagne:

This noodle didn't go to the hairdresser; it got cut by a ravioli wheel (also known as "fluted pastry cutter"), a widely-available & easy-to-use gadget.

If you intend to cook the pasta soon after you cut it (ie, if you're not planning to dry it for longer-term storage), store it temporarily on a lightly-floured tea towel, either in the refrigerator or at room temperature. If you intend to dry it for storage, use a wooden pasta-drying rack (available in "Cuisine" stores), or makeshift a facsimile thereof. (In Italy, a broom handle is commonly used.) After it is dry, store it in a sealed plastic bag.

To cook fresh, soft pasta, all it takes is 1-2 minutes in a generous quantity of rapidly boiling water. Drain and serve right away.

Pesto

Sweet Basil.

If you have never had cause to be glad you have a nose, pesto might lift you to new realms of nasal appreciation. One of the most aromatic of human concoctions, pesto is to your kitchen as the first hyacinth of spring is to your garden.

Pesto is a powerful mash of fresh basil and garlic, moistened with olive oil, sparked by sharp cheese, and subtly textured by pulverized nuts. It is commonly used as a sauce for pasta, yet its thick, pastelike consistency makes it readily usable as a seasoning in the preparation of other dishes (see index). It stores well in the refrigerator or freezer, so you can keep it on hand for a quick pasta dinner - or for whatever other special dish you might want it for.

This recipe makes about 2½ - 3 cups - plenty for 6-8 servings of pasta.

3 packed cups fresh basil leaves (no stems)

3-4 healthy cloves of garlic

¼ - ½ tsp. salt

¾ cup freshly-grated parmesan cheese

¼ cup pulverized nuts

½ cup olive oil

½ cup (packed) fresh parsley ⎫

¼ cup melted butter ⎬ optional

freshly-ground black pepper ⎭

1) Purée everything together in a blender or a food processor fitted with the steel blade - until it becomes a uniform paste, OR

2) Use a mortar & pestle, and coarse salt to pound the basil and garlic together. Stir in remaining ingredients.

FOR PASTA: Toss room temperature pesto with hot, drained pasta (about ¼ cup pesto per serving - more or less, to taste).

STORE IN A TIGHTLY-LIDDED JAR.

Pasta Primavera ("spring pasta") refers to the combination of pasta with delicately-cooked fresh early vegetables. Together, pasta and vegetables produce a wonderful complementarity of texture and soul.... as you discover the possibilies for combining them, new Quick-But-Elegant dinners will enter your repertoire. The recipe below is one example of a pasta primavera. Try it, and then experiment with different vegetables: ideally, what is just appearing – in slender, young form – at your produce stand (or, whatever is just dawning in your garden)....Zucchini, green beans, fresh herbs, asparagus...

Confetti Spaghetti

45 minutes to prepare.   4·5 servings.

This version of pasta primavera bears the colors of the Italian flag.

3 Tbs. each: butter and olive oil
1 cup minced onion
3-4 cloves garlic, minced
½ tsp. salt
lots of freshly-ground black pepper
1 tsp. dried basil
2 stalks broccoli – chopped
2 cups small cauliflowerettes

¼ lb. mushrooms, chopped
2 cups raw peas (fresh or frozen)
1 medium-sized red bell pepper, diced
3 Tbs. tamari sauce
1 lb. spaghetti or linguine
4-6 scallions minced
1 packed cup finely-minced parsley
2 packed cups grated cheddar

(1) In a large, heavy skillet, cook the onions and garlic in combined butter and olive oil, with salt, pepper, and basil, until the onions are soft (5-8 minutes).
(2) Add broccoli, cauliflower and mushrooms. Stir, cover, and reduce heat to medium-low. Let cook until the broccoli and cauliflower are just tender (8-10 minutes).
(3) Add peas and diced red pepper. Stir and cook over medium heat for just a few minutes – until the peas and pepper are just heated through. Remove from heat, and stir in tamari sauce. Set aside in a warm place, and cover it.
(4) Cook the pasta in plenty of boiling water until al dente. Drain, transfer to a large bowl, and immediately add the sauté with all its liquid. As you toss the mixture together, sprinkle in the scallions, parsley and cheese. Serve immediatamente!

Marinated Tomato Sauce

3 large (3" diameter) ripe tomatoes

¼ cup olive oil
½ tsp. salt

about 12-15 leaves of fresh basil
1 large clove of garlic, minced

lots of fresh black pepper
½ lb. mozzarella cheese, in small cubes

(1) Cut the tomatoes into 1-inch chunks.

(2) Using a sharp heavy knife or cleaver, mince the fresh basil leaves.

(3) Combine all ingredients in a bowl, and let it stand at room temperature for about 1 hour before cooking the pasta.

(4) Cook ½ lb. spaghetti or linguine in plenty of boiling water until <u>al dente</u>. Drain, transfer to a serving bowl, and immediately add the room temperature sauce.

Toss briefly and serve promptly.

Pepper Sauce

20-25 minutes to prepare.

sauce for 1 lb. of pasta. (6 servings)

Note: The ideal coordination between pasta and sauce preparations is to have your pasta water boiling as you start the sauce. Cook the pasta as you sauté the peppers. They should be ready at the same time.

6 medium-sized sweet peppers
4 Tbs. olive oil
1 large clove of garlic, crushed
½ tsp. salt
½ tsp. oregano

½ tsp. dried basil
lots of fresh black pepper
½ tsp. crushed red (hot) pepper
4 Tbs. red wine vinegar

(1) Cut the peppers in half lengthwise. Remove seeds and stems. Slice peppers into thin strips. Set aside.

(2) In a large, heavy skillet, begin cooking the crushed garlic in the olive oil, with salt, pepper, and herbs — over a medium flame. Do this for only about 1 minute.

(3) Add the peppers, and sauté them until tender-but-not-mushy (5-8 minutes).

(4) Remove from heat; stir in the vinegar. Toss with hot, drained pasta as soon as possible.

Pasta with Brussels Sprout, Mushroom & Cheese Sauce

30 minutes
to prepare.

...for ½ lb.
of pasta

(serves 3-4)
(easily doubled)

½ lb. (approximately 10 large) Brussels sprouts
½ cup chopped onion
½ lb. chopped mushrooms
2 Tbs. butter
¼ tsp. salt (more, to taste)
lots of freshly-ground black pepper

½ tsp. dill weed
½ tsp. dried tarragon
½ tsp. dry mustard
1 Tbs. flour
1 cup hot milk
½ tsp. prepared horseradish
1 packed cup grated cheddar

(1) Cut the Brussels sprouts into quarters, and put them up to steam for 10-15 minutes.

(2) Cook the mushrooms and onions together in butter, with salt, until the onions are soft (8-10 minutes over medium-low heat). Add herbs as they cook.

(3) Sprinkle in the flour, stirring as you sprinkle. Cook a few minutes more, stirring.

(4) Gradually drizzle in the hot milk. Stir with a wooden spoon. Cover, and cook over very low heat —stirring intermittently— for 5-8 minutes.

(5) Stir in the horseradish (increase, to taste, if desired), the cooked Brussels sprouts, and the cheese. Set aside while you cook your pasta.

Pasta with Marinated Artichoke Hearts

15-20 minutes
to prepare.

sauce for ½ lb. pasta
(3-4 servings)
(easily doubled)

1 6-oz. jar marinated artichoke hearts
1 Tbs. olive oil
1 Tbs. butter
1 cup sliced onions
1 tsp. dried basil

½ cup sour cream
½ cup cottage cheese
salt, pepper,
cayenne,   } to taste
parmesan cheese

(1) Drain the liquid from the marinated artichokes into a skillet. Slice the drained hearts into bite-sized pieces.

(2) Add the olive oil and butter to the drained-off marinade in the skillet. Heat this mixture, add the onions, and sauté them until soft (5-8 minutes). Add the artichoke hearts and basil. Sauté 3-5 more minutes.

(3) Remove from heat; stir in remaining ingredients. Cook and drain the pasta, and toss immediately with the still-warm sauce.

Lasagna al Pesto

.... all green.

1 lb. fresh spinach

1 cup minced onion

3 Tbs. olive oil

salt & pepper, to taste

½ cup grated parmesan

1 cup pesto (p. 161)

2 lbs. (4 cups) ricotta cheese

¼ cup toasted sunflower seeds

20-24 green lasagna noodles

1 lb. mozzarella cheese, in thin slices

~ extra olive oil for the top ~

The Filling:

1. Clean and stem the spinach. Chop it very fine. Set aside temporarily.
2. In a large, heavy skillet, sauté the onions in 2 Tbs. of the olive oil (save the other Tbs. of oil for the noodles) — until the onions are soft (5-8 minutes). Add salt and pepper in moderate quantities. Remove from heat.
3. Stir the raw spinach into the hot onions. Transfer to a large-ish bowl.
4. Add half the grated parmesan, the pesto, the ricotta, and the sunflower seeds. Grind in some extra black pepper. Mix thoroughly.

To Assemble:

1. a) If you are using fresh, soft home-made noodles (pp. 158-160), you won't need any precooking. b) If you are using dried noodles, boil them ever-so-briefly (about 2 minutes), then rinse them under cold water, and drizzle them with that leftover Tbs. of olive oil.
2. Place a layer of noodles in the bottom of your oiled 9 X 13- inch pan.
3. Spread ⅓ of the filling onto the noodles. Place ⅓ of the mozzarella over that.
4. More noodles. 5. Another ⅓ of the filling. 6. ⅓ more of the mozzarella.
7. Yet more noodles. 8. Remaining filling. 9. Remaining mozzarella.
10. One final layer of noodles. 11. Remaining parmesan. *And Finally:* 12. Drizzle the top w/ extra olive oil.

Cover with foil and bake for 35-40 minutes.

Hot Marinated Cauliflower
(((((& Macaroni)))))

50 minutes to prepare.   4 servings.

½ cup olive oil
2 large cloves garlic, crushed
2 cups chopped onion
½ tsp each: oregano
            basil
            thyme
            rosemary
1 tsp. salt
1 tsp. whole peppercorns
2 bay leaves

¼ lb. mushrooms – quartered
1 medium head cauliflower
⅓ cup wine vinegar
⅓ cup dry red wine
2 Tbs. tomato paste

1 12-oz. package elbow macaroni

½ cup freshly-grated parmesan
freshly-minced parsley
   (and, if available, a minced
       fresh basil leaf or 2)

(1) In a large, heavy saucepan, cook the garlic, onion, and herbs in olive oil over medium heat, until the onions are soft and translucent (5-8 minutes).

(2) Break the cauliflower into medium-sized flowerettes. Add these and the mushrooms to the sauté. Stir until well-mixed. Turn the heat to medium-low and cook, covered, for about 8 more minutes, stirring occasionally from the bottom.

(3) Add the vinegar, wine, and tomato paste. Stir until well-blended. Continue to cook – covered, and over low heat – until the cauliflower is just tender.

(4) Just before serving, cook the macaroni in plenty of boiling water until <u>al dente</u>. Drain well and mix with the hot sauce. (If you made the sauce earlier, you may want to heat it –gently– while the macaroni cooks.)

(5) Serve topped with parmesan (or any other sharp cheese of your choice) and freshly-minced parsley (and, if available, <u>basil</u>, for an additional Heavenly Quality).
   → If you have any of this left over, it is also good cold.

Cauliflower Paprikash

50 minutes to prepare.   4 servings.

2 Tbs. butter
1 cup chopped onions
2 Tbs. flour
1 tsp. prepared horseradish
1 cup sour cream
1 cup yogurt
2 tsp. mild paprika

½ tsp. salt
black pepper
1 12-oz. pkg. egg noodles
2 Tbs. poppyseeds
2 Tbs. each~freshly-minced
   dill & chives (or 2 tsp.
   each, if using dried herbs)

1 medium-sized cauliflower

(1) In a medium-sized, heavy saucepan, sauté the onions in 1 Tbs. of the butter, until the onions are soft (5-8 minutes). Sprinkle in the flour, mix well, and continue to stir and cook over low heat about 2 more minutes.

(2) With a wire whisk, beat in the horseradish, sour cream, and yogurt. Cook, stirring, over low heat another 5 minutes. Add paprika, and salt and pepper to taste.

(3) Break the cauliflower into small flowerettes. Steam them until tender. Add them ~still hot~ to the sauce.

(4) Just before serving, cook the noodles in plenty of boiling water until <u>al dente</u>. (If necessary, heat the sauce while the noodles cook. Heat it VERY GENTLY!) Drain the noodles, and transfer to a large serving bowl. Toss them immediately with 1 Tbs. butter and the poppyseeds.

(5) Spoon the hot sauce over the hot noodles. Top with dill, chives, and extra paprika.

Lukshen Kugel

5-6 servings.
Butter a 9x13" pan.
Preheat oven to 375°.

"Lukshen" means "noodles" in Yiddish. I call this by its Yiddish name to distinguish it from numerous other noodle kugel recipes, because this one is unusual: it contains no cheese. Its flavor has a provocative sweet/tart tension.

> Serve this as a summer
> luncheon entrée:
> with sour cream or yogurt,
> an Israeli salad (p.60)
> and Fresh Strawberry Mousse
> (p.263)

4 Tbs. butter
3/4 cup sliced almonds
3/4 tsp. cinnamon
1/2 cup chopped, pitted prunes
1/2 cup sliced dried apricots
2 Tbs. honey
1 12-oz package wide egg noodles

4 large eggs, well-beaten
1 tsp. salt
1 20-oz. can crushed pineapple ✳
   (packed in unsweetened juice)

1/2 cup wheat germ
extra cinnamon

(1) Melt 2 Tbs. of the butter in a medium-sized pan. Sauté 1/2 cup of the almonds with cinnamon for several minutes over medium-low heat — until the almonds are nicely-toasted. Stir in the prunes, apricots and honey. Cook just a minute or two more. Remove from heat.

(2) Cook the noodles in plenty of boiling water until only about 2/3-cooked (i.e., softened, but still pronouncedly al dente). Drain, and transfer to a bowl. Immediately add the sautéed almonds & fruit (be sure to scrape in all the butter) and mix well.

(3) Add salt and eggs. Mix well with a wooden spoon. Add the entire contents of the can of pineapple - liquid included. Mix well. Spread into your buttered 9x13" pan.

(4) Top with:
~remaining almonds
~wheat germ
~ a fine cloud of cinnamon
~ the remaining 2 Tbs. of
   butter, here & there, in
   thin slices ("dots").

(5) Bake uncovered
~35 minutes at 375°F.

✳ Believe it or not,
canned pineapple
is actually preferable
to fresh in this
recipe.

EGG STRAVAGANZA

Soufflés

Soufflés, elegant and elusive ~ and deceptively filling ~ have long been a source of intimidation for novice cooks. The accumulation of mystique surrounding this baked Egg Puff (which is basically what a soufflé is) has led many people to believe that only Official Gourmets have the license to concoct one. I would like to deflate this mystique (without deflating the Soufflé), and to encourage all mortal beings to understand just how the making of This Thing can be accessible to us.

There are only a few things you need to know how to do — and an equally few things you need to be Fussy about.

You need to know:

(1) how, in many cases, to make a basic white sauce, which involves melting some butter, whisking some flour into it to make a smooth paste (called a "roux"), and slowly pouring in some hot milk as you whisk to keep it smooth;

(2) how to gently cook this sauce until it thickens; and you need the moderate amount of patience required to watch over it, stirring;

(3) how to separate eggs, remembering to put your eggwhites in a large-enough bowl, as when you beat them they will greatly (7-8 times!) increase their volume;

(4) how to beat eggwhites, using a wire whisk or an electric mixer, until they are Stiff-But-Not-Dry. The little peak of eggwhite on the tip of the beater should be able to point upward with no outside assistance; AND

(5) how to fold eggwhites into a batter, using a rubber spatula and a firm-but-gentle cutting, lifting & side-of-bowl scraping motion, which will effectively incorporate air into the mixture.

Things you need to be Fussy about:

(1) Use a straight-sided soufflé dish.

(2) Butter above dish absolutely All Over the inside surface (you are not required to butter the outside surface).

(3) Use an oven thermometer; be sure you preheat your oven accurately.

(4) Separate your eggs earlier in the day, then cover the bowls and leave them to come to room temperature. (It is easier to separate cold eggs than room temperature eggs.)

(5) You will need the restraint necessary to Not Open the oven door for even the briefest of Peeks during the baking, plus

the ability to not jump rope or dance the jig on the kitchen floor while the soufflé is baking.

(6) MOST IMPORTANT OF ALL:

You need punctual guests, who will be seated and ready before the soufflé emerges from the oven. The average puff-span of a soufflé is approximately 1½ minutes, after which interval it will collapse into partial oblivion (although the flavor will still be intact).

In other words, do not plan to serve a soufflé when you are inviting chronically-late types of people to dinner.

Or, you can invite these people, and plan to serve a soufflé, but tell them the wrong time to arrive, like, for example, an hour early.

Tempus Fugit.

SO, these are the main things you need to know. You do not need to consciously apply any Magic.... the ingredients will contribute their own, if handled with loving attention and care.

Ricotta & Pesto Soufflé

♪Note: This recipe requires PESTO SAUCE (p.161), and assumes you have some on hand, in which case the PREPARATION TIME, including baking, is approximately 1½ hours.

⚜Generously butter a medium-sized soufflé dish, and sprinkle it with parmesan cheese.

⚜Preheat oven to 375°F.

⚜ 6 large eggs, separated, and at room temperature
⚜ 1 cup whole-milk ricotta cheese
⚜ 3 Tbs. melted butter
⚜ ¼ cup unbleached white flour
⚜ ½ tsp. salt
⚜ lots of freshly-ground black pepper
⚜ ¼ cup freshly-grated parmesan cheese
⚜ ½ cup pesto sauce (recipe on p.161)

(1) In a medium-sized saucepan combine the egg yolks, ricotta, butter, and flour. Whisk together until smooth. Cook over low heat, whisking, about 10 minutes.

(2) Remove the saucepan from the heat; add salt, pepper, parmesan, and pesto. Whisk well. Set aside to cool until it reaches room temperature. Transfer to a large mixing bowl.

(3) Beat the eggwhites until stiff but not dry. Gently, but persuasively, fold the whites into the room temperature ricotta mixture. Use a firm rubber spatula, and turn the bowl as you fold. Transfer the batter into your buttered soufflé dish.

(4) Without a moment's hesitation, enter the soufflé into the preheated oven, and immediately reduce the temperature to 350°F. Let it bake undisturbed for 40 minutes. As usual, serve it 0.0 minutes after removal from the oven.

Apple & Cheddar Soufflé

1½ hours to prepare
(including baking)

Preheat oven to 375°F.

Butter a medium-sized
soufflé dish.

1 cup milk
4 Tbs. butter
5 Tbs. flour
½ tsp. cinnamon
dash of nutmeg
½ tsp. salt

1 Tbs. honey
6 eggs, separated, and
   at room temperature
1 packed cup grated cheddar
2 cups grated tart apple
½ cup finely-minced walnuts

(1) Heat the milk slowly in a heavy saucepan. Remove from heat just <u>before</u> it boils.

(2) Melt the butter in a medium-sized saucepan. Whisk it, as you gradually sprinkle in the flour, and keep cooking and whisking the resulting roux for another 5 minutes.

(3) Still whisking the roux, drizzle in the still-hot milk. Cook over low heat, stirring steadily (use a wooden spoon) until the sauce thickens (8-10 minutes). Remove from heat.

(4) Stir in the spices, salt, and honey. Pre-beat the egg yolks, and drizzle them into the hot mixture, beating constantly. Transfer the whole thing to a large bowl (you can save on dishwashing if you just re-use the egg yolk bowl). Stir in the cheese, apple, and walnuts. Let cool to room temperature, stirring occasionally.

(5) Beat the eggwhites until stiff but not dry. Fold them gently and quickly into the sauce. Turn the soufflé into its baking dish.

(6) Place it in the preheated oven, turn the temperature down to 350°F, and leave the soufflé to bake in total concentration for 40 minutes. Remove and serve immediately.

FOR BRUNCH

Apple-Cheddar Soufflé
WITH sour cream OR yogurt
AND Grape Nuts Muffins
(p.115).

Cauliflower & Sour Cream Soufflé

About 1¼ hours
to prepare;

40 minutes
to bake.

Preheat oven
to 375°F.

Butter a medium
soufflé dish.

5 large eggs, separated, and at room temperature

2 Tbs. butter
1½ cups finely-chopped onions
¾ tsp. salt
lots of freshly-ground black pepper
1 tsp. caraway seeds

2 Tbs. fresh lemon juice
4 Tbs. unbleached white flour
1 cup sour cream (room temperature)
2 tsp. prepared horseradish (white)
1 medium head of cauliflower

(1) In a heavy saucepan cook onions in butter over medium heat, stirring. Gradually (over the first few minutes of cooking) add salt, pepper, caraway seeds, and lemon juice. Keep cooking and stirring for about 5 minutes.

(2) When the onions appear to have wilted considerably, turn the heat to Low, and begin to gradually sprinkle in the 4 Tbs. of flour. Keep cooking and stirring.

(3) Beat well together the egg yolks, sour cream, and horseradish. Add this mixture to the first mixture in the saucepan soon after step (2). Stir well, turn the heat to Very Low, and let it cook with great subtlety for 8-10 minutes. Stir with a wooden spoon from time to time. Remove from heat. Transfer to a large bowl.

(4) Break or chop the cauliflower into small flowerettes. Steam these until tender, then add them to the sour cream mixture.

(5) Beat the egg whites until stiff. Fold these assertively-but-compassionately into the first mixture. Transfer the soufflé into your prepared pan immediately, and pop it right into your preheated oven. Turn the dial down to 350°F. and let the soufflé bake in privacy for 40 minutes. Have your plates ready......

Dilled Asparagus Soufflé

About 1¼ hours to prepare;

40 minutes to bake.

Preheat oven to 375°F.

Butter a medium soufflé dish.

5 large eggs, separated, and at room temperature

1¼ lbs. fresh asparagus
3 Tbs. butter
½ cup minced onion
½ tsp. salt; black pepper to taste
¼ tsp. dry mustard

1 tsp. dill weed
½ tsp. crushed, dried tarragon
4 Tbs. unbleached white flour
1½ cups hot milk
½ cup (packed) grated mild cheddar

(1) Break off the tough first-inch-or-so of each asparagus spear. Chop the spears into ½-inch sections — on the diagonal, if possible. Steam until <u>just</u> tender. Rinse under cold water; drain well and set aside.

(2) In a heavy, medium-sized saucepan cook the onion in butter with salt and seasonings, until the onion is soft and translucent.

(3) Turn the heat way down, and gradually sprinkle in the flour as you stir constantly with a wire whisk. The resulting roux will be very thick. Keep cooking it another 5 minutes anyway, stirring intermittently with a wooden spoon.

(4) Keep that wooden spoon moving, and drizzle in the hot milk. Continue to stir and cook over very low heat another 8-10 minutes ~ until you have a uniformly-blended and nicely-thickened sauce. Remove from heat.

(5) Beat the egg yolks. Add a little of the hot sauce, beating well, then beat all the yolk-mixture back into the sauce. Stir in the cheese and asparagus. Set aside to cool to room temperature. Transfer to a large bowl.

(6) Beat the whites until stiff. Fold them into the first mixture, using a firm rubber spatula and quick, decisive strokes. Enter the soufflé into its awaiting dish - and bake it immediately for 40 minutes (turn the oven temperature down to 350°F. after it goes in). Serve <u>tout de suite</u>!

Cheddar Spoonbread

Spoonbread is a soufflé made with corn meal. In its basic form, it is a traditional American dish, often served for lunch, brunch or a light supper, with a sweet accompaniment, such as fruit preserves, honey or maple syrup. This version is augmented by fresh corn and cheddar cheese, making it a more substantial dinner-dish than the traditional version. Try serving it with cinnamon applesauce, home-made bread, and a leafy green salad.

6 large eggs, separated and at room temperature
2 cups milk
2 Tbs. butter
3 cups fresh corn (approximately 3 ears'worth)
½ tsp. salt
1½ cups yellow corn meal
1½ packed cups grated medium-sharp cheddar

(1) Heat the milk in a small saucepan until it just reaches the boiling point. Remove it from the heat before it boils. (This is called "scalding".)

(2) In a deep skillet — or a medium-sized saucepan — sauté the corn in the butter. Add salt. Stir and sauté over medium heat for a few minutes.

(3) Add the cornmeal to the corn. Stir and sauté them together for 5 minutes.

(4) Drizzle the hot milk into the sautéed corn & meal. Remove from heat. Transfer to a large bowl. Stir in the cheese, and beat in the egg yolks. Let the mixture cool to room temperature.

(5) Beat the eggwhites until stiff. Fold them into the corn mixture with a rubber spatula, combining the 2 mixtures as well as possible without deflating the whites. Transfer to the soufflé dish, pop it into the 400° preheated oven, and turn the temperature down to 375°F. Bake 35-40 minutes. Serve, pronto!

Pesto-Polenta Spoonbread

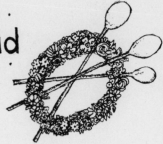

Polenta is a cheese-flavored corn meal mush, traditionally served as a pasta course in Northern Italian cuisine. Pesto sauce, also a traditional Italian specialty, is often served on or with polenta.

Serve this with crusty Italian bread, and cold, marinated cauliflower (p.57).

Pesto recipe is on p.161.

Preparation Time= 1¼ hours (includes baking, but assumes your pesto is made.)

Butter a medium soufflé dish.

Preheat oven to 400°F.

5 large eggs, separated and at room temperature

1½ cups yellow corn meal

2 cups water

¼ tsp. salt

¼ cup freshly-grated parmesan cheese

⅔ cup pesto sauce (recipe, p.161)

(1) Place corn meal and water together in a saucepan. Mix until well-blended, using a wooden spoon. Add salt. Heat this mixture until it comes to a boil. Lower heat.

(2) Cook over a low flame for 5-8 minutes, stirring frequently to prevent lumps. It will be very thick.

(3) Remove from the heat, and vigorously beat in the egg yolks. Stir in the parmesan and the pesto. Transfer to a large bowl, and set aside to come to room temperature.

(4) Beat the eggwhites until stiff but not dry. Fold them quickly-but-carefully into the first mixture, and transfer the whole affair to your well-buttered soufflé dish. With reasonable haste, place it in the oven, and turn the temperature down to 375°F. Let it bake in peace for 35-40 minutes, at which point it should be served without further ado.

Cheese  Soufflé

1¼ hours to prepare;
40 minutes to bake.

Butter a medium
soufflé dish.

4·5 servings.

Preheat oven
to 375°F.

6 eggs, separated
3 Tbs. butter
3 Tbs. flour
2 tsp. dry mustard
1¼ cups milk, scalded & still hot

1½ packed cups (approximately ½ lb.)
    grated sharp cheddar cheese
½ tsp. salt
black pepper ⎱
cayenne pepper ⎰ to taste

(1) Separate the eggs; put both yolks and whites in large bowls, cover them, and let them come to room temperature.

(2) In a medium-sized saucepan, melt the butter. Sprinkle in the flour and the dry mustard, whisking constantly as you sprinkle. Cook this roux all by itself, over low heat — still whisking- for a minute or two.

(3) Slowly add the hot milk, a little at a time, whisking vigorously during and after each addition, so that the mixture stays smooth and uniform. Cook this sauce over a low flame, stirring intermittently with a wooden spoon, for about 8-10 minutes. Remove from heat, stir in the cheese, and season with salt and pepper(s). Let come to room temperature, stirring every now and then, as it cools.

(4) Beat the egg yolks, then beat them into the cooled sauce. Then, return the mixture to the large egg-yolk bowl.

(5) Beat the whites until stiff. Fold them swiftly and adeptly into the first mixture, transfer the batter to the prepared Dish, and place it in the preheated oven. Bake for 40 minutes, undisturbed, and serve it posthaste to your already-seated-and-patiently-although-eagerly-awaiting Guests.

Omelettes

Everyone seems to have a personal method for making omelettes, and few of these personal methods would be considered "correct" according to French Haute Cuisine. But unless you intend to cook professionally in a French café —or in some other gourmet establishment specializing in omelettes— I don't think you need to struggle with learning <u>The</u> classic method. If you are comfortable with the way you already make omelettes, the only extra consideration you need take into account is the personal taste of whoever will be eating the result. But if you are NOT comfortable with your omelette-making, here are some pointers which may help to improve things for you:

1) Always let the eggs come to room temperature first (as ← illustrated).

2) Invest in a good, heavy omelette pan, 6-7 inches in diameter, with sides that angle outward.

3) Keep the pan seasoned: scrub it with water and salt (no soap) after use. Dry it by heating it; brush it with oil while it is still hot. Keep it oiled until its next use.

4) Heat the pan gradually, until it is good and hot, <u>before</u> adding the beaten egg. Use about 1 Tbs. butter for each 2-egg omelette. Let the butter melt. It will begin to make a crackling/sizzling noise when it is finished melting. As soon as it <u>stops</u> making the noise, that is the precise perfect moment to add the egg. Keep the heat constantly strong as you cook it, and work quickly, lifting the omelette sides and tilting the pan to let the uncooked egg flow into contact with the hot pan. (Don't leave your in-process omelette unattended while you go read the newspaper.) As soon as all the egg is set, apply the filling, fold it over, and slip (or flip) it onto a plate.

5) Have your filling ready <u>before</u> cooking the omelette (if it needs to be hot, have the filling heated).

6) Have your plates ready (and warmed, if possible).

7) Have your guests ready (if the omelette has to sit and wait, it will take insult and toughen).

❊ Some Omelette Fillings ❊

NOTE: When making multiple omelettes you can a) Make one big one and split it -OR- b) have 2 frying pans going at once -OR- c) work quickly, turn your oven to low, and use Momentary oven Storage until everyone's omelette is ready.

1. Spanish Omelette:

(sauce for 2; 15-20 minutes to prepare.)

½ cup minced onion
1 medium clove garlic, crushed
1 Tbs. olive oil
¼ tsp. salt
½ tsp. each: basil and oregano
black pepper & cayenne, to taste

1 small bell pepper, in very thin strips
1 medium-sized ripe tomato, chopped
4-6 green olives, minced
2 Tbs. dry red wine
2 Tbs. tomato paste

1) In a medium skillet, sauté onion and garlic in olive oil with salt, herbs, and pepper, until the onion is soft (5 minutes).

2) Add remaining ingredients, mix well, and cover. Cook over low heat another 8-10 minutes. You can either make your omelettes immediately, or store the filling for up to several days. Reheat gently before using.

2. Persian Omelette:

(sauce for 2-3; 15 minutes to prepare.)

1 Tbs. butter
½ cup chopped onion
¼ tsp. salt (more, to taste)
¼ tsp. each: cumin, cinnamon, turmeric, dry mustard,
                                      and thyme
black pepper and cayenne
6 large mushrooms, sliced
¼ cup slivered toasted almonds
1 small (6") banana, sliced

1) In a medium skillet, sauté onion in butter, with salt and spices, until the onion is soft (5 minutes).

2) Add the mushroom slices, and sauté another 5-8 minutes. Remove from heat; stir in almonds and banana slices. Make your omelettes right away; put some finely-chopped parsley into the beaten egg.

3. **Sherried Mushroom Omelette:**   (sauce for 2; 20 minutes to prepare.)

> 1 Tbs. butter
> about a dozen large mushrooms, sliced
> 2 tsp. unbleached white flour
> ¼ tsp. salt (more, to taste)
> lots of black pepper
> ¼ tsp. each: thyme, dill weed
> ¼ cup dry sherry
> 1 finely-minced scallion (include green part)
> 2 Tbs. sour cream

1) In a medium skillet, cook the mushrooms in butter for several minutes.
2) Add flour, salt, and seasonings, stirring well as you sprinkle them in. Keep stirring, and cook over low heat 5 minutes.
3) Add sherry. Stir and cook over low heat 5 minutes more. Remove from heat; stir in minced scallion and sour cream. Proceed to make your omelettes.

4. **Gourmet Quickies:**   (uncooked)
   a) **Mexican:** Canned green chilies, jack cheese plus sliced avocado. Sprinkle a little ground cumin and basil into the beaten egg.

   b) **Marinated Artichoke Hearts with Järlsberg Cheese:** Use your favorite brand of marinated artichoke hearts, let them come to room temperature, slice them into manageable pieces. Cut the cheese into strips. Beat a little horseradish and dry mustard into the eggs.

   c) **Ricotta Cheese with Parmesan and Pesto:** The pesto recipe is on p. 161. (It's nice to keep some on hand for quick pasta dinners, or for omelettes, such as this one.) Make sure your ricotta is room temperature. There are no rules about amounts or proportions—use your taste as a guide.

5. It just so happens that **Enchilada Fillings** #1, 2 or 4 (pp. 144-145) double beautifully as omelette fillings. If you cut the amounts by half, you'll have enough of each to fill 3 or 4 omelettes.

6. **Leftovers:** Many of the casseroles in this book, if left over, would make fascinating omelettes. Experiment boldly (especially if you only have a little bit of something left over, and you're eating alone); you might Discover Something.

HUEVOS RANCHEROS

Traditionally, this dish consists of fried eggs nestled in a crispy corn tortilla, covered with a tomato & pepper sauce. This version substitutes corn bread for the tortilla, and thus becomes more substantial as a supper (rather than breakfast) dish. The corn bread soaks up the spicy sauce quite nicely.

If you don't have the time or the desire to bake the corn bread, use crispy tortillas (or even tortilla chips, if you are in a hurry, and you happen to have some on hand) instead.

Green Chili & Cheese Corn Bread (p. 111)

2 medium-large (3" diameter) tomatoes
½ cup chopped onion
½ cup chopped green bell pepper
1 Tbs. olive oil
1 Tbs. red wine vinegar
½ tsp. salt
lots of fresh black pepper
¼ cup diced canned green chilies
↳ (and/or ½ tsp. crushed red hot pepper)

4 large eggs
butter for frying

½ cup (packed) grated jack cheese
(or any mild white cheese)

(1) Combine all the sauce ingredients in a blender or a food processor fitted with a steel blade. Purée, and transfer to a saucepan.

(2) Heat the purée to boiling point. Cover, reduce heat, and simmer 10 minutes.

(3) Cut 2 generous squares of cornbread, and slice them in half lengthwise. Place them in the toaster, and fry the eggs in butter as the bread toasts. Place 2 bread-halves on each plate, place and egg on each piece, and pour sauce over the top. Sprinkle with cheese, and serve right away.

Eggs Florentine

In French cooking, "Florentine" means: on a bed of spinach.

(ORIGIN: In the 16th century, when Catherine de Medici married the King of France, she brought with her her personal chefs from Florence. It was in France that they encountered spinach for the first time... apparently with great enthusiasm....)

45 minutes to prepare; 20-25 minutes to bake.

4-5 servings

Butter a 9x13" pan.

Preheat oven to 375°F.

1½ cups chopped onion

2 Tbs. butter

½ lb. mushrooms, sliced

1 tsp. salt

2 lbs. fresh spinach - cleaned, stemmed, & chopped

3 Tbs. butter

3 Tbs. flour

3-4 Tbs. dry sherry

1½ cups hot milk

1 Tbs. Dijon mustard

¼ tsp. salt (more, to taste)

black pepper

8 small pats of butter

8 eggs

½ cup (packed) grated Swiss cheese

nutmeg

paprika

(1) In a very large skillet, begin cooking the onions in butter over medium heat. After several minutes, add the mushrooms and salt. Sauté about 5-8 minutes, or until the onions are very soft. Add the spinach gradually (it won't fit all at once) and keep stirring over low heat until all the spinach is in and just slightly cooked (not more than 5 minutes). Remove from heat, and spread into a buttered 9x13" pan.

(2) In a saucepan, melt the 3 Tbs. butter and whisk in flour. Whisk and cook this roux over low heat for a minute or 2, then add the sherry, and cook another few moments. Drizzle in the hot milk, whisking constantly. Add mustard, salt, and pepper. Stir and cook over low heat until smooth and slightly thickened (10-12 minutes). Set aside.

(3) Place 8 pats of butter symmetrically on top of the spinach bed. Break an egg onto each pat. Carefully spoon the sauce over and around the eggs. Sprinkle the top with grated Swiss cheese, and small amounts of nutmeg and paprika. Bake uncovered for 20-25 minutes. Let stand 5 minutes before serving.

Poached Eggs
on a bed of Vegetables

30 minutes to prepare.

2 servings (easily multiplied)

This is a colorful, easy one-dish supper. It lends itself nicely to 2 servings (enough, but not too much... perfect with a tossed salad and some cooked grains), and it can easily be doubled to serve 4.

The vegetables are sautéed first, and the eggs are then poached directly on top of the sauté. Bring the whole pan to the table, so your eating partner(s) can see how attractive the dish looks before it is served.

1 Tbs. butter
½ cup minced onion
a large handful of mushrooms, sliced
2 small stalks of broccoli (about 2 cups, chopped)
½ tsp. salt
lots of fresh black pepper
a few dashes of cayenne
½ tsp. each: basil and dill weed
1 small red or green bell pepper, diced
1 medium tomato, chopped
1 cup freshly-chopped spinach
¼ cup sour cream
4 large eggs

(1) In a large (10") cast iron skillet, begin cooking onion in butter over medium heat. After a few minutes, add the mushrooms, broccoli, and salt. Continue to cook and stir about 5 minutes.

(2) Add herbs, bell pepper, and tomato. Cook and stir 5 minutes. Stir in spinach and sour cream, and turn the heat up to medium-high. With a large spoon, indent 4 little beds for the eggs.

(3) Break the eggs into their beds. Cover, and poach about 5 minutes, or until <u>just</u> set. Bring to the table, and serve immediately.

1 Frittata:

35 minutes to prepare
4 servings.
Preheat oven to 350°F.

* 2 Tbs. olive oil
* 1 Tbs. melted butter
* 1 small onion, minced
* 1 small clove garlic, minced
* ½ tsp. salt
* freshly-ground black pepper
* ½ tsp. each: basil, oregano
* ¼ tsp. each: thyme, rosemary

* 5-6 mushrooms, sliced
* 1 small (5") zucchini, sliced
* 1 small bunch of spinach or swiss chard, chopped
* 1 small bell pepper.
* 5 large eggs, well-beaten
* a few slices of mozzarella
* grated parmesan

(1) In a 9-or 10-inch cast-iron skillet, cook the onion and garlic with salt and herbs in combined olive oil and butter, 5-8 minutes.

(2) Add remaining vegetables, and cook quickly over medium-high heat until the vegetables are tender (8-10 minutes).

(3) Turn the heat way up, wait just a minute (to be sure it's good and hot), and pour in the beaten eggs. Cook on the stove-top for several minutes, lifting the edges, and letting the uncooked egg flow underneath the cooked egg (as you would for an omelette). Turn the heat back to medium as you do this.

(4) As soon as the egg appears set, place a few pieces of mozzarella here and there on its top surface, and sprinkle with parmesan. Place it in the oven for 12-15 minutes (until it is firm, and the cheese is melted and about to brown). Remove and serve in wedges – hot or room temperature.

→ Cold frittata wedges make wonderful sandwich fillings (with fresh spinach and home-made mayonnaise – p. 79.)

2 Savory French Toast:

10-15 minutes to prepare.

SERVING
* 1 egg, beaten
* ½ cup milk
* 2-3 slices of bread
* a few dashes of salt

* black pepper
* a few slices of sharp cheddar cheese

* optional: a few dashes of basil

* – butter – *

(1) Beat together the egg and milk with salt, pepper, and optional basil.

(2) Soak the bread in the custard, and fry it on both sides in butter. (It helps to get your skillet Very Hot first.) After you turn it over, place pieces of cheese on the cooked side. Let it melt. Serve hot. Good with _applesauce_.

3 Fancy Scrambled Eggs

10 minutes to prepare.

* Beaten eggs & butter for frying
* → FRESH chives
* → FRESH parsley
* → FRESH basil and/or marjoram
* small cubes of cream cheese
* small chunks of fresh tomato
* salt and pepper, to taste

Normal scrambled egg procedure, with the following changes   1) With a scissors, snip fresh herbs into the beaten egg 2) Add cubes of cream cheese when the eggs are about half-done and 3) Add chunks of tomato at the very end.

4 Curried Eggs

15-20 minutes to prepare / 4 servings / Preheat broiler..

* 6 eggs - boiled for 6 minutes
* 3 Tbs. butter
* ½ tsp. mustard seeds
* ½ tsp. each: cumin & turmeric
* ¼ tsp. each: salt, cayenne, ground cloves & ginger
* ½ cup sour cream
* ½ cup yogurt
* ¼ cup sesame seeds

1) Brush a pie pan with 1 Tbs. melted butter.
2) Peel the eggs, slice them in half lengthwise, and place them face-up in the pie pan.
3) Melt the other 2 Tbs. butter in a small pan. Add the mustard seeds, and cook them a few minutes - until they pop. Add all other spices.
4) Beat together the sour cream & yogurt. Add the spiced butter. Mix well, and spoon this on top of the eggs. Sprinkle with sesame seeds and broil for 5 minutes - or until bubbly.

5 Broiled Eggs

15 minutes to prepare.   / Preheat broiler.

* Thick slices of French or Italian bread
* Butter, and a clove or 2 of garlic
* Fried Eggs, with salt, pepper & oregano
* Slices of your favorite cheese

1) Crush garlic into the butter. Spread this onto both sides of the bread slices.
2) Fry the bread on both sides until crisp.
3) Place the bread in a shallow pan. Place a fried egg on each slice, and cover the egg with cheese. Broil until the cheese melts.

TOFU

SO WHAT IS THIS STUFF CALLED TOFU? (Are you afraid to ask, because it seems that Everyone Else Knows, and they'll think you aren't cool?)

I am happy to offer a few words on behalf of tofu, having been completely won over by the charms of this humble and versatile substance. Whether you are a vegetarian, or you would just prefer to consume less meat, there may come a time when you need a change from eggs and dairy products as your main protein alternatives. Here is where tofu steps in to answer your prayers.

Tofu is soybean curd, made from soy milk (a non-dairy substance made from soy beans). It is prevalent, in many forms, in East Asian cuisines. Soft, cheese-like, and bland in its basic form, tofu lends itself beautifully to seasonings. Its texture can be altered in many ways through various cooking and pressing techniques. Tofu is high in protein, low in calories and carbohydrates, and has no cholesterol. It is also inexpensive, especially when purchased at specialty tofu shops or made at home. If there is no tofu shop near you, and you don't wish to make your own, look for tofu in natural food or whole-grain stores, Japanese or Chinese food markets, and in the produce sections of more progressive supermarkets (its availability increases with its fame). It is usually sold by the pound (in a solid block, or in "cakes"~usually 4 per pound), packed in water in sealed plastic containers. Refrigerate it and change its water daily, and tofu will keep up to a week.

Tofu is so adaptable, you can choose to feature it (as in the following recipes), or to use it more anonymously as a protein & texture booster for salad dressings, casseroles, soups, breads, etc. (It mashes and purées easily for anonymity.) If you marinate it you'll have great snack or hors d'oeuvres material, or a condiment to other dishes. Furthermore, tofu makes wonderful baby food. It is soft and digestible (the crude soy fiber is left behind in the making), and very nutritious. In addition to protein, it has calcium, iron, vitamin E, and magic healing and comforting powers. Tofu can be mashed and flavored with just about anything. (see "Tofu for Children", p.198.)

The following recipes feature tofu in main dishes. Look in the index for a list of all the other places in this book where tofu appears.

For further ideas and a wealth of information (including detailed instructions for making tofu at home), the definitive work is <u>The Book of Tofu</u>, by William Shurtleff and Akiko Aoyagi.

Sweet & Sour Tofu with Mushrooms & Cashews

Marinate the tofu earlier in the day (or the day before).

The remaining preparation takes only about ½ hour.

4 Servings.

→ Don't forget to start cooking your rice about 20 minutes in advance of beginning the stir-fry. (2 cups brown rice: 3 cups water.)

1 lb. tofu, cut into small cubes	Freshly-ground black pepper
¼ cup fresh lemon juice	2 tsp. peanut oil
¼ cup tamari sauce	8 scallions, minced (whites plus greens)
6 Tbs. water	1 green bell pepper } in strips
¼ cup tomato paste	1 red bell pepper } in strips
2 Tbs. honey	1 lb. mushrooms ∿ quartered
1 tsp. freshly-minced ginger	½ tsp. salt
4 medium cloves of garlic, crushed	1 cup toasted cashew pieces

(1) Cut the tofu, and set aside.

(2) Combine the next 8 ingredients in a bowl, and mix until well-blended. Add the tofu to this marinade, stir gently, and let it marinate, covered, for several hours. (It can be refrigerated and marinated overnight ∿ or all day.)

(3) About 10 minutes before serving time, set up your wok (or skillet) over a flame, and let it heat up for a minute or two. Add the oil to the hot wok, and immediately add the vegetables and the salt. Stir-fry very quickly over high heat. After several minutes, add the tofu plus all its marinade. Lower the heat to medium, and continue to stir-fry another several minutes (until everything is hot and bubbly). The total stir-frying time should not exceed 10 minutes. Remove from heat, and stir in the pre-toasted cashews.

Serve immediately, over rice.

Broccoli & Tofu

... in spicy peanut sauce

4-5 servings.

Vegetable & Sauce preparation time = 20-30 minutes.

Stir-frying Time = 15-20 minutes.

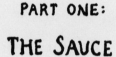

PART ONE:

THE SAUCE

½ cup good, unprocessed peanut butter
½ cup hot water
¼ cup cider vinegar

2 Tbs. tamari sauce
2 Tbs. blackstrap molasses
¼ - ½ tsp. cayenne pepper

(1) In a small saucepan, whisk together the peanut butter and the hot water until you have a uniform mixture.

(2) Whisk in the remaining ingredients. Set aside.

(Don't forget to start cooking rice about 10 minutes before you begin your stir-fry.)

PART TWO:

THE SAUTÉ

1 1-lb. bunch of fresh broccoli
3 Tbs. peanut oil
2 tsp. freshly-grated ginger root
4 medium cloves garlic, minced
1 lb. tofu, cut into small cubes

-a few dashes of salt-
2 cups thinly-sliced onion
1 cup coarsely-chopped raw peanuts
2-3 Tbs. tamari sauce
2 freshly-minced scallions

(1) Cut off the bottom half-inch of the broccoli stems. Shave off the tough outer skins of the stalks with a sharp paring knife or a vegetable peeler. Cut the stalks diagonally into thin slices. Coarsely chop the flowerettes. Set aside.

(2) Begin heating the wok (or a large, heavy skillet). When it is hot add 1 Tablespoon of the peanut oil. Add half the ginger and half the garlic. Salt lightly. Sauté over medium heat for 1 minute, then add the tofu chunks. Turn the heat up a little, and stir-fry the tofu for 5-8 minutes. Transfer it, including whatever liquid it might have expressed, to the saucepanful of peanut sauce. Mix together gently.

(3) Wipe the wok with a paper towel, and return it to the stove to begin heating once again. Add the remaining 2 Tbs. of oil to the hot wok, and follow suit with the remaining ginger and garlic. Salt lightly. Add the onions, and grind in some fresh black pepper. Sauté, stirring frequently, over medium heat, until the onions are soft (about 5 minutes).

(4) On another burner, begin heating the peanut-tofu sauce on a very low flame. It shouldn't actually cook – it only needs to be warmed through.

(5) Add the broccoli and the chopped peanuts to the wok. Add 2-3 Tbs. tamari sauce, and stir-fry over medium-high heat until the broccoli is bright green and just tender (about 5 minutes).

(6) Pour the heated peanut sauce over the sauté. Toss gently until everything is coated with everything else. Sprinkle in the minced scallions as you toss.

Serve over rice, and pass around some additional tamari, hot sauce, and even more chopped peanuts, if desired.

These are very
easy and simple.

About 4 servings.

45 minutes to
prepare (including
the rice-cooking);
30 more minutes
to cook.

Tofu-Nut Balls

½ cup raw brown rice
1 cup water
2 Tbs. tamari sauce
a generous ½ cup finely-ground almonds
½ lb. tofu, mashed
½ cup wheat germ

(1) Place the rice, plus 1 cup of water, in a small saucepan. Bring to a boil, cover, and lower the heat to a simmer. Cook until very soft - about 30 minutes.

(2) Place half the tofu in the jar of a blender, along with the tamari sauce and about 3/4 of the cooked rice. Blend to a thick paste.

(3) Mash the remaining tofu with a fork. Add the mixture from the blender, along with all the remaining ingredients. Mix well.

(4) Use your fingers to make the batter into a series of 1-inch balls. At this stage, you can either refrigerate the balls up to 24 hours before cooking, or cook them right away.

(5) To cook, either 1) Deep-fry in hot (360°F) oil until crisp. Drain.
or 2) Bake on a lightly-greased tray - 30 minutes at 350°F.

⇨SERVE: 1) As an hors d'oeuvre, on toothpicks, to your bewildered, but polite (and ultimately delighted) guests; 2) In tomato sauce with pasta, 3) With french fries and ketchup 4) With Mushroom-Tahini Sauce (p.232).

HOT TOFU AND SESAME NOODLES

¾ cup good, unprocessed peanut butter

1¼ cups hot water

3 Tbs. cider vinegar

1½-2 Tbs. tamari sauce

¾ cup toasted sesame seeds

4½ Tbs. Chinese sesame oil

½ tsp. crushed hot red pepper

½ lb. tofu (cut into small chunks)

2 pkgs. ramen noodles ↓

[These are available in most Asian
(and some American) groceries ~ in
small, cellophane-wrapped units.

If you can't find them, substitute
a half-pound of vermicelli noodles.]

1 medium cucumber

4 scallions, finely minced

¾ cup finely-chopped cashews or peanuts

(1) In a medium-sized saucepan, combine the peanut butter and the hot water, stirring with a whisk until they form a smooth mixture.

(2) Add the vinegar, tamari, sesame seeds, sesame oil, crushed red pepper (or cayenne) and tofu chunks. Stir until blended. Set aside for now.

(3) Open your package of ramen noodles, discover the enclosed tiny envelope of "flavor mix", and throw it away in the garbage. Set the noodles aside.

(4) Begin boiling about a quart and a half of water in a large saucepan.

(5) Take the medium cucumber, peel it if necessary (i.e., if it's waxed), and cut it lengthwise down the center. Remove and discard the seeds. Slice (or coarsely grate) the cucumber into very thin strips.

(6) Heat the peanut sauce over a low flame, and add the noodles to the boiling water. Boil them for 3 minutes only, then drain well, and mix with the sauce.

(7) Serve in individual bowls, topped generously with strips of cucumber, minced scallion, and chopped nuts.

Tofu, Spinach & Walnut Loaf

40 minutes to
to prepare;
I hour to bake.

...with Dilled Horseradish Sauce

4-6 servings

Preheat oven to 350°F.

I.

2 Tbs. butter or oil
1½ cups minced onion
½ lb. mushrooms, minced
1 cup ground walnuts

2 lbs. fresh spinach, chopped
⅓ cup dry sherry
1 Tbs. worcestershire sauce
½ tsp. salt

1 Tbs. tamari sauce
½ lb. tofu, mashed
1½ cups wheat germ
black pepper & nutmeg

(1) In a deep skillet, saute' the mushrooms and onions in butter or oil until the onions are soft (about 5 minutes). Add the nuts, spinach, sherry, worcestershire sauce and salt. Stir and cook over medium heat another 5-8 minutes, or until the vegetables are just-cooked-through, and everything is well-mingled.

(2) Add remaining ingredients (black pepper and nutmeg to taste), and stir until very well-combined. Spread into an oiled, medium-sized loaf pan. Bake, uncovered, for I hour at 350°. Serve hot, with the following sauce (which you can prepare as the loaf bakes):

II.

2 Tbs. butter
2 Tbs. flour
1¼ cups hot milk

1 Tbs. prepared horseradish
1 tsp. tamari sauce (more, to taste)
½ tsp. dill
½ tsp. mild paprika

(1) In a medium-sized saucepan, melt the butter. Whisk in the flour. Continue to whisk and cook the roux over low heat for a minute or 2.

(2) Drizzle in the hot milk, whisking constantly. Whisk and cook over medium-low heat 5-8 minutes, or until smooth and nicely-thickened. Stir in remaining ingredients; cover, and set aside until serving time. Don't cook the sauce any further; just heat it gently before serving.

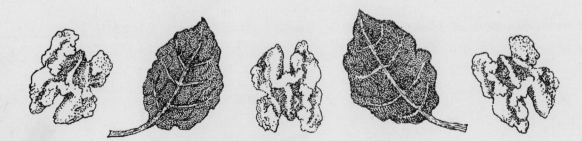

About 40 minutes
to prepare.

(Quite Easy!)

Tofu Sukiyaki

4 servings

Before you begin: put up 2 cups brown rice
to cook in 3 cups of water. Bring to
a boil, cover, and lower heat to a simmer.

¼ cup tamari sauce
1 cup water
3 minced scallions
1 large clove of garlic, sliced
1½ tsp. freshly-grated ginger
1 Tbs. cider vinegar
1 Tbs. honey

1-2 Tbs. dry sherry
1 lb. tofu
½ lb. fresh mung bean sprouts
1 stalk celery
1 large carrot
1 large green bell pepper
⅓ lb. fresh green beans

(1) In a large saucepan, combine the tamari sauce, water, scallions, garlic, ginger,
vinegar, honey, and sherry.

(2) Cut the tofu into small (1-inch) cubes, the celery and carrot into thin diagonal
pieces, the bell pepper into strips, and the green beans (make sure you
remove their stems and strings!) in half lengthwise (to make long, thin strips).
You will need a good, sharp knife or cleaver for all this.

(3) Place all the items from step (2) into the saucepanful of liquid (step (1)). Bring
to a boil, then cover, and lower the heat to a simmer. Cook until all the vegetables are tender (10-15 minutes), but not mushy. Serve over rice, in bowls,
including some of the broth with each serving.

Szechwan Tofu Triangles
in Triple Pepper Sauce

45 minutes to prepare.

(You may wish to put up some rice 25-30 minutes before wok time)

4 servings.

3 firm cakes (¾ lb.) tofu
½ cup peanut oil (or vegetable oil)

1 large green bell pepper ⎫ in thin
1 large red bell pepper ⎭ strips
4 large scallions, minced
1 Tbs. peanut -or vegetable- oil

⅓ cup dry sherry or rice wine
tamari sauce (see step 4)
1½ cups water
3 cloves garlic, crushed
1½ tsp. dry mustard
½ tsp. crushed dried red hot pepper
¼ tsp. freshly-ground black pepper
2 Tbs. cornstarch

(1) Cut the tofu cakes into triangles, as illustrated: 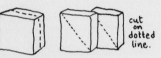 cut on dotted line.

(2) Heat the ½ cup oil in a wok or a deep skillet ~ until the oil is hot enough to instantly bounce a drop of water on contact. Fry the tofu triangles until their outer surface crispens (a few minutes on each side). Use additional oil, if necessary. Drain the triangles on paper towels, and keep them warm in a low oven.

(3) Prepare the bell peppers and scallions (cut the peppers into strips; mince the scallions). Set aside.

(4) In a 1-cup liquid measure, pour some wine up to the "⅓-cup" mark. Add enough tamari sauce to make ½ cup of liquid.

(5) Combine tamari-sherry mixture with water, garlic, mustard, & red-hot and black peppers. Place the cornstarch in a bowl. Whisk the liquid into the cornstarch.

(6) Heat your wok or skillet. Add 1 Tbs. oil, and sauté the bell peppers and scallions, stirring over medium heat, for 3-4 minutes. Pour in the sauce, turn the heat up a little, and stir-fry about 5-8 more minutes. Add the triangles, stir gently, and serve immediately.

Tofu Marinades

Tofu is an excellent absorber of marinades. With the discovery of this special tofu trait, the world of simple tofu meals takes on a new dimension: FLAVOR. (Add this to the list of tofu's more obvious attributes: softness, substantiality, innocence....)

Once you get into the habit of marinating tofu, you will be able to design more satisfying meals around brown rice, green salads, and steamed or sautéed vegetables.... and you might find yourself actually looking forward to these very simple meals.

FOR SALADS: Cut a couple of small cakes of tofu into tiny cubes, and place them in a jar with your favorite vinaigrette salad dressing (figure on one cake of tofu per ½ cup of salad dressing). Do this at least several hours ahead of serving time (or, the night before), and simply pour the whole jarful onto your salad before tossing it.

FOR BROWN RICE: For each serving, cut one medium-sized cake of tofu into medium-sized chunks. Place them in a bowl with a tablespoon of tamari sauce and a teaspoon of Chinese sesame oil. Add a Tablespoon of vinegar, a few teaspoons of toasted sesame seeds, some freshly-ground black pepper, and a minced scallion. (Optional: a few drops of hot sauce.) Let this marinate for several hours or overnight. Mix it in with your rice just before you eat it.

FOR STEAMED OR SAUTÉED VEGETABLES: For every 2 servings, cut 2 medium-sized cakes of tofu into medium-sized chunks. Add 3 Tbs. tamari sauce, a crushed clove of garlic, juice from a lime or from half a lemon, black pepper, and a teaspoon of honey. (Optional additions: a tablespoonful of Chinese sesame oil, some toasted cashews, a little mustard or worcestershire sauce.) Let it stand for several hours, and add it to steamed or sautéed vegetables just before serving.

TOFU FOR CHILDREN

Many parents wish they could somehow cause their young children to become more readily attracted to tofu, especially since it is so nutritious and inexpensive. The truth is, children often have an innate appreciation of tofu:

→ They enjoy the sensation of picking it up with their bare hands and squeezing it until it oozes out between their fingers.

→ They like to chase it around on their plate with a spoon.

→ They derive pleasure from throwing it on the floor and stepping on it.

→ They also like to eat it.

Here are a few quite-successful approaches:
(good luck!)

(1) Heat ½ inch of vegetable or peanut oil in a heavy skillet. Cut tofu into small (½-inch) cubes, and dust them lightly with sifted cornstarch. When the oil is hot, fry the tofu cubes until crisp. Drain on paper towels, and sprinkle with a little tamari sauce. This makes a great snack!

(2) Mash some tofu with a ripe banana. Add a little bit of honey and some raisins and toasted sunflower seeds. Eat it with a spoon....wash it down with a glass of apple juice.

(3) Cook some egg noodles. Drain the noodles and immediately add some cottage cheese and tofu, cut into half-inch cubes. Sprinkle with tamari sauce and a few drops of Chinese sesame oil.

(4) Sneak some mashed tofu into mashed potatoes. (This method is for the most stubborn of resisters...)

(5) Make Tofu-Nut Balls (p. 192), and serve them with Lots of Ketchup.

Casseroles, Mélanges,

...and other groupings

Escalloped Apples au Gratin

45-50 minutes to prepare;
40 minutes to bake.

4 servings.

Preheat oven to 375°F.

<u>A Request</u>: Please don't be deterred by the presence of sauerkraut in this recipe. Even if it seems strange, give it a chance – it is really good! (I've served this dish to sauerkraut haters without forewarning them. They've loved it... and have not believed me when I've revealed the Secret Ingredient, it blends in so well.)

1 2-lb can sauerkraut

6 heaping cups peeled, sliced tart apples (about 6-8 large apples'- worth)

2 Tbs. flour

½ tsp. cinnamon

a dash of : cloves, nutmeg, and salt

2 Tbs. honey

2 Tbs. butter

1 cup chopped onions

½ tsp. dry mustard

½ lb. mild cheddar cheese, grated

¾ cup fine bread crumbs

¾ cup finely-chopped walnuts or almonds

(1) Place the sauerkraut in a colander or strainer, and rinse it well under cold tap water. Squeeze it dry.

(2) Toss together the apple slices, flour, and spices. Drizzle in the honey, and mix well.

(3) Sauté the onions in the butter until clear and soft (5-8 minutes). Add the dry mustard and the sauerkraut, and cook another few minutes over medium heat. Remove from heat.

(4) Take half the grated cheese, and combine it with the breadcrumbs and chopped nuts. Leave the other half of the grated cheese to stand alone.

(5) Now for the fun part: in your buttered deep-dish casserole, make the following pattern of layers : 1st, a layer consisting of half the apple mixture; next, half the onion - sauerkraut mixture; 3rd, the plain, grated cheese; 4th the Remaining Apples, followed by the Remaining Onion/Sauerkraut mix; and FINALLY, the Nut-Crumb-Cheese Topping! Cover, and bake for 20 minutes, then <u>un</u>cover, and bake 20 minutes more.

Mushroom Mystery Casserole

This recipe is fashioned after one of my mother's specialties, which she calls: "Mush-Mosh."

1 Tbs. butter
1 cup chopped onion
3/4 tsp. salt
2 stalks celery, minced
1/4 tsp. each - dry mustard,
                    thyme
2 lbs. mushrooms, coarsely chopped
lots of freshly-ground black pepper
2 Tbs. unbleached white flour
2-4 Tbs. dry sherry
4 healthy slices crisp, buttered whole-grain toast,
       ↳ cut into cubes ↙
1/2 cup (packed) grated sharp cheddar cheese

4 large eggs
1 cup milk
paprika...for the top

(1) In a large, heavy skillet, sauté the onions and celery in butter with salt and herbs, until the onions are clear and the celery just tender (5-8 minutes).

(2) Add mushrooms and black pepper. Continue sautéing over medium heat, stirring frequently, for about 5 minutes.

(3) Gradually sprinkle in the flour, mixing constantly. Keep mixing, and cook 5 minutes more over low heat. Add sherry, stir, and cook an additional 5 minutes - low heat.

(5) Spread the sauté in your buttered casserole dish. Sprinkle the toast cubes on top, and follow suit with the grated cheese.

(6) Beat together the eggs and milk (for extra froth, whip them in the blender), and pour this custard over the top. Dust generously with paprika, and bake uncovered for about 45 minutes, or until firm and nicely-browned.

Vegetable Upside-Down Cake

4-6 servings.

Preheat oven to 350°F.

PART I.

4 Tbs. butter

3 Tbs. wheat germ

1 cup chopped onion

small pieces {
2 cups chopped broccoli
1½ cups chopped cauliflower
1 large, chopped carrot

1 minced green bell pepper

1 cup raw corn (fresh or frozen)

¼ tsp. salt (to taste)

lots of freshly-ground black pepper

1 packed cup grated sharp cheddar
         or Swiss cheese

(a) Melt 3 Tbs. of the butter. Pour it into a 9 x 13-inch pan, distribute it evenly, and sprinkle in the wheat germ.

(b) With the remaining Tbs. of butter, sauté the onion in a large skillet for about 5 minutes. Add the next 3 vegetables; continue sautéing until they're tender.

(c) Add green pepper, corn, and seasonings. Sauté a few minutes more.

(d) Spread the still-hot vegetables into the buttered, wheat-germed pan. Sprinkle the cheese over them ~ it will melt nicely. Let this stand while you prepare PART II.

PART II.

1 cup unbleached white flour

¾ cup whole wheat flour

1½ tsp. baking soda

½ tsp. salt

½ tsp. each ~ basil, thyme,
          oregano, dill

¼ cup grated parmesan cheese

½ cup wheat germ

2 large eggs, beaten

¾ cup buttermilk

¼ cup melted butter

(a) Sift together flours, soda, salt, and herbs. Stir in parmesan and wheat germ. Mix well, and make a well in the center.

(b) Beat together the eggs, buttermilk, and melted butter.

(c) Pour the liquid mixture in the well in the center of the dry ingredients. Mix until well-combined, being sure to scrape the bottom and sides of the bowl.
→ THE BATTER WILL BE VERY STIFF! Undauntedly —and carefully— spread it over the cheese-coated vegetables. Use a blunt knife and/or a rubber spatula to distribute it as evenly as possible.

(d) Bake, uncovered, 30 minutes. Have ready a serving tray slightly larger than the baking pan. Invert the hot cake firmly and carefully onto the tray, and Voilà!

Shepherd's Pie

... a deep-dish casserole: vegetable hash on the bottom, and a potato crust on top.

1¼ hours to prepare;
35 minutes to bake.

4-5 servings.
Preheat oven to 350°F.

salt and pepper, to taste
½ cup yogurt
½ cup freshly-minced chives
½ cup freshly-minced parsley

I. { 2 large potatoes
1 Tbs. butter

1½ Tbs. butter
1½ cups chopped onion
1 large clove garlic, crushed
1 tsp. salt
black pepper
1 stalk finely-minced celery
12 oz. chopped mushrooms

1 1-lb. eggplant, in small cubes
1 green bell pepper, minced
¼ tsp. thyme
½ tsp. each: basil, oregano
1 cup raw (fresh or frozen) peas
½ cup (packed) grated cheddar
3 Tbs. wheat germ
1 Tbs. cider vinegar

(1) Cook the potatoes (in their skins) in boiling water, until soft. Drain, and mash with all ingredients from "I". Set aside.

(2) In a large, heavy skillet, sauté the onions and garlic in 1½ Tbs. of butter, with salt and pepper, until the onions are soft (5-8 minutes).

(3) Add the celery, mushrooms, and eggplant. Cook over low heat, stirring occasionally. When the eggplant is cooked through (and this will happen more quickly if you cover the skillet between stirrings), add green pepper, herbs, and peas. Continue cooking about 5 minutes longer.

(4) Remove from heat; toss with cheese, wheat germ, and vinegar. Spread this mixture into your buttered deep-dish casserole. Spread the mashed potatoes on top, as a crust. OPTIONAL (and OPTIMAL): Sprinkle extra cheese plus some paprika on top. Bake uncovered, 35 minutes.

Tsimmes

40 minutes
to assemble;
2 hours
to bake.

4-6 servings
(Depending
on what else
gets served)

Tsimmes is a festive Jewish dish that combines vegetables and fruit, savory and sweet... all baked together. This version is 98% traditional; its 2 points of departure are the omission of a few chunks of meat, and the optional addition of cheese in the topping. Serve it with the Spinach Kugel (see opposite page), and a freshly-baked challah (p.97) for a warming winter supper.

I.
- 2 lbs. sweet potatoes
- 2 large carrots, sliced
- 1 large (3-4 inch diameter) tart apple, sliced
- 1 heaping cup chopped onion
- 20 large, pitted prunes
- juice of 1 large lemon
- 1 tsp. salt
- ¼-½ tsp. cinnamon (to taste)
- ⅔ cup fresh-squeezed orange juice

II.
- 2 eggs, beaten
- ¼ cup wheat germ, matzo meal or fine crumbs
- ½ tsp. salt
- (optional: ½ cup [packed] grated mild cheddar)
- 3 Tbs. butter, cold, and in thin slices

(1) Take half the sweet potatoes and grate them coarsely. Set these aside. With the other half, cut bite-sized slices or small chunks.

(2) In a deep-dish casserole, combine the sweet potato chunks with all the other ingredients in List I. Toss until nicely-mixed.

(3) Mix together the grated sweet potato with the other ingredients from List II. Pat this into place on top of the first mixture in the casserole. Dot the top with the butter slices.

(4) Cover tightly and bake for 1 hour. Remove the cover, and bake another hour, until the top is brown and crisp.

Vegetable Kugels

A kugel (which, in loose translation from the Yiddish, means a "pudding") (which translation is so loose as to be downright Vague) is a Basic Item of Jewish cuisine. So what is it already? .... easier to describe than to define: Generally, a kugel is a baked shallow casserole, consisting of a bunch of small units of food (ie- noodles, or a finely-chopped or grated vegetable) held together with beaten egg. It is cut into squares, and the top surface is usually crisp.

The classic vegetable kugel is Potato (p.207), and here, in addition, are 2 others: one for spinach, and one for carrots and zucchini. [There is also a Noodle ("Lukshen") Kugel recipe on p.168.]

Spinach Kugel

30 minutes to prepare; 45 minutes to bake.

4-5 servings.

Preheat oven to 375°F.

Butter a 9×13-inch pan.

2 lbs. fresh spinach ~ chopped
6 oz. (¾ cup) cream cheese
1 lb. (2 cups) cottage cheese
4 large, well-beaten eggs
1 cup matzo meal

¾-1 tsp. salt (to taste)
¼ tsp. nutmeg (more, to taste)
lots of fresh black pepper
1½ Tbs. fresh lemon juice
paprika ~ for the top

(1) In a heavy skillet, cook the spinach quickly – with no added water— over medium heat, stirring until it just begins to wilt (about 4-5 minutes). Remove from heat, and cut in the cream cheese while the spinach is still hot. Mix well, until the cheese is melted and well-distributed.

(2) Add all remaining ingredients, except ¼ cup of the matzo meal, and beat well.

(3) Spread into your prepared pan, and sprinkle the ¼ cup matzo meal over the top. Dust with paprika. Bake, covered (you can use foil) for 35 minutes, then uncover it and let it bake 10 minutes more.

Carrot-Zucchini Kugel

45 minutes to prepare;
1¼ hours to bake.

4-6 servings.

Butter a 9x13" pan.

Preheat oven to 375°F.

6 packed cups coarsely-grated zucchini
    (approximately 3-4 medium zucchini)
3 cups finely-minced onion
3 Tbs. butter
¾-1 tsp. salt
3 packed cups coarsely-grated carrot
    (approximately 5 medium carrots)
3 large eggs, beaten
¾ cup matzo meal, fine breadcrumbs,
        or wheat germ
6 Tbs. flour
1 tsp. baking powder
freshly-ground black pepper

dots of butter for the top (about 2-3 Tbs.)

1) Place the grated zucchini in a colander over a sink or a bowl. Salt it lightly, and let it stand 15 minutes. Squeeze out all excess moisture.

2) In a heavy skillet sauté the onions in 3 Tbs. butter with ¾ tsp. salt over medium heat, until the onions are soft and translucent (5-8 minutes). Remove from heat.

3) In a large bowl mix together the zucchini, sautéed onions, and grated carrot. Beat in the eggs and the matzo meal (or crumbs or wheat germ).

4) Sift in the flour and baking powder. Grind in a generous amount of fresh black pepper. Mix well.

5) Spread the batter into a well-greased 9 x 13-inch baking pan. Place thin slices of butter here & there on the top surface. Bake 1¼ hours, uncovered.

Tante Malka's Potato Kugel Deluxe

40 minutes to prepare;
1-1¼ hours to bake.

4-6 servings.

Butter a 9x13" pan.

Preheat oven to 375°F.

4 medium (4" long, or so) potatoes
3 cups chopped onion
4 Tbs. butter
1¼ tsp. salt
½ lb. mushrooms, chopped
black pepper, to taste
¾ tsp. dill weed

4 large, beaten eggs
1½ cups sour cream
½ cup matzo meal or wheat germ
   (or fine crumbs)

paprika

(1) Scrub and coarsely grate the potatoes. Set aside.

(2) Sauté the onion in butter, with salt, for about 5 minutes over moderate heat. Add mushrooms, black pepper, and dill. Sauté another 5-8 minutes.

(3) Combine the raw grated potatoes with the sauté in a large bowl. Beat in the eggs, sour cream, and matzo meal (or wheat germ, or crumbs).

(4) Spread evenly into a well-greased 9x13-inch baking pan. Dust the top with paprika. Bake 1-1¼ hours, uncovered, at 375°F – until crisp on top.

For a Delicious & Inexpensive Supper:
* Swedish Cabbage Soup (p.31)
* The Above Kugel (serve with a little
   extra sour cream on top)
* Applesauce (add cinnamon & walnuts)
* Vegetables Rémoulade (p.15)
* Whole Wheat Poppyseed Cookies (p.279)

Humble Vegetable Casserole

1¼ hours to prepare;
½ hour more to bake.

4 servings.

Preheat oven to 350°F.

2 Tbs. butter
½ cup sliced onion
½ lb. sliced mushrooms
1 large stalk of broccoli, chopped
2 medium-sized potatoes, thinly-sliced
¾ tsp. salt
black pepper, to taste
½ tsp. dill weed

2 hard-boiled eggs, chopped
½ cup chopped sweet pickle
1½ packed cups grated cheddar
1 tsp. caraway seeds

¾ cup milk
paprika

(1) In a large, heavy skillet, cook the onions over very low heat, in the butter, until they begin to soften (3-5 minutes).

(2) Add the mushrooms, broccoli, potato slices, and salt. Stir and cover. Continue cooking over medium-low heat until the potato slices are just tender (8-10 minutes). Don't overcook, as this will cause the vegetables to become Boring.

(3) Season the cooked vegetables with black pepper and dill, stirring to well-acquaint everything with everything else.

(4) In a separate bowl, toss together the chopped egg, pickle, grated cheese and caraway seeds.

(5) Spread half the cooked vegetable mixture into the bottom of your buttered deep-dish casserole. Sprinkle half the egg-cheese mixture over the vegetable layer, distributing it evenly and unimaginatively.

(6) Repeat step (5) [see directly above], only this time use the other half of each mixture. Pour the milk over the top of the casserole, and dust with paprika. Cover, and bake for 30 minutes at 350°F.

Carrot~Cashew Curry

45 minutes
to prepare.

4 servings.

4 Tbs. butter
3-4 cloves garlic, crushed
1 tsp. freshly-minced ginger
1 tsp. mustard seeds
1 tsp. ground cumin
1 tsp. ground coriander
1 tsp. dill weed
1 tsp. turmeric

2 cups sliced red onion
1½ tsp. salt
2 small potatoes, thinly-sliced
4 large carrots, thinly-sliced
2 cups orange juice
cayenne pepper, to taste
2 red bell peppers, thinly-sliced
1½ cups toasted cashew pieces

1 cup yogurt

(1) If you plan to serve this over rice, put up the rice to cook before you begin. 3 cups of water to 2 cups of rice: bring to a boil together, cover, and turn heat to low. It will be done 20-30 minutes later.

(2) Melt the butter in a large, deep skillet. Add the garlic, ginger, and mustard seeds. Sauté over medium heat until the seeds begin to pop (3-5 minutes).

(3) Add the remaining spices, and the onions, salt, potatoes, and carrots. Keep sautéing and stirring another 5-8 minutes. Add the orange juice. Cover, turn the heat to medium-low, and simmer until the potatoes are edibly tender (10-15 minutes).

(4) Add the cayenne, the bell pepper slices, and the cashews. Cover, and let it stew another few minutes — until the peppers are just barely cooked.

(5) Stir the yogurt into the hot curry just before serving.

Serve over rice, with a sweet chutney, OR: see page 210.

* Potato, Panir & Pea Curry *

30 minutes to prepare.   4 servings.

1 Tbs. butter	a pinch of thyme
1 tsp. mustard seeds	½ tsp. salt
½ tsp. caraway seeds	black and cayenne pepper
2 cloves garlic, crushed	2 large potatoes—thinly-sliced
1 Tbs. sesame seeds	½ cup water (approximately)
½ tsp. ground cumin	¼ cup fresh-squeezed lemon juice
½ tsp. turmeric	3 cups raw peas (fresh or frozen)
½ tsp. ground cloves	1½ cups large curd cottage cheese

(1) In a large, heavy skillet, melt the butter, and add the seeds, the garlic, and all the spices, except the salt and pepper(s). Cook, stirring, over medium-low heat, for several minutes, or until the mustard and sesame seeds start to pop.

(2) Add the thinly-sliced potato, along with the salt and black and cayenne peppers. Keep the heat to medium-low, and stir the potatoes until they are thoroughly coated with all the buttery seasonings.

(3) Add ½ cup of water, and cover the skillet. Let it cook – disturbing it every now and then to stir it – until the potatoes are tender. (You might need to add small amounts of extra water if sticking occurs.) Be careful not to let the potatoes get too mushy.

(4) Add the lemon juice, peas, and cottage cheese about 5-10 minutes before serving time, as the peas should be just barely cooked. Stir well, and keep the heat fairly low.

For a memorable Indian meal, with wonderful contrasting textures, serve Potato, Panir & Pea Curry with *Indian Eggplant Salad (p. 64) and *Carrot-Cashew Curry (p. 209).

Eggplant-
Pecan
Curry

1 hour to prepare.

4 servings.

2 Tbs. butter
3 medium cloves crushed garlic
1 tsp. freshly-grated ginger root
1½ cups minced onion
¾ tsp. salt
1 tsp. dry mustard
1½ tsp. turmeric
½ tsp. cayenne pepper
1 tsp. ground cumin

½ tsp. allspice
2 Tbs. flour (unbleached white)
water, as needed to prevent sticking
↳(about ½ cup)
1 1-lb. eggplant, in 1-inch cubes
1 red bell pepper, sliced
1 cup chopped, toasted pecans
⅔ cup half & half - or evaporated milk
1 medium-sized ripe tomato, chopped

(1) In a very large, heavy skillet, cook garlic, ginger, and onion in butter, with salt, over medium heat. Stir frequently, and cook for 5 minutes.

(2) Add spices, and gradually sprinkle in the flour. Continue stirring and cooking another 5-8 minutes. Add water, a little at a time, if needed to prevent sticking.

(3) Add eggplant, stir well, and cover. Lower the heat, and let it cook about 10-15 minutes. Interrupt it every so often for a stir, and to see if perhaps it needs even a little more water to further prevent sticking.

(4) When the eggplant is tender, add the remaining ingredients. Cook and stir over low heat another 5-8 minutes.

Savory Vegetable Cheesecake

Butter a 10" springform pan. Sprinkle in a small handful of fine breadcrumbs.

6-8 servings.

50 minutes to prepare; 1½ hours to bake and rest before serving.

Preheat oven to 375°F.

3 cups (packed) coarsely-grated zucchini

3 Tbs. butter

1 cup minced onion

2-3 cloves garlic, crushed

½ tsp. salt

1 cup grated carrot

3 Tbs. flour

½ tsp. each: basil, oregano

¼ cup (packed) freshly-minced parsley

1 Tbs. fresh lemon juice

3 cups ricotta cheese

1 packed cup grated mozzarella cheese

½ cup freshly-grated parmesan cheese

4 large eggs (at room temperature)

freshly-ground black pepper

2 medium-sized tomatoes, sliced into rounds, then each round sliced in half (into "D"s). Dredged in:

3-4 Tbs. fine breadcrumbs.

(1) Set the grated zucchini in a colander over a sink or a bowl. Salt lightly, and let stand 15 minutes. Squeeze out all excess moisture.

(2) In a large, heavy skillet, sauté the onions in butter with ½ tsp. salt. After several minutes, add garlic, carrots, zucchini, flour, and herbs. Keep stirring, and cook over medium heat 8-10 minutes. Remove from heat; stir in parsley and lemon.

(3) Beat together cheeses and eggs (the best result comes from using an electric mixer at high speed), until very well-blended. (Use a LARGE BOWL for this!) Add the sautéed vegetables and mix well. Season to taste with black pepper (and more salt, if necessary).

(4) Turn into the above-described Prepared Pan. Bake uncovered - at 375°F- for ½ hour. Then, interrupt its baking experience momentarily, to decorate it with the above-mentioned Dredged Tomato "D"s, distributing them like so:

Tomato Arrangement.

(5) Return the cake to the oven, reduce the heat to 350°F, and bake another 30 minutes. Turn off the oven, open the door, and leave the cake in there for 15 additional minutes. Then let it cool 10-15 minutes more—out of the oven— before cutting and serving.

influenced vegetable stew

... similar to a Greek "stifado", but meatless,
and containing more vegetables...

About 2 hours
to prepare.

4 servings.

³/₄ cup raw kidney beans } soaked overnight, then cooked in
boiling water until tender (1½-2 hours),
and drained

3 Tbs. olive oil
4 medium cloves crushed garlic
1½ cups chopped onion
1¼ tsp. salt
1 cup thinly-sliced potatoes
1 tsp. cinnamon
1 tsp. ground cumin
lots of fresh black pepper
crushed red hot pepper, to taste
juice from 1 large lemon
2 large carrots, sliced
1 small cauliflower, broken into small flowerettes
4 medium-sized fresh, ripe tomatoes, cubed
2 tsp. honey

(1) In a very large skillet, sauté the onions and garlic in olive oil, with salt, for
5 minutes, or until the onions are soft and translucent.

(2) Add potatoes, spices, and lemon juice. Cover and cook 8-10 minutes, stirring
occasionally. (Add small amounts of water, if it appears to be sticking.)

(3) Add remaining ingredients, except beans. Cover, and let it stew over medium heat
about 30 minutes, stirring occasionally.

(4) Add the cooked beans, stir, cover, and let it simmer about 10 minutes more.

serve with Tsatsiki (cucumber salad) (p.62)
and Greek Olives,
a Crusty Bread,
and Amaretto Cheesecake (p.276)

Persian Eggplant

1 hour to prepare;
35-40 minutes to bake.

4-5 servings

Oil a 9x13" baking pan.

Preheat oven to 350°F.

3 Tbs. olive oil
2 large cloves of garlic, crushed
1 cup chopped onion
½ lb. chopped mushrooms
1 1½-lb. eggplant - in 1" cubes
½ tsp. dill weed
½ tsp. ground cumin
¾-1 tsp. salt
black and cayenne peppers

juice from 1 medium lemon
½ packed cup dried currants
½ cup raw bulghur wheat
1 tsp. honey

2 Tbs. butter
2 Tbs. flour
1¾ cups hot milk
2 hard-boiled eggs, grated

(1) In a very large, heavy skillet (or Dutch oven-type saucepan) sauté the onions and garlic over moderate heat for several minutes. Then stir in the mushrooms, eggplant, seasonings, and lemon juice. Keep cooking and stirring over medium heat for about 5-8 more minutes.

(2) Add the currants, bulghur (raw), and honey. Stir well, and cover. Simmer over medium-low heat about 10-15 minutes, stirring intermittently. When the eggplant is edibly-tender, remove from heat, and spread it into an oiled 9x13" pan.

(3) In a small saucepan, melt the butter over low heat. Sprinkle in the flour, whisking constantly. Continue to whisk, and cook this roux gently for 3-5 minutes. Gradually drizzle in the hot milk - still whisking. When all the milk is added, graduate from whisk to wooden spoon, and stir and cook about 5-8 minutes more - until smooth and slightly-thickened. Remove from heat, and stir in the grated hard-boiled eggs.

(4) Pour this sauce over the eggplant mixture, and spread it as evenly as possible. Dust the top with paprika, and bake, uncovered, for 35-40 minutes at 350°F.

Spicy Baked Beans with Rum & Molasses

1½ hours ~ bean-cooking time
(during which, one
can prepare the rest)
& 1½-2 hours more to bake.

4 main-dish servings
(more yield if it's a
side dish)

2 cups raw pea (navy) beans

3 Tbs. butter

2 cups chopped onion

3 cloves crushed garlic

¾ tsp. salt (more, to taste)

2 tsp. dill weed

1 tsp. allspice

lots of fresh black pepper

4 Tbs. dark (Dijon or Poupon) mustard

4 Tbs. dark molasses

3 cups tomato juice

¾ cup dark rum

2 tsp. tamari sauce

1 cup water

2 Tbs. fresh lemon juice

1-2 diced carrots

1-2 stalks minced celery

1 chopped bell pepper

(optional: 1 tsp. freshly-grated ginger)

~ Sour cream for the top of each serving ~

(1) Place the beans in a large kettleful of water. Bring to a boil, then partially cover, and cook over medium heat until the beans are tender (1-1½ hours). Check the water level from time to time during cooking. Drain, if necessary.

(2) (You can do this while the beans are cooking...) In a large saucepan, sauté the onions and garlic in the butter, with salt, until the onions are soft (5-8 minutes).

(3) Add all remaining ingredients, except the beans, vegetables and sour cream, to the onions. Simmer, covered, for about 45 minutes.

(4) Preheat the oven to 300°F. Combine the cooked beans, the sauce, and the raw, chopped vegetables in a large casserole. Cover tightly, and bake about 1½-2 hours.

Serve topped with sour cream, accompanied by a green, leafy salad and Green Chili & Cheese Corn bread (p.111).

Frijoles con Queso, Etc. Casserole

This is a 3-layer casserole ~ almost like a cobbler ~ with spicy, cheesy beans on the bottom, vegetables in the middle, and a crusty cornbread topping. Soak your beans well in advance, and prepare other parts of the casserole as the beans cook. (1½ hrs. to prepare; 40 min. to bake)

1½ cups raw pinto beans
4 oz. (½ cup) cream cheese
1 cup firm yogurt
½ cup (packed) grated mild white cheese
1 Tbs. olive oil
1½ cups chopped onion
2-3 large cloves crushed garlic
¾ tsp. salt

½ tsp. ground cumin
½ tsp. dried basil
lots of black and cayenne pepper
{ 1 medium (7") zucchini, in chunks
{ 2 medium-sized tomatoes, chopped
{ a few dashes each: salt, pepper,
                          oregano,
                          basil

(1) Soak the pintos in plenty of water ~ for several hours (overnight is best). Cook them in twice as much water until tender (approximately 1½ hours). Drain, and immediately cut in the cream cheese, so it will melt nicely into the still-hot beans. Mix in the yogurt and cheese. Set aside.

(2) YOU CAN DO THIS WHILE THE BEANS COOK: Sauté the onions and garlic in olive oil with ¾ tsp. salt, the cumin, the ½ tsp. basil, and the black & cayenne pepper... about 5-8 minutes. Add this sauté to the bean/cheese mixture. Mix well, and transfer to a buttered 2-quart, deep casserole.

(3) In the same skillet you used to sauté the onions, etc., pan-fry the zucchini chunks (you don't need to add extra oil if you're careful) with a little salt, pepper, basil and oregano. Use medium heat, and stir constantly. Cook them for only about 3 minutes, then add the chopped tomato, turn the heat up a little, and continue to stir and cook another 5 minutes. Spread this mixture on top of the beans.

⌥CORNBREAD TOPPING⌥

⌥1 cup yellow corn meal
⌥½ cup unbleached white flour
⌥½ tsp salt
⌥1 tsp. baking powder
⌥½ cup yogurt
⌥1 large egg

(1) Combine the 4 dry ingredients. Preheat oven to 375°F.
(2) Beat together the yogurt and egg, and stir into the dry mixture until well-mixed.
(3) Spread this batter on top of the zucchini/tomato layer of the casserole. Bake 40 minutes at 375°F ~ uncovered. Serve immediately.

Broccoli & Buckwheat Godunov

Buckwheat...

...and its groats.

About 40 minutes to prepare;
35-40 more minutes to bake.

4 servings.

I.

1 cup (raw) buckwheat groats ("Kasha")

1½ cups water
½ tsp. salt
1 Tbs. butter

1 cup sour cream
1 cup yogurt
2 beaten eggs

Bring the water to a boil in a large saucepan. Add groats, cover, and cook over low heat 5 minutes. Remove from heat, and fluff with a fork. Add remaining ingredients, and mix well.

II.

3 Tbs. butter
2 cups chopped onion
½ lb. chopped mushrooms
1 1-lb. bunch broccoli,
    chopped fine

1 tsp. salt
½ tsp. dill weed
½ tsp. caraway seeds
black pepper ~ lots ~
1 Tbs. lemon juice

Preheat oven to 350°F.
In a large skillet, sauté onions in butter until soft. Add mushrooms and broccoli. Cover, and cook 5-8 minutes (until broccoli is just tender.) Add remaining ingredients; mix well.

NOW: Combine the buckwheat mixture ("I") with the broccoli mixture ("II"), and mix well. Spread into a buttered 9 x 13-inch pan. Bake 35-40 minutes, uncovered. Serve hot, with the following topping (which you can prepare while the casserole bakes):

III.

unnecessary

3 hard-boiled eggs, grated
¼ cup freshly-minced parsley
2 tsp. dried (or 2 Tbs. fresh) dill

Combine eggs, parsley, and dill in a small bowl, and pass it around for Individual Portion-Top Sprinklings.

Risotto alla Milanese

serve Risotto alla Milanese
with
a Cream of Tomato Soup variation (p.26),
Italian Eggplant Salad (p.65),
and Coconut-Almond Macaroon Torte (p.271).

50 minutes
to prepare;
30 minutes
to bake.

4 servings.

Preheat oven
to 325°F.

Butter
a deep-dish
casserole.

2 cups (raw) brown rice
3 cups water
¼ tsp. saffron threads

½ lb. mushrooms, coarsely chopped
¾ cup marsala or dry sherry

1½ Tbs. each: butter,
olive oil
4 medium cloves of garlic, crushed
2 cups chopped onion

1 tsp. salt
½ cup toasted pine nuts
½ tsp. dried basil
lots of black pepper
1 cup raw peas (fresh or frozen)
1 medium-sized red bell pepper,
cut in thin strips

⅓ cup freshly-grated parmesan

(1) Combine rice, water and saffron in a saucepan. Bring to a boil, cover, and lower heat to a simmer. Cook 20-30 minutes ~ until tender. Fluff it with a fork after cooking, to release trapped steam, thus warding off mushiness.

(2) While the rice cooks, combine the raw mushrooms with the marsala. Let them marinate 30 minutes.

(3) Sauté the garlic and onions with salt in combined butter and olive oil until the onions are soft and translucent.

(4) Combine everything, except the parmesan cheese, and mix well. Spread into a buttered deep-dish casserole, and sprinkle the cheese on top. Bake uncovered, about 30 minutes, at 325°F.

sweet & pungent
Fried Rice

4 servings

1ST DO-AHEAD:

2 cups raw brown rice *cooked in* 3 cups water *until* done *(20-30 minutes)*

2ND DO-AHEAD:

½ lb. cubed tofu	8 minced scallions	Combine, and
¼ cup tamari sauce	3-4 slices of ginger	let marinate
¼ cup wine vinegar	1 clove garlic, crushed	20-30 minutes.

1 Tbs. peanut oil	1 stalk broccoli, chopped
1 Tbs. sesame seeds	1 green bell pepper, in thin strips
1 large clove garlic, crushed	1 cup mung bean sprouts
1 heaping tsp. freshly-minced ginger	¼-½ cup dry white wine (to taste)
½ tsp. salt	2 beaten eggs
1 stalk celery, chopped	½ cup chopped, toasted cashews
1 large carrot, diagonally-sliced	[Chinese sesame oil & extra tamari]

(1) Do the above mentioned Do-Aheads. Meanwhile: chop the vegetables and likewise get everything else ready. Assemble your Wok (or set up your large, heavy skillet).

(2) Begin this process approximately 20 minutes before you plan to serve: Heat the wok or skillet, then add the oil. Sauté the sesame seeds, garlic, and ginger, with salt, over medium heat, for a minute or two.

(3) Add the vegetables, and stir-fry another 5-8 minutes. Add the wine, and stir-fry about 5 minutes more.

(4) Add the rice, and keep stir-frying a few minutes, then add the tofu plus all its marinating companions, and the beaten eggs. Keep stir-frying another 5 minutes, or until everything is heated through, and the eggs are set. Top with cashews, and sprinkle each serving with a few drops of sesame oil (& extra tamari, to taste).

Spanish Rice

A warming dinner for a cold, rainy night:

Galician Garbanzo Soup (p.34),
Spanish Rice
Green Salad
Sweet Zucchini-Spice Bread (p.110)
and Fresh Fruit

1 hour to prepare.

4-6 Servings.

1½ cups chopped onion
2 large cloves crushed garlic
¼ cup olive oil
½ tsp. salt
1¾ cups raw brown rice
2 chopped green bell peppers

½ tsp. each: oregano & basil
to taste { freshly-ground black pepper
cayenne pepper
2¼ cups tomato juice
2 small fresh tomatoes, chopped
½ cup chopped green olives

freshly-chopped parsley
1 packed cup grated sharp cheese

(1) In a large, heavy saucepan, sauté the onions and garlic in olive oil with salt ~ until the onions are soft (5-8 minutes).

(2) Add the raw rice, green peppers, and spices. Sauté over medium heat another 5-8 minutes, stirring frequently.

(3) Add tomato juice. Bring to a boil. Turn the heat way down, cover, and let simmer 15 minutes.

(4) Add the tomatoes and the olives. Stir, and cover again. Continue simmering until the rice has absorbed all the liquid (about 15 minutes more). Remove from heat.

(5) Fluff the cooked rice with a fork and transfer to a serving bowl. Garnish with grated cheese and chopped parsley, and serve immediately.

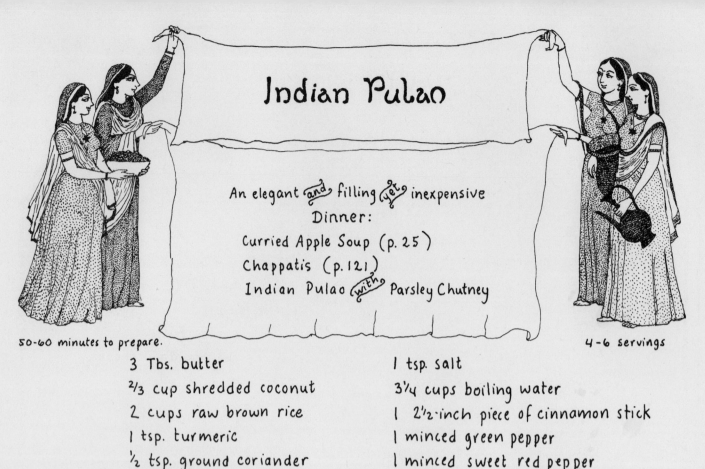

Indian Pulao

An elegant and filling yet inexpensive
Dinner:
Curried Apple Soup (p. 25)
Chappatis (p. 121)
Indian Pulao with Parsley Chutney

50-60 minutes to prepare. *4-6 servings*

3 Tbs. butter
²/₃ cup shredded coconut
2 cups raw brown rice
1 tsp. turmeric
½ tsp. ground coriander
2 medium-sized carrots, diced

1 tsp. salt
3¼ cups boiling water
1 2½-inch piece of cinnamon stick
1 minced green pepper
1 minced sweet red pepper
½ cup raisins

1½ cups chopped, toasted nuts (for extravagance, try pistachios)

(1) Melt the butter in a large, heavy saucepan. Add the coconut, rice, turmeric, coriander, carrots and salt. Stir and cook these all together over a medium-low flame for 5-8 minutes.

(2) Add the boiling water and cinnamon stick. Stir, cover, and let simmer (low heat) for 15 minutes.

(3) Stir in the peppers and the raisins, cover, and let it simmer until the rice is tender (approximately 15-20 minutes more). Transfer to a serving bowl; top with nuts.

PARSLEY CHUTNEY ... pungent & potent....

2 packed cups freshly-minced parsley
½ tsp. salt
1½ tsp. grated fresh ginger root
4-6 (that's right) cloves crushed garlic
3 Tbs. crushed dried mint
2 Tbs. fresh lemon juice
½ cup firm yogurt
cayenne pepper

Combine everything in a blender,
or a food processor fitted with
its steel blade.

Purée.

Cover tightly and refrigerate.

Spiced Lentil Dinner

Total Preparation
Time =
About 2 hours.

4-6 servings

1. Date & Orange Chutney

1 whole seedless orange, chopped

1 packed cup chopped, pitted dates

1 heaping tsp. freshly-minced ginger

⅓ cup water

⅓ cup cider vinegar

1-2 Tbs. honey

[OPTIONAL] { ¼ cup raisins

crushed red hot pepper, to taste

Combine everything in a saucepan. Partially cover, and cook over medium-low heat for 20-30 minutes, stirring intermittently. Cool, cover tightly, and refrigerate until cold. (This chutney can be made way in advance; it keeps for several weeks.)

2. Chappatis

(Recipe, p.121. Wrap them in a damp tea towel, and keep them warm in a 250°F oven, while you prepare the lentils and the yogurt.)

3. Spiced Lentils

1½ cups raw lentils

2 Tbs. butter

2 large cloves of garlic, crushed

1 cup minced onion

1 large stalk celery - chopped

1 tsp. salt

1 cup shredded coconut

½ tsp. powdered ginger

½ tsp. turmeric

½ tsp. cinnamon

½ tsp. ground coriander

a few Tbs. of water, as needed

freshly-grated black pepper, to taste

juice from 1 large lemon

2 cups chopped tart apple (approx. 2 large ones)

cayenne pepper, to taste

(1) Cook the lentils in 2¼ cups water (bring to boil, then cover and lower heat to simmer) 30-40 minutes, or until tender. (2) Meanwhile, cook everything else - except the apples - until tender (use a deep, heavy skillet), adding water, if necessary, to avoid sticking. (3) Add the apples to the sauté, cook 10 minutes more (covered), and then combine this mixture with the lentils in a casserole. Cover, and keep warm in a 250°F oven.

4. Yogurt Sauce ("Raita")

{ 2 cups yogurt

½ tsp. whole cumin seeds

scant ½ tsp. salt

½ cup finely-minced cucumber

½ cup finely-minced bell pepper

2 Tbs. finely-minced red onion }

Combine all of these; stir, and serve.

PLAIN
GRAINS

Don't overlook the possibility of eating a simple supper of plain, cooked grains every now and then. It can be a refreshing change from sophistication. It can also be delicious, warming, and peaceful. Add a little extra depth with minimal Touches, like a handful of toasted sunflower seeds or nuts — or some chunks of tofu, plain or marinated (p. 197). Have it with a green salad; you'll be surprised at how complete it can help you to feel.

Some people have trouble cooking grains to the perfect consistency (i.e., tender, fluffy, not mushy — but not too crunchy either). The tendency is to end up with one large gooey unit, rather than with separate, delicate morsels. This problem could be the result of using too much water. The idea is to get away with the smallest possible amount of water.

1. Brown Rice

Thirty minutes is all it takes to cook long or short-grain brown rice. The trick is to let it cook in privacy; if you keep interrupting it to see if it is still there, you will set loose the steam necessary to cook the rice with a minimum of water. So promise yourself you will only check the rice once or twice — and briefly at that, just to give it a stir — and not every 3 minutes, okay? (But this will require that you have Faith that your rice will not disappear if you turn your back on it for 15 minutes at a time.)

What is the difference between long-grain and short-grain brown rice? Nutritionally, there is negligible difference. Also, you cook them in exactly the same way. (You can cook them together.) The taste and texture is where the big difference occurs: long-grain is lighter and fluffier; short-grain is denser, chewier and sweeter. Take your pick.

To cook brown rice:

⅟₂ Use 2 parts raw rice to 3 parts water. Figure on at least ½ cup raw rice for each portion (depending, of course, on what else is being served). Sample ratios, for math-haters: 1 cup rice: 1½ cups water 2 cups rice: 3 cups water, and so on.

⅟₂ Place both rice and water in a saucepan. Cover and bring to a boil. Uncover just slightly (one small vent) and simmer, low-keyed, for 25-30 minutes.

⅟₂ Stir once or twice during cooking. Replace cover immediately. It's best not to add salt or butter to rice until <u>after</u> it's cooked.

2. Millet:

This is one of the more mush-inclined grains, but if you follow these directions, you stand a good chance of having differentiated millet particles instead of paste.

⅟₂ Again, the ratio is 2 parts raw grain : 3 parts water. (see brown rice ratio, above.) In addition, add 1 tsp. butter or oil for each cup of raw millet.

⅟₂ Bring the water to a boil by itself first. Then add butter or oil, and sprinkle in the millet. Stir briefly, and partially cover. Turn heat to low.

⅟₂ Cook the millet for <u>15-20 minutes only</u>! Stir with a fork halfway through cooking and again, at the end. This time, it is desirable that the trapped steam escape, otherwise it will keep cooking the millet even after it is removed from direct heat. So fluff it with a fork a <u>lot</u> after it's cooked, and leave it uncovered. This is the best deterrent to mushiness. Add salt after it is cooked.

3. Bulghur:

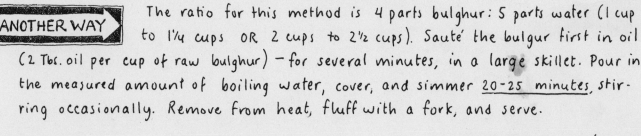

ONE WAY ▶ The ratio is still 2 parts grain : 3 parts water. Place the raw bulghur in a saucepan. Boil water separately. Pour the measured amount of boiling water over the bulghur, cover, and let it steep <u>15 minutes</u>. At this time place the saucepan, still-covered, over very low heat, and simmer <u>10 more minutes</u>. Remove from heat, fluff with a fork, and serve.

ANOTHER WAY ▶ The ratio for this method is 4 parts bulghur : 5 parts water (1 cup to 1¼ cups OR 2 cups to 2½ cups). Sauté the bulgur first in oil (2 Tbs. oil per cup of raw bulghur) — for several minutes, in a large skillet. Pour in the measured amount of boiling water, cover, and simmer <u>20-25 minutes</u>, stirring occasionally. Remove from heat, fluff with a fork, and serve.

✿ ✿ ✿ ✿ ✿ ✿ ✿ ✿ ✿ ✿ ✿ ✿ ✿ ✿ ✿ ✿ ✿ ✿ ✿

Chickpea & Vegetable Stew

4 servings.

✿

2 Preliminaries::

1. You will need **2 cups cooked chickpeas** (garbanzo beans). So you have to plan in advance. Soak <u>1 cup raw</u> overnight, then cook the chickpeas in plenty of boiling water until tender (1-1½ hours).

2. You will need **4 cups cooked millet** So, as you begin to cook the stew, put up <u>2 cups raw</u> in <u>3 cups of boiling water</u>. It will take about 20 minutes. (For more detailed millet-cooking instructions, see p. 225.)

2 Tbs. olive oil
2 Tbs. butter
1 heaping cup chopped onion
1 tsp. salt
1 lb. fresh mushrooms, chopped
3 Tbs. fresh lemon juice
1 1-lb. bunch fresh broccoli, chopped
½ cup (packed) currants
black pepper ⎫
cayenne   ⎭ to taste
½ tsp. mild paprika
1½ cups chopped, toasted cashews

(1) Cook the onion in combined olive oil and butter, with salt, in a large, heavy skillet. Keep the heat medium-low, and cook about 5 minutes, or until the onion begins to get tender.

(2) Add mushrooms, lemon juice, and broccoli. Cover, and cook over medium-low heat until the broccoli is bright green and j<u>ust</u> tender (8-10 minutes).

(3) Add cooked drained chickpeas, and all remaining ingredients, and simmer, covered, another few minutes. Serve over millet.

A very nice way to serve this stew is on a platter, with the stew in the center, and the millet arranged around its edge, like a frame.

✿ ✿ ✿ ✿ ✿ ✿ ✿ ✿ ✿ ✿ ✿ ✿ ✿ ✿ ✿ ✿ ✿ ✿ ✿

Featuring:

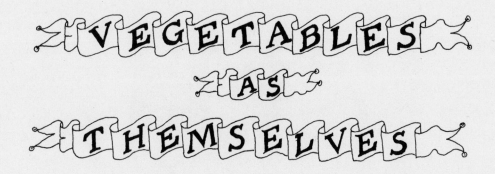

VEGETABLES AS THEMSELVES

Brazilian Stuffed Peppers

40 minutes
to prepare;

30 minutes
to bake.

4 servings.

Preheat oven
to 350°F.

4 large, able-to-stand, perfectly-formed Bell Peppers

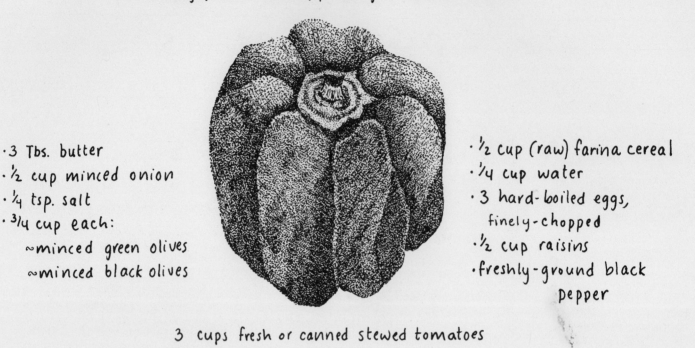

- 3 Tbs. butter
- ½ cup minced onion
- ¼ tsp. salt
- ¾ cup each:
  ~minced green olives
  ~minced black olives

- ½ cup (raw) farina cereal
- ¼ cup water
- 3 hard-boiled eggs, finely-chopped
- ½ cup raisins
- freshly-ground black pepper

3 cups fresh or canned stewed tomatoes

(1) Slice across the tops of the peppers, about ½-inch from the tips. Discard the tops, and remove the seeds.

(2) Drop the peppers into a large kettle of boiling water, and leave them there (over a flame, to keep the water boiling) only about 3-5 minutes. Remove as soon as they're slightly tender (but still feisty), and rinse immediately in cold water. Drain well by turning them upside down and placing them in a colander for a while.

(3) In a medium-sized skillet, sauté the onions in butter, with salt, until soft. Add the olives and farina. Continue to sauté (medium heat; stirring) another 5-8 minutes. Add water; mix well. Continue stirring and cooking over medium heat another 5 minutes. Remove from heat.

(4) Add eggs, raisins, and black pepper. Mix well. Stuff the peppers.

(5) Spread the stewed tomatoes into a shallow baking pan. Arrange the peppers so that they stand, wading in the tomatoes. Cover loosely with foil.
Bake 30 minutes at 350°F.

THE ENCHANTED BROCCOLI FOREST

50 minutes to prepare;
30 minutes more to bake.

Preheat oven to 325°F.

4 servings.

Butter a 10×6-inch pan,
(or its approximate
equivalent)

1 1-lb. bunch of broccoli	Cut off bottom-several-inches of stalk. Shave off the tough outer skin, and cut the broccoli into spears (these will be the Trees).
2 cups (raw) brown rice 3 cups water	Combine in saucepan. Bring to a boil, lower heat, and cover. Cook until just done (20-30 minutes). Fluff with a fork.

Meanwhile:

1 Tbs. butter 1 cup chopped onion 1 large clove crushed garlic ½ tsp. salt ½ tsp. dill weed lots of black pepper ¼ tsp. dried mint cayenne pepper, to taste	Sauté all of these together over medium heat, stirring, until the onions are soft and translucent (8-10 minutes) Add to the above Cooked Rice. Mix well.
3 large eggs ¼ cup freshly-minced parsley 1½ packed cups grated cheddar or Swiss cheese	Beat together well, then beat into the rice mixture. Spread evenly into your buttered 10×6-inch pan.
The above-described Broccoli Trees Juice from one Lemon combined. 2 Tbs. melted butter	Steam the broccoli until bright green and just tender. Rinse immediately in cold water; drain. Arrange these broccoli trees upright in the bed of rice- mixture (as depicted above) and drizzle the trees with lemon-butter.

—Cover gently, but firmly as possible, with foil. Bake 30 minutes.

STUFFED ARTICHOKES

Preliminaries = 1 hour
Filling = 45 minutes
Oven time: 30 minutes
→ Total = 2¼ hours

4-6 servings
Preheat oven to 325°F.

1st Preliminary:

Cook 6 artichokes as you normally would, for normal consumption.
(Usually this involves boiling or steaming them for about 35 minutes, or until leaves come out easily.)
Drain the artichokes (turn upside down in a colander) and cool until handle-able.

2nd Preliminary:

To hollow out the artichokes for stuffing:
(1) Grab hold of the central leaf-cluster (at the tip), and yank it out.
(2) Reach into the cavity with a regular spoon, and with a few masterful strokes, scrape out the choke (inedible fuzz) and discard it.

The Walnut Stuffing:

2 Tbs. butter
1½ cups minced onion
1 large clove of garlic, crushed
1½ cups finely-minced walnuts
½ cup wheat germ
½ tsp. salt
freshly-ground black pepper

½ cup dry white wine
¼ cup freshly-minced parsley
¼ tsp each: thyme,
　　　　　　　　paprika
½ tsp. dry mustard
1½ packed cups grated mild cheddar
2 Tbs. fresh lemon juice

(1) In a large, heavy skillet, cook the onions and garlic in the butter over medium-low heat, until the onions are soft (5-8 minutes).

(2) Add walnuts, wheat germ, salt, and pepper. Continue to stir and cook over low heat another 5-8 minutes.

(3) Add wine and herbs. Keep cooking gently another 10 minutes or so.

(4) Remove from heat. Stir in the cheese and lemon juice — mix well.

5) Divide the stuffing evenly among the 6 artichokes. Fill each cavity firmly. Place the stuffed artichokes in a shallow baking dish, standing them upright. (You may need to cut off their stems to stabilize their posture.) Cover the pan loosely with foil, and place it in a 325°F. oven for about 30 minutes, so that all elements heat through nicely.

REBAKED POTATOES

Initial bake = 45 min.
Preparation = 10 min.
Final bake = 35 min.
 TOTAL = 1½ hours.

2-4 servings,
depending on
what else is
served.

Preheat oven to 375°F.

This dish is substantial and satisfying enough to be a main course. Figure on one medium-sized potato per person. The following recipe is for two, but it can easily be multiplied.

2 fist-sized potatoes
3 Tbs. mayonnaise
½ cup cottage cheese
1 hard-boiled egg, finely-chopped
½ tsp. salt
½ tsp. dill weed

½ packed cup cheddar cheese
¼ tsp. cayenne pepper
lots of freshly-ground black pepper
2 tsp. prepared mustard
one medium-sized tomato
paprika and extra cheddar

DO AHEAD: Bake the potatoes as you normally would for Baked Potatoes. (About 45 minutes at 375°F.) When they are cool enough to handle, slice them in half laterally, and scoop out the insides, leaving the skins intact.

(1) Place the potato innards in a bowl, and mash them with the mayonnaise and the cottage cheese. Add all remaining ingredients, except the tomato, paprika, and extra cheddar. Mix well.

(2) Divide the filling evenly among the potato skins. Slice the tomato into rounds, and place these slices decoratively on top of each stuffed potato. Sprinkle some extra cheese over the tomatoes, and dust on some paprika. Place the potatoes in a shallow baking dish.

Bake for 35 minutes at 375°F.

Eggplant Rollatini

- 2 medium-sized (4 inch-diameter at widest point) eggplants
- salt
- olive oil

Mushroom-Tahini Sauce:

- 4 tsp. butter
- 4 tsp. olive oil
- 1½ cups minced onion
- 2 large cloves garlic, crushed
- 12 oz. mushrooms, chopped

- ¾ tsp. salt (more, to taste)
- fresh black pepper, to taste
- cayenne pepper, to taste
- 1 tsp. dill weed

- 2 Tbs. unbleached white flour
- ½ cup sesame tahini
- 2 tsp. honey
- 2-3 cups hot water
- a few drops of tamari sauce

Filling:

- 3 cups firm cottage (or pot) cheese
- ½ cup wheat germ

- a liberal amount of fresh black pepper
- 3 scallions — whites and greens, finely-minced

(1) Slice the unpeeled eggplants lengthwise, at ½-inch intervals: ...etc.

(2) Salt the open eggplant surfaces lightly, and let them sit about 10 minutes, to sweat out some of their bitter humors. Rinse the slices, spread them on an olive oiled baking tray (or 2), and bake them in a 350°F. oven until they are supple and rollable (about 30-35 minutes). Remove, and allow to cool.

(3) Prepare the sauce while the eggplant bakes:
  a- In a medium-sized saucepan, cook the onions, garlic, and mushrooms in combined butter and olive oil with salt, until the onions are soft (5-8 minutes).
  b- Sprinkle in herbs and flour, mixing constantly. Keep cooking over lowered heat, 1-2 minutes. Stir in tahini and honey. Cook a few more minutes.
  c- Add water (more or less, depending on desired thickness) and tamari. Stir and cook over low heat an additional 8-10 minutes.

(4) Combine the cottage cheese and wheat germ with black pepper and scallions. Place about ¼ cup (rounded) at the base of each eggplant slice, spread it around a little, and roll up the eggplant. Place the completed rolls in an oiled baking pan, standing on end, and leaning up against each other. Pour the sauce over the top, cover, and bake 30 minutes at 350°F.

The Various Cuts
of Vegetables

For many people, a major deterrent to the use of fresh (as opposed to frozen or canned) vegetables is an aversion to chopping. This aversion seems to be either a) fear of inconvenience – or– b) fear of injury. Some people have begun to use fresh vegetables more frequently with the acquisition of food processors, as these helpful machines have a slicing attachment which, in a matter of minutes, can render a whole soup's-worth of vegetables into diminutive units. However, the food processor cannot give you the variety of shapes and dimensions procurable by hand (provided the owner of said hand has a good, sharp, appropriate knife, an attention span of at least 10 minutes, and a little practice). The more shapes and sizes you can carve out of a vegetable, the more possibilities you will find for preparing it. You will discover, for example, that a potato, yam, or winter squash can be <u>sautéed</u> instead of baked or boiled, acquiring new texture and flavor. You will find that a variety of vegetables can be stir-fried together, with none of them compromising its texture (see pp. 238-40). You will find, as you learn to slice thinly, a whole new world of <u>raw</u> vegetable possibilities, and your salads will soar (see p. 81).

The key to good vegetable-chopping lies in one's relationship with a chosen knife or cleaver. Shop carefully, and find one you feel personally drawn to, and with which you are comfortable. Keep it <u>sharp</u> (the sharper, the safer), and take good care of it.

The key to safety is <u>attention</u>. ALWAYS KEEP YOUR EYES ON YOUR HANDS WHILE YOU CHOP! Most cuts occur from simply not paying attention.

NOTE ABOUT KNIVES: For most vegetables you need a <u>straight-edged</u>, wide blade. Use serrated knives only for acidy fruits and vegetables (citrus, tomatoes, peppers).

The following 4 pages provide some cutting guidelines →

When should (or shouldn't) which vegetables get peeled, and why? (or why not?)

BEETS - as a rule, should be peeled. However, don't bother to use your peeler. It is much easier to remove their skins if you blanch them first - for about 10 minutes in boiling water. The skins will then <u>rub</u> off.

CARROTS- Always try to scrub them instead. But peel them if the skin is exceedingly unacceptable. The same goes for: POTATOES, SWEET POTATOES, YAMS, TURNIPS, RUTABAGAS, CELERY ROOT, PARSNIPS, AND OTHER ROOT VEGETABLES.

WINTER SQUASH- Peel, if you intend to slice them thinly for sautéing. But if you plan to boil or bake them, they will readily volunteer departure from their natural encasements after they're cooked.

SUMMER SQUASH AND ZUCCHINI- Only peel these if the skin is: a) overly tough or: b) disgusting (sometimes the skin can look bad, but the insides can be just fine.)

CUCUMBERS Peel if they're waxed or if they taste bitter. Otherwise, don't.

EGGPLANT - unnecessary to peel if the skin is smooth and tight. However, some people will not be convinced that eggplant skin is <u>ever</u> edible. If these people are coming to dinner, peel.

BROCCOLI STALKS- It's a good idea to use a peeler on these, as it gets off the tough outer skin, without losing too much of the tender insides.

<u>DON'T PEEL</u> fresh, unscathed garden vegetables, especially your own home-grown cucumbers. Get a good scrub brush, and become accustomed to using it. The clean skins of fresh vegetables have Illustrious Minerals, not to mention interesting textures and fine personalities.

Cutting Each Vegetable......

First, a ground rule for safety: Try, at all times, to place the vegetable in the most stable position possible. This usually means flatside-down. Since most vegetables are curved, a flat surface must be introduced by an Initial Cut somewhere (often down the center). Thereafter, this flat surface — plus the firm hold of your free hand — will help prevent the vegetable from rolling out from under your knife, causing its escape to parts unknown and/or the accidental chopping of your knuckles.

. . . .

A LITTLE-KNOWN FACT ABOUT <u>GARLIC</u>: The easiest way to peel garlic is to lay it down on its side (one or two cloves at a time), and whack it firmly with the flat side of a large knifeblade. The garlic skin, after this treatment, will magically loosen.

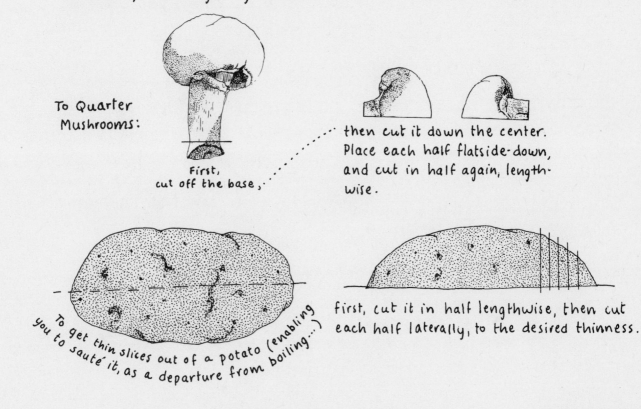

To Quarter Mushrooms:

First, cut off the base,

then cut it down the center. Place each half flatside-down, and cut in half again, length-wise.

To get thin slices out of a potato (enabling you to sauté it, as a departure from boiling...)

first, cut it in half lengthwise, then cut each half laterally, to the desired thinness.

The base of an asparagus stalk will detach just where it's supposed to, if snapped gently by hand.

An effective cut for asparagus, especially if it's to be used for a vegetable sauté, is <u>diagonal</u>, at 1½-inch intervals. Start from the base, and work toward the tip, turning the asparagus ¼-turn after each slice.

This technique can also be used for carrots and broccoli stalks.

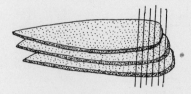

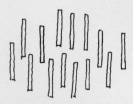

To cut matchstick (or "julienne") pieces of zucchini, eggplant or carrot, the first step is to cut the vegetable into thin slices <u>lengthwise</u>. The easiest way to do this is to cut one slice first, making

one flat surface. Then you can lay the vegetable down on this surface while you cut the remaining length-wise slices, and the whole cutting process will be more stable.

After the lengthwise slices

are cut, pile them up, and begin cutting width-wise strips, as illustrated. (Don't pile all the slices at once— do it in 2 or 3 batches.)

And this is how one makes matchsticks – or julienne strips.

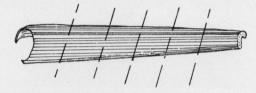

For Celery Matchsticks: Cut each stalk at approximately 2-inch intervals. Then cut each interval thinly, into lengthwise strips.

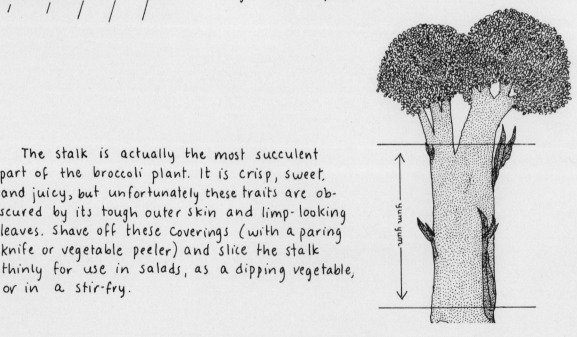

The stalk is actually the most succulent part of the broccoli plant. It is crisp, sweet, and juicy, but unfortunately these traits are ob-scured by its tough outer skin and limp-looking leaves. Shave off these coverings (with a paring knife or vegetable peeler) and slice the stalk thinly for use in salads, as a dipping vegetable, or in a stir-fry.

Cauliflower can be sliced into thin "trees" with a knife. In this form it can be sautéed very quickly, and it is lovely in salads. Also, you can break cauliflower into chunkier "flowerettes" by hand.

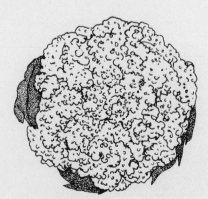

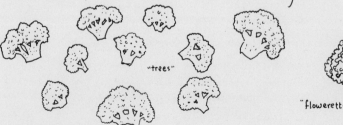

"trees"

"flowerette"

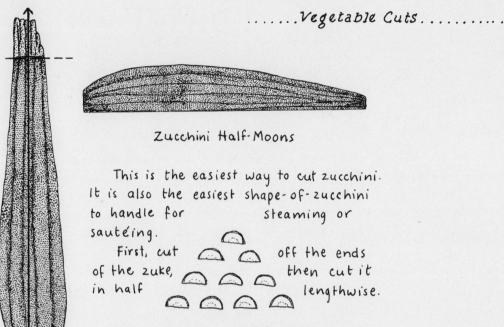

Zucchini Half-Moons

This is the easiest way to cut zucchini. It is also the easiest shape-of-zucchini to handle for   steaming or sautéing.

First, cut   off the ends of the zuke,   then cut it in half   lengthwise.

Then, place each half flatside-down, and slice across at whatever interval you choose for more or less thickness.

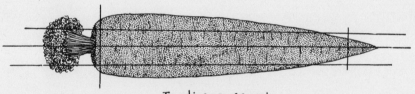

To dice a carrot:

First, make some nice, uniform carrot sticks,

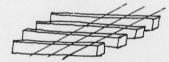 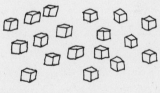

then line them up, and cut across to make little cubes.

There are no clever tricks for carving elaborate shapes out of a bell pepper. Usually one is called upon to render this vegetable into strips or mincedness.

Here are a few tips:
~ Cut the pepper down the center first - lengthwise. Remove all seeds and core.
~ Use a serrated knife. It will grip the pepper well, cutting more precisely than a straight-edged blade.

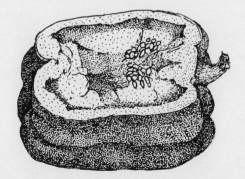

A Dinner of
Sautéed Vegetables

People who love to cook tend to search for increasingly exotic and complex ideas with which to experiment. Very few enthusiastic gourmets will probe in the opposite direction, toward simplicity. Yet the search for the simple can be engaging and challenging, and the results can be inspiring.

You can quickly, easily, inexpensively, and pleasurably prepare a meal of stir-fried vegetables, and if you follow only a few certain guidelines your creation can be surprisingly elegant and satisfying. I would like to dispel the common notion that a meal consisting primarily of cooked vegetables is necessarily (a) underseasoned and mushy; (b) inadequate, both nutritionally and quantitatively; (c) depressing; and (d) just generally low class. How you cook a vegetable, how fresh and lovely it is in its raw state, and how you cut the vegetable prior to cooking it — attention to these variables makes all the difference.

Here is the brief list of Essential Efforts which, if heeded, will readily separate the ho-hum vegetable dinner from the sensually thrilling one:

Effort #1: Become the proud owner of a real Chinese wok.

Effort #2: Practice your vegetable chopping to the point where you are able to cut any vegetable to exactly the size and shape you want it to be. (See pp. 233-37.)

Effort #3: Find a local produce merchant who sells the finest, freshest vegetables possible at all times, and adopt this merchant as your very own. Take the slight, extra trouble of shopping carefully and frequently, buying vegetables closest to the prime of their season.

Effort #4: Follow the cooking method described on the following 2 pages. There is no particular skill or talent required here — just pay careful attention to what you are doing.

Basic Trick: To group the vegetables, after they are cut, according to their respective cooking times, so that none will over- or under-cook. You accomplish this by adding the slower-cooking vegetables to the wok earlier than the quicker-cooking ones.

Heat the wok alone first - for up to a minute. Then add a little oil (vegetable or peanut), and if you are using onions, add them now, and sauté them alone first. If not, add whatever "group 1" vegetables you are using, and sauté them until they are partially-done.

Then add "group 2", and sauté until everything is <u>almost</u> done. "Group 3" comes in right at the very end. These vegetables cook practically on contact with the other hot vegetables.

Group 1	Group 2	Group 3
potatoes, sliced thin	mushrooms	GREENS:
celery	peppers	(spinach
carrots	zucchini	chard
broccoli	summer squash	escarole,
cauliflower	asparagus (if thin)	etc.)
cabbage		scallions
eggplant		bean sprouts
winter squash		
asparagus (if thick)		

Plan on about ¾-1 lb. raw vegetables per serving.

You don't have to use all of these vegetables. You can use just some, or even just one. It's easier, and a good way to practice if you're new at this.

Remember: The more thinly a vegetable is sliced, the more quickly it cooks.

Basic Goal: To cook the vegetables quickly (over high heat, stirring almost constantly) so that each vegetable is done to its own individual perfection.

Good Things to Do: 1) Hover over the wok as you sauté. <u>Stir</u> <u>Very</u> <u>Much</u>.
2) Have everything all ready beforehand, and within arm's reach of the stove.
3) Keep the heat high, and keep the vegetables moving in the wok. Work quickly.

Try one or several of these in your sauté. Have all extras prepared beforehand, and add them during the last few minutes of the cooking.

Extras

chopped, toasted nuts
pieces of tofu (plain or marinated - see p. 197)
sliced water chestnuts
cooked noodles (rinsed and drizzled with sesame oil)
sesame seeds
soaked, sliced black mushrooms

SEASONINGS: wine
tamari sauce
crushed garlic
grated ginger
crushed hot pepper
Chinese sesame oil
OR, a combination,
such as:

Hal's Special Sauce

10 minutes to prepare.   Enough for 3-4 servings.

½ cup orange juice*
¼ cup tamari sauce
1 Tbs. grated fresh ginger
2-3 cloves garlic, crushed
1-2 Tbs. honey
2 tsp. Chinese sesame oil
2 Tbs. cornstarch

1) Combine the 1st 6 ingredients.
2) Place the cornstarch in a bowl; whisk the liquid mixture into it.
3) Set aside, but keep the whisk handy, as you will need to whisk the sauce again just before you pour it into the sauté.

*optional: pineapple juice, instead of orange.

Add this sauce (don't forget to whisk it from the bottom just before, to redistribute the settled cornstarch) to the wokful of vegetables about ⅔ of the way through the cooking. Once it is in the wok, stir the sauté from the bottom constantly, so the sauce gets to coat all the vegetables evenly, and so it won't stick to the bottom.

Light Meals for Nibblers

Light Meals for Nibblers:
Table of Contents

Light meals

are growing in popularity. People seem to have less time and money to spend, and increasingly, elaborate meals are being relegated to Special Occasion status. So in between these special occasions, how can a busy person eat well without feeling deprived and on the brink of moving into the parking lot of a fast food enterprise? I don't know, but this chapter contains some suggestions. With a little foresight, some organized shopping, and a strong will Not to become a fast food addict (I know the temptation can be powerful), light meals can come into your life —into your own home! — with variety, validity, and delight.

The main emphasis of this chapter is on dips and spreads. If you get into the habit of keeping your house well-stocked with fresh vegetables and good bread, a dip is all you need to transform these into a light supper. The dips are all easy to prepare, and they keep for several days.

Following the dips are several recipes for cheese-based dinners. They are all quickly prepared, except the Mushroom-Cheese Pâté, which needs baking. This can be prepared in the evening or on a weekend, and then kept for up to a week, if well-wrapped and refrigerated, for some high-class nibbling.

I hope this brief chapter will encourage busy people, single people, and people who just want lighter eating to <u>enjoy</u> your meals. I hope that your imagination is sparked beyond these suggestions, and unleashed for the benefit of your own nourishment.

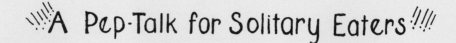 A Pep-Talk for Solitary Eaters

Hello, single eaters.

Do you regularly miss out on the pleasures of Dining, because it doesn't seem worth the trouble to make things Nice if they're only for you (and the 6 o'clock news announcer, who is your steady dinner companion)? Perhaps you can be convinced that you, yes you, are indeed deserving of good food and a little extra attention. Try these suggestions, and dinner with your Self can become something you eagerly anticipate, and for which you'll even dress up and light candles..... a Pleasurable Experience.

Set aside a block of time once a week for a cooking session. Prepare one soup and one casserole-type entrée. Bake or cook the entrée to completion, then divide it into single portions, pack them into airtight containers, and freeze them. On days when you'll want a portion for dinner, take it out of the freezer in the morning, and heat it in the oven just before you want dinner. Keep a steady supply of fresh fruits and vegetables around, and prepare yourself a spectacular salad while your entrée heats. On alternate nights, have the soup, with raw vegetables and one of the many dips from this chapter. Also, don't forget about omelettes (pp. 179-181) and quick egg suppers, most of which can be made easily and in single portions. Try baking bread once a week, too. You deserve such a luxury, even if no one else is available to share it with you. Besides, it's nice to get it all to yourself.

Think of yourself as your own guest (a favored one, who laughs with sincerity at all your jokes). Set an attractive place for yourself, and <u>sit</u> <u>down</u> <u>to</u> <u>eat</u>! I once knew an old woman who had lived alone for many years, and had really mastered the fine art of eating alone. She would never eat while standing halfway into her refrigerator, poking her fork into random jars. She always set a place for herself, sat down, and dined elegantly, if simply. She wouldn't even munch on pickles without first arranging them on an attractive little serving plate. This woman insisted that to treat oneself in this fashion was to live a longer, happier life. I believed her and still do.

DIPS

Dips: things mashed up with other things to a harmonious consistency; readily spreadable, or pick-upable with raw vegetables or crackers or chips. Dips as snacks, as hors d'oeuvre.... dips as _dinner_. Most of these are very easy to make, and even easier to eat.

Almond Orange Dip

25 minutes to prepare, plus time to chill.

Yield: about 2½ cups

1 cup blanched almonds chopped
2 Tbs. butter

⅓ cup fresh-squeezed orange juice

1 cup firm yogurt
a pinch of ground ginger (more, to taste)
¼ tsp. tamari sauce
2 Tbs. freshly-minced parsley
2 Tbs. finely-minced fresh chives
a rounded ¼ tsp. orange rind
salt and pepper, to taste
cayenne, to taste

(1) Sauté the almonds in the butter, stirring over low heat for about 5 minutes, or until the almonds are nicely, lightly toasted. Remove from heat.

(2) Transfer the sautéed almonds to the jar of a blender. Add the orange juice, and purée. Transfer to a bowl.

(3) Add all remaining ingredients, and mix very well — until uniform (you can use a whisk). Season to taste, cover well, and refrigerate until cold.

Tofu Guacamole

1 large (5" long) ripe avocado

2 cakes (½ lb.) medium-soft tofu

½ tsp. salt

black pepper ⎫
⎬ to taste
cayenne ⎭

1 medium clove of garlic, crushed

¼ tsp. ground cumin (more, to taste)

3-4 Tbs. fresh lemon juice

chopped parsley – for the top.

(1) Mash all ingredients, except parsley, with a fork.

(2) After mashing, beat well with fork (vigorously!) or whisk, until smooth and uniform.

(3) Arrange nicely in a serving bowl. Top with parsley. Cover tightly and chill.

Avocado-Tofu-Egg Dip

3 Tbs. cider vinegar

3 Tbs. cold water

1 cake (¼ lb.) tofu

1 medium (4" long) ripe avocado

2 hard-cooked eggs

½ tsp. Dijon mustard

½ tsp. prepared horseradish

½ cup very finely-minced red onion

salt ⎫
⎬ to taste
black pepper ⎭

(1) Place vinegar, water, tofu and avocado in the jar of a blender – or a food processor fitted with the steel blade attachment. Purée until smooth. Transfer to a bowl.

(2) Coarsely grate or finely chop the hard-cooked eggs. Stir these, plus all remaining ingredients, into the purée. Cover tightly and chill.

Orange Humus

Pre-soaked chick peas
need to cook 1½-2 hours.

After that, 10 minutes
to prepare.

Yield: about 3 cups.

1½ cups raw chick peas

¼ tsp. each: ground cumin
ground coriander
ground ginger
dry mustard
turmeric
paprika

½ cup orange juice
¼ cup tahini
1½ - 1¾ tsp. salt
1-2 Tbs. cider vinegar
3 medium garlic cloves, crushed
3 scallions, finely-minced (whites and greens)
1-2 tsp. tamari sauce

(1) Soak the chick peas overnight. Cook in a large kettle, in plenty of boiling water, until very soft (1½-2 hours). (The softer they are, the easier they'll mash.) Drain and mash well.

(2) Combine the mashed chick peas with all remaining ingredients. Cover and chill.

Mexican Bean Dip

(same preparation time as above)

1 cup raw pinto beans

Yield: 2 cups

2 medium garlic cloves,
½ cup finely, finely minced raw onion
¾ tsp. salt
black pepper
crushed red hot pepper   } to taste
¼ tsp. each: ground cumin
dry mustard
dried basil

(1) [The soaking and cooking procedures for the pinto beans are exactly the same as those for the chick peas above.]

(2) Combine the mashed pinto beans with all remaining ingredients. Cover and chill.

Avocado-Egg Dip

15 minutes to prepare
(if eggs are pre-cooked)

Yield: about 1 cup

1 medium-sized (4" long) ripe avocado

3 Tbs. cider vinegar

2 large scallions, finely-minced (whites and greens)

8 green pimiento-stuffed olives, minced

4 hard-cooked eggs

salt
black pepper } to taste

(1) Mash the avocado well with the vinegar.

(2) Stir in the minced scallions and olives.

(3) Coarsely grate — or finely chop— the hard-cooked eggs. Stir these in, and add
salt and pepper. Cover tightly and chill.

Avocado-Tahini Dip

10 minutes to prepare

Yield:
about 1 cup

1 medium-sized (4" long) ripe avocado

¼ cup fresh lemon juice

⅓ cup tahini

1 medium-sized clove of garlic, crushed

1 cup firm yogurt

2 scallions, finely-minced (whites and greens)

salt
black pepper } to taste
cayenne

(1) Mash the avocado well with the lemon juice.

(2) Add the tahini, and beat for several minutes (either with a fork, vigorously,
or with a whisk). Beat in the garlic and yogurt.

(3) Stir in scallions and seasonings. Cover well and chill.

Tofu-Sesame Dip

2 Tbs. cider vinegar

2 Tbs. water

1 Tbs. tamari sauce

1 Tbs. Chinese sesame oil

1 small clove of garlic, crushed

1 Tbs. fresh lemon juice

1 cake (¼ lb.) tofu

¼ cup tahini

1 scallion, finely-minced (whites and greens)

¼ cup (packed) finely-minced parsley

salt

black pepper ⎫
            ⎬ to taste
cayenne   ⎭

(1) In the jar of a blender – or in a food processor fitted with the steel blade – combine the first 7 ingredients. Purée until smooth.

(2) Beat the tahini for a few minutes (use a whisk). Beat this into the purée. Stir in remaining ingredients. Cover well and chill.

Pesto-Bean Dip

15 minutes to prepare
(if pesto and beans
are ready)

Yield: 3 cups

    This recipe requires 2 preliminary preparations, after which the rest is very simple. The preliminaries are: (1) *Pesto Sauce* (p. 161) and (2) *Cooked White Pea Beans*. To cook white pea beans, soak 1 cup of them in water for about 3 hours. Place soaked beans in a saucepan, cover them with plenty of water, and cook until very soft (1½-2 hours) covered, over low heat.

2 cups cooked (1 c. raw) white pea beans

½ cup pesto sauce

½ cup cottage or ricotta cheese

approximately 6 Tbs. milk (as needed)

salt and pepper, to taste

(1) Drain the cooked beans, and mash very well. Let cool to room temperature.

(2) Mix in pesto and cottage or ricotta cheese. As milk, as needed, to moisten.

(3) Season to taste with salt and pepper. Cover well, and chill.

PEANUT DIP WITH TOFU

10 minutes to prepare.   Yield: 1½ cups

⅓ cup good peanut butter
¼ cup boiling water

½ lb. (usually 2 cakes) firm tofu
1 tsp. cider vinegar
2 tsp. tamari sauce

¼ tsp. ground ginger
½ cup finely-chopped toasted peanuts

optional: cayenne, to taste
           freshly-minced chives, to taste

(1) Place the peanut butter in a medium-sized bowl. Add the boiling water, and mix until they combine to make a smooth, soft paste.

(2) In a separate small bowl, mash the tofu well, together with the vinegar and tamari. Mix until it is a uniform mash.

(3) Add the tofu mash to the peanut paste. Beat until smooth.

(4) Stir in ginger and peanuts (and optional additions). Cover and chill.

Tahini Dip

10 minutes to prepare.   Yield: 1½ cups

1 cup sesame tahini   ½ tsp. salt
⅓ cup apple juice   ½ tsp. cumin
3 Tbs. cider vinegar   ¼ tsp. cinnamon
2 medium cloves of garlic, crushed   ¼ tsp. cayenne pepper

(1) Place the tahini in a medium-sized bowl. Beat it at high speed with an electric mixer for 5 minutes. Gradually drizzle in apple juice and vinegar, as you beat it.

(2) Stir in remaining ingredients. Serve with raw vegetables, crackers, or pieces of toasted pita bread.

30 minutes to prepare
plus
about 2-3 hours to chill.

PURÉED VEGETABLE DIP

2 Tbs. olive oil
2 cups chopped onion
½ tsp. salt
lots of black pepper
¼ tsp. thyme
½ tsp. basil
1 large clove garlic, crushed
1½ cups chopped broccoli
1 cup chopped yellow summer squash
1 medium green bell pepper, chopped
2 Tbs. red wine vinegar

¼ cup each: toasted sunflower seeds
toasted sesame seeds
1 cup finely-minced pitted black olives

(1) In a very large skillet, begin sautéing the onion in olive oil, with salt, pepper, and herbs.

(2) After a few minutes, add the garlic, broccoli, squash, and bell pepper. Stir well, cover, and cook over medium heat 10-15 minutes, stirring occasionally.

(3) Remove from heat, stir in vinegar, and let it cool to room temperature.

(4) Purée the sauté (include all its liquid – whatever there is of it) in a food processor fitted with the steel blade. (You can also use a blender or a food mill.)

(5) Return the purée to a bowl, mix in the toasted seeds and minced olives, and chill, covered, until cold. Serve with bread, crackers, or chips.

Heated Cheeses

Plain, good, cold or room temperature cheese is a noble food, both simple and sophisticated at once. Take this same plain, good, cold or room temperature cheese, and HEAT it—either to meltedness or just to slightly-warmed softness — and it acquires the elusive ability to transmit feelings of Psychological Comfort to its eater. Cold cheese feels like a snack, but warmed cheese feels like a <u>meal</u>. Melt cheese on bread or steamed vegetables or cooked grains, OR, melt it by itself, and dunk bread into it (see Greek Melt, below). Even semisoft cheeses, like brie, camembert, or rondelé, can be heated gently in their little foil containers (in a very low oven, for about 10 minutes), and then served with wedges of fresh fruit (try cantaloupe or ripe pears).

When you have little else but cheese in the house, and you begin to sense that feeling of deprivation coming on, the answer is: heat it. There is a good chance you will feel much better.

GREEK MELT

15-20 minutes to prepare.   2 servings; easily multiplied.

2 Tbs. butter
½ lb. medium-sharp cheese, cubed
1 medium clove of garlic, crushed
1 Tbs. fresh lemon juice
~ some warm, crusty bread~

(1) Melt the butter in a small, heavy skillet. (Cast-iron is best.)

(2) Add the cubes of cheese, distributing them as evenly as possible over the melted butter. Melt the cheese over gentle heat, until it starts to bubble at the edges.

(3) Sprinkle the top of the cheese with crushed garlic and lemon juice. Bring the whole skilletful right to the table,* and serve it immediately, with warm crusty bread (use the bread to scoop it up).

*Don't forget, the skillet is <u>hot</u>! Put it on a (trivet.

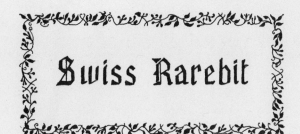

Swiss Rarebit

50 minutes to prepare

4 servings

3 Tbs. butter
3 Tbs. flour

1½ cups dry white wine
12 oz. mushrooms, chopped
½ tsp. salt
½ tsp. crushed tarragon

8 medium scallions, minced (greens and whites)
1 firmly-packed cup grated Swiss cheese

Thick slices of fresh pumpernickel bread
freshly-grated nutmeg
freshly-ground black pepper

(1) In a large, heavy saucepan, melt the butter over very low heat.

(2) Gradually sprinkle in the flour, whisking constantly. Cook this roux, whisking for about 1 minute.

(3) Slowly pour in the wine, continuing to whisk constantly until all the wine is added. Continue to cook over medium-low heat, stirring occasionally with a wooden spoon, for 5 minutes.

(4) Add mushrooms, salt, and tarragon. Cover, and simmer 15 minutes, stirring occasionally.

(5) Stir in the minced scallions and the grated Swiss cheese. Keep cooking over low heat, stirring frequently, for another 5 minutes.

(6) To serve, place 4 generous slices (toasted or not) of pumpernickel bread on 4 separate plates (or in shallow soup bowls). Spoon the rarebit over the top. Grind on some fresh nutmeg and black pepper, and serve.

Mushroom & Cheese Pâté

30 minutes to prepare; 1¼ hours to bake.

...and it also needs time to chill.

Either 2 medium loaf pans— or 1 deep-dish casserole's-worth.

Preheat oven to 400°F.

4 Tbs. butter
3 cups chopped onion
1 lb. mushrooms, coarsely-chopped
½ tsp. salt (more, to taste)
1 tsp. dry mustard
½ tsp. dill weed
black pepper, to taste

cayenne, to taste
3 Tbs. dry white wine
¼ cup wheat germ
8 oz. (1 cup) neufchatel or cream cheese
1 lb. (2 cups) ricotta cheese
(paprika
(freshly-minced parsley

(1) In a large, heavy skillet begin cooking the onions in butter over medium heat, stirring occasionally.

(2) After about 5 minutes, when the onions are soft, add the mushrooms, salt, dry mustard, dill, black pepper, and cayenne. Stir well, and cook uncovered over moderate heat, stirring intermittently, for another 5 minutes.

(3) Add the wine, and stir. Continue to cook for 5 more minutes.

(4) Sprinkle in the wheat germ, stirring the mixture as you sprinkle. Stir and cook 1-2 minutes more, then remove from heat.

(5) Cut the neufchatel or cream cheese into the hot mixture.

(6) Use a blender or a food processor fitted with a steel blade to purée the mixture. Transfer the purée to a large mixing bowl. Whisk in the ricotta.

(7) You can bake the pâté in a buttered casserole, or in 2 loaf pans. If baked in a casserole, it will be softer, and you can serve it in mounds on greens, or as a spread (great on crackers!). If baked in a loaf, it will be sliceable, perfect for an hors d'oeuvre. (When you use loaf pans, butter them, and line them with buttered wax paper. Cool it in the pan, then remove it, and peel off the paper. In either case, chill before serving.)

→Sprinkle with paprika and parsley. Baking time = 1¼ hours, uncovered, at 400°F.

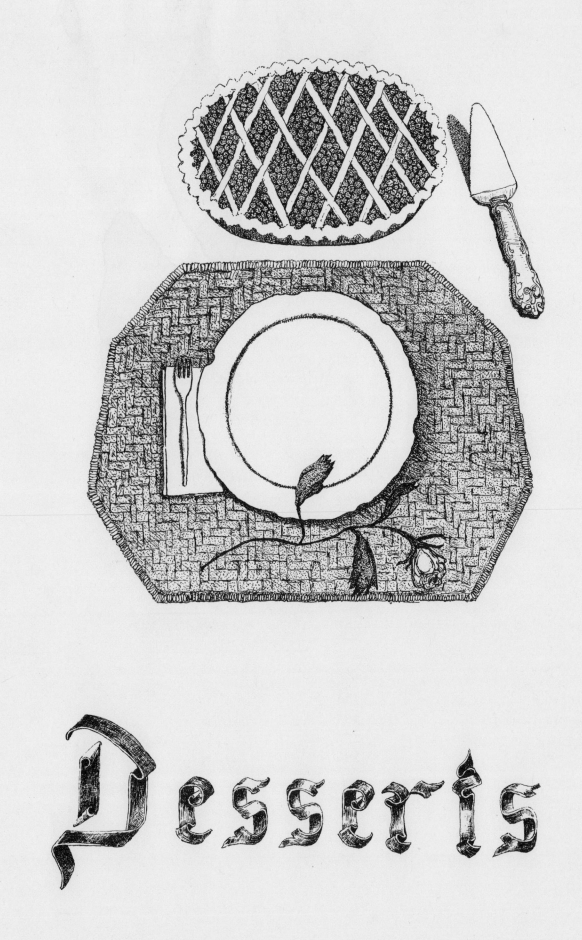

Desserts

DESSERTS:
Table of Contents

It is with great pleasure that I present you with these dessert recipes.

The sugar content is kept to a minimum wherever possible, and for those of you who seek such things, there are several cakes (and other desserts) sweetened with honey instead.

If you prefer honey to sugar, but you are not sure which kind of honey to use, the general rule-of-thumb is: the lighter the color, the milder the flavor. I think it desirable to use the lightest-possible honey, so its flavor won't dominate the entire dessert. Shop for honey discriminately, and always try to get a taste of it before you buy it. You'd be amazed at the variety of flavors different honeys have, and you should be sure you buy one you like.

If you don't care how your dessert is sweetened as long as it tastes good, then you have quite a list of things to choose from here. Don't forget, desserts are not restricted to after-dinner fare. Many of these recipes are lovely additions to afternoon tea or Sunday brunch. I hope they serve to sweetly expand your repertoire.

Peach & Rum Puddingcake

30 minutes to prepare;
35 minutes to bake.

Butter a 9x13" pan.
Preheat oven to 350°.

2 cups unbleached white flour

2 tsp. baking powder

½ tsp. salt

1 tsp. cinnamon

½ tsp. allspice

2 eggs

1 packed cup brown sugar

½ tsp. vanilla extract

2 Tbs. rum

2 Tbs. melted butter

2½ cups fresh peach slices

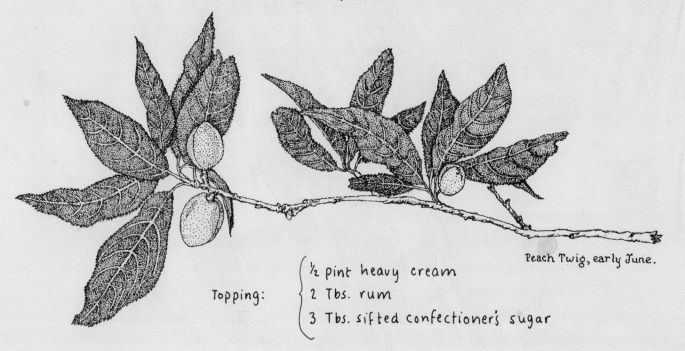

Peach Twig, early June.

Topping:
½ pint heavy cream
2 Tbs. rum
3 Tbs. sifted confectioner's sugar

(1) Sift together the flour, baking powder, salt and spices — into a mixing bowl.

(2) In a separate bowl, beat together the eggs and brown sugar. Use an electric mixer, and beat well at high speed for several minutes.

(3) Beat the vanilla, rum, and melted butter into the sugar & egg mixture.

(4) Stir the wet ingredients into the flour mixture. Add the peaches. Use a wooden spoon, and try to combine everything well with just a few swift strokes.

(5) Spread the mixture into your buttered 9x13" pan. Bake 35 minutes at 350°F.

(6) Whip the heavy cream, sprinkling in the rum and confectioner's sugar. Serve the puddingcake hot or warm, in squares, laced with topping.

Spicy Gingerbread

25 minutes to prepare;
30-35 minutes to bake.

Preheat oven to 350°F.
Butter an 8-inch square
pan (or its equivalent).

...loved by Gingerbread friends
and enemies alike...

1) 5 Tbs. butter
    3 Tbs. freshly-grated ginger root
    } Sauté together lightly, about 3-4 minutes. Remove from heat.

2) ½ cup light honey
    ½ cup light molasses
    } Beat together vigorously for 5 minutes. Beat in above ginger plus all its butter.

3) ½ cup firm yogurt
    1 large egg
    } Beat well together. Combine with above, and set aside.

4) 1 cup whole wheat flour
    1 cup unbleached white flour
    1½ tsp. baking soda
    ¼ tsp. salt
    1 tsp. dry mustard
    ½ tsp. ground cloves or allspice
    ½ tsp. cinnamon
    ¼ tsp. nutmeg
    } Sift together thoroughly, into a large mixing bowl.

5) Make a well in the center of the dry mixture.

6) Add the wet mixture. Mix thoroughly, but minimally.

7) Spread the batter into a nicely-buttered pan.

8) Bake 30-35 minutes in a 350°F oven. It's done when the top surface is springy to the touch, or when a toothpick inserted into the center comes out clean.

Cream-Filled Carob Fudge Torte

I. The Cake

30-40 minutes to prepare.
20-30 minutes to bake.

Preheat oven to 350°F.
Butter 2 9-inch rounds.

- ½ cup soft, sweet butter
- ¾ cup light honey
- 2 large eggs
- ½ cup carob powder } blended together
- ½ cup hot coffee or water } to a smooth paste
- 2 cups unbleached white flour
- 1 tsp. soda
- ½ tsp. salt
- ⅔ cup firm yogurt
- 1½ tsp. pure vanilla extract

(1) Cream together butter and honey. Beat at high speed for 5 minutes.

(2) Add eggs, one at a time, beating well after each.

(3) Beat in carob paste until uniformly blended.

(4) Sift together dry ingredients. Stir them into the carob-butter mixture alternately with the yogurt (flour/yogurt/flour/yogurt/flour). Mix just enough to combine after each addition. (Overmixing toughens the texture of a cake.)

(5) Stir in the vanilla.

(6) Divide the batter evenly between the cake pans. Bake 20 to 30 minutes, or until a toothpick inserted into the center comes out clean.

(7) Cool 10 minutes in the pans, then remove carefully (rap pans sharply, then invert onto dinner plates). Cool thoroughly before assembling.

II. The Filling

- 8 oz. (1 cup) softened cream cheese
- ½ cup firm yogurt
- 1 tsp. pure vanilla extract
- ½ tsp. freshly-grated lemon rind
- 3-4 Tbs. honey

- a few toasted sunflower seeds
- extra carob powder

[OPTIONAL VARIATION: Reduce the cream cheese by half, and add ½ cup ricotta cheese.]

(1) Combine everything except sunflower seeds and carob powder. Beat until fluffy and smooth.

(2) Spread half the filling between the layers, and spread the rest on top.

(3) Sprinkle the top with sunflower seeds and a little bit of sifted carob powder. Chill before slicing.

Oatmeal-Yogurt Cake

15 minutes to prepare;
25 minutes to bake.

Butter a 9x13" pan.
Preheat oven to 350°F.

1 packed cup light brown sugar
½ cup melted butter
2 eggs
⅔ cup firm yogurt
½ tsp. vanilla extract
1 cup unbleached white flour
1 cup whole wheat flour
1 tsp. baking soda

1 tsp. baking powder
½ tsp. salt
½ tsp. cinnamon
½ tsp. allspice
¼ tsp. nutmeg
¼ tsp. ground ginger
1½ cup raw rolled oats
½ cup fresh-squeezed O.J.

optional: ½ cup dark raisins

1) In a large mixing bowl combine brown sugar and melted butter. Beat well.

2) Add the eggs, one at a time, beating very well after each.

3) Beat in the yogurt and vanilla until well-blended.

4) Sift together flours, soda, powder, salt, and spices.

5) Add half the flour mixture and all the oats to the butter mixture. Stir until well-mixed.

6) Add half the orange juice, stirring.

7) Alternately add remaining flour mixture and orange juice, and stir just enough to blend after each addition. Add raisins with last bit of orange juice.

8) Turn into a well-buttered 9x13-inch oblong pan. Spread into place, and bake 25 minutes, or until a probing knife comes out clean.

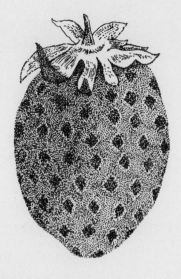

Fresh Strawberry Mousse

4-6 servings

Separate the eggs earlier, so they can come to room temperature.

4 hours to prepare, including chilling.

3 large eggs
1 quart fresh strawberries
4 Tbs. light honey
2 Tbs. kirsch (or a similar fruity liqueur)

¼ tsp. salt
3 Tbs. cornstarch

½ pint heavy cream (cold)

1) Separate the eggs. Cover each container tightly; allow to come to room temperature.

2) Wash and hull the strawberries. Pick out the 3 largest and Most Gorgeous, and save these for the Decoration. Place the runners-up in a saucepan with the honey, the kirsch, and the salt. Cover and cook 10-15 minutes over low heat.

3) Strain out some of the hot liquid from the cooked mixture, and add it to the cornstarch in a small bowl. Mix until smooth, and return this paste to the strawberry mixture. Mix thoroughly.

4) Beat a spoonful of the hot strawberries into the egg yolks, then return the yolks to the strawberries. Beat with a wooden spoon for about 2 minutes. Cool to room temperature.

5) Beat the eggwhites until stiff. Fold into the strawberry mixture. Chill for about 1 - 1½ hours.

6) Whip the cream until it is fairly firm. Fold this into the chilled mousse. Refrigerate until completely set (2 hours or so). Garnish with slices of those above-reserved Select Strawberries.

Apple~Port~Cheese Pie
with Almond Crust

1½ hours to prepare; 2 hours to chill.

1 9" pie.

I. THE CRUST: ~preheat oven to 375°F~

½ cup (1 stick) cold butter   ¼ cup finely-ground almonds
1 cup unbleached white flour   3-4 Tbs. cold water

(1) Use a pastry cutter or a food processor to cut together the butter and flour until they become a uniform mixture resembling coarse corn meal. Mix in the almonds.

(2) Sprinkle in the water, mixing quickly to form a firm, cohesive ball of dough.

(3) Roll out, and apply to a 9-inch pie pan, forming a Nice Edge. Weight it down by placing a piece of foil with a handful of dry beans right on the crust. Bake for 15 minutes at 375°F. Remove foil and beans, and bake 15 minutes longer. Cool.

II. THE APPLES & PORT:

1½ cups port wine   \   1 stick cinnamon   \ ½ tsp. grated lemon rind
3 large, tart apples, peeled & sliced \   ⅓ cup light honey   \ dash of salt

(1) Combine port, apples, and cinnamon stick in a saucepan. Bring to a boil, turn down heat, cover, and cook 10 minutes (or, until apples are just tender). Remove from heat, and discard cinnamon stick.

(2) Strain, reserving both apples and liquid. Add honey, lemon rind, and salt to the liquid. Mix well, and set aside.

III. THE CHEESE FILLING:

4 oz. softened cream cheese   \ ¼ tsp. vanilla extract \ ¼ tsp. almond extract
¼ cup of the Reserved Liquid (just above) \ 1 Tbs. honey \ 3 Tbs. yogurt

(1) Combine all ingredients and beat very well. Spread evenly onto cooled crust.

(2) Arrange apple slices on top in a Lovely Pattern.

        ....and finally:

IV. THE GLAZE:

3 Tbs. cornstarch   PLUS   The remaining port liquid

(1) Place cornstarch in a small saucepan. Whisk in the liquid. Keep whisking, and cook over medium heat until thick and glossy (approximately 5-8 minutes).

(2) Without waiting for it to cool, pour it over the top of the Arranged Apples. Chill until cold and firm.

Cherry-Berry Pie

50 minutes
to prepare;
45 minutes
to bake.

1 9" pie

CRUST
{ ½ cup cold butter
2 cups unbleached white flour

¼ tsp. salt
approximately 6 Tbs. cold milk

1) Use a pastry cutter or a food processor (steel blade) to cut the butter and flour together until the mixture is uniform, resembling coarse corn meal.

2) Add salt. Begin adding the milk, a tablespoon at a time, mixing with quick strokes (use a fork). As soon as the dough is cohesive, push it together — into itself — in the center of the bowl to make a ball. Divide the dough into two moderately unequal portions. Roll one portion out (using as much flour-coating as necessary) and fit it into a 9-inch pie pan. Roll the second portion, and cut it into about 10 strips, ½-inch by about 12 inches. Wrap these carefully in waxed paper, and refrigerate until later.

FILLING
{ 2 cups fresh blueberries ~ or sliced strawberries
2 cups fresh sweet cherries - stemmed and pitted
3 Tbs. unbleached white flour
2 Tbs. fresh lemon juice   optional: ½ tsp. freshly-grated lemon rind

½ cup light honey
½ tsp. cinnamon
freshly-grated nutmeg

{ ~ confectioners' sugar ~ } for the top.

1) Gently toss together the berries and the cherries in a bowl.
2) Gradually sift in the flour as you toss.
3) Keep tossing, and drizzle and/or sprinkle in remaining ingredients.
4) Deposit the filling in the faithfully-waiting crust. Now you have a choice of styles for gracing the top with those above-mentioned strips of dough:
CHOICE A: You can weave the strips into a lattice. (did you weave potholders on a small metal loom, as a child? Yes? Then, same principle. Press strip-ends firmly into edges of crust. No? Then, proceed to choice B.

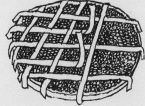

CHOICE B: Just lay the strips on top of the pie ~ lay them flat, or twist them. Press the ends to the pie-edges.
5) Bake at 450°F. for 10 minutes. Turn the temperature down to 350°F, and bake another 30-35 minutes. Sift confectioners' sugar over the top as soon as the pie comes out of the oven. Eat it hot, warm, or cold.

Orange-Filled Chocolate Crêpes with Fudge Sauce

Make the filling and the pancakes early in the day, and refrigerate them.

One hour before serving time, begin the final 2 steps.

4-6 luxurious servings.

I. The Filling

4 seedless (navel) oranges
1/3 cup orange liqueur
1/4 cup orange marmalade
1/2 cup chopped, toasted walnuts

(1) Peel and section the oranges. Place them in a bowl with the liqueur, and let them marinate for several hours. Strain, and reserve all the liquid.

(2) Mix in marmalade and walnuts. Cover, and set aside.

III. Assembly

(1) Preheat oven to 300°F.

(2) Divide the filling evenly among the cooked crêpes. Place the filling near one edge of each crêpe, and roll it up. Place the filled crêpes on a lightly-buttered tray. Cover loosely with foil.

(3) Heat for 15-20 minutes.

~ Prepare the sauce while they heat. ~

II. The Pancakes

1 cup unbleached white flour
2 medium eggs
a dash of salt
1 cup milk
1 Tbs. unsweetened cocoa
2 Tbs. confectioner's sugar

} Whip together in a blender.

(1) Use a 6- or 7-inch crêpe pan –high heat!– to make very thin pancakes (use just enough batter to coat the pan.) Oil the pan lightly, and cook the crêpes on both sides until just dry.

(2) Stack the cooked crêpes on a plate.

IV. The Sauce

2 Tbs. butter
4 oz. semisweet chocolate
The reserved liquid from "I."
3-4 Tbs. confectioner's sugar

(1) Melt butter and chocolate together in a double boiler.

(2) Heat the reserved liquid. Add it to the chocolate, along with the sugar. Cook, stirring, 10-12 minutes (low heat!). Serve hot over the crêpes.

Russian Coffeecake

30 minutes to prepare.
50-60 minutes to bake.

Preheat oven to 350°F.
Generously grease a 10" tube pan.

1 cup (2 sticks) butter (softened)
1 packed cup light brown sugar
4 large eggs
1 tsp. pure vanilla extract
1 cup buttermilk (room temperature)

2 cups unbleached white flour
1 cup whole wheat flour
3 tsp. baking powder
1 tsp. baking soda
½ tsp. salt

FILLING
{
a heaping ½ cup semisweet chocolate chips
a heaping ½ cup whole almonds
a heaping ½ cup shredded, unsweetened coconut
a generous ½ cup peach or apricot jam
½ cup sliced dried apricots
}

1) Cream the butter and sugar together until light and fluffy. Add the eggs one at a time, beating well after each. Stir in the vanilla.

2) Sift together the flours, baking powder, soda and salt.

3) Add the dry mixture and the buttermilk alternately to the butter mixture. Use a wooden spoon, and mix just enough to blend after each addition.

4) Place the chocolate chips and almonds in blender jar. Whirl together at high speed for about 20-30 seconds (until pulverized but not mushy). Combine with the coconut.

5) Spoon half the batter into the prepared pan, gently spreading it until even. Spoon dollops of jam here and there onto batter (don't try to spread it-just leave it in little blobs), and sprinkle on the apricots and about ⅔ the chocolate-nut mix.

6) Add the remaining batter, distributing it nicely. Sprinkle the top with the remaining chocolate-nut mix, and bake the cake for 50-60 minutes (until a probing knife comes out clean). Cool completely before removing from pan.

Stuffed Baked Apples

· ·

· Preparation time:
about 1 hour,
including baking.

· 4 servings ·
Preheat oven
to 375°F.

You can put
these into the oven
just as you're sit-
ting down to your
meal. The apples
will be ready in
time to be served
fresh fresh & hot
for dessert.

4   2½-inch-diameter
    tart cooking apples

¼ cup Grape Nuts cereal
¼ cup finely-minced walnuts
¼ tsp. cinnamon
a small handful of raisins
                or currants
2 Tbs. honey

Try serving
these as a brunch
dish, accompanied
by a wedge of
cheddar cheese, or
topped with yogurt.
For dessert, they
are really good
with that old
standby, vanilla
ice cream.

(1) Carefully remove the cores from the apples, using an apple corer
(highly-specialized gadget), a vegetable peeler, or a paring knife. Try
to get all the seeds out of there, as well as anything else you'd rather
not bite into inadvertently.

(2) Combine the remaining ingredients, and fill each apple. (If you are
a Filling Enthusiast, you can make the cavities larger, and increase the
filling amounts.)

(3) Place the stuffed apples in a shallow baking dish, and add about
¼ inch of water. Bake, uncovered, for 40 minutes.

Serve hot, room-temperature, or cold.

Sourcream · Apple Pie
with Oatmeal Cookie Crust

CRUST:

1½ cups raw rolled oats
¼ cup sesame seeds
½ cup whole wheat flour
½ tsp. salt
½ tsp. cinnamon
¼ cup finely minced nuts
½ tsp. vanilla extract
½ cup sweet butter ⎫ melted
3 Tbs. honey   ⎬ together

Combine all ingredients, and mix well. Press firmly and evenly into bottom and sides of a 9-or 10-inch pie pan.

FILLING:

5 cups sliced tart cooking apples
juice and rind of 1 average lemon
¼ cup light honey (or maple syrup)
2 Tbs. unbleached white flour
½ tsp. cinnamon
¼ tsp. nutmeg
1 large egg
½ cup sour cream

(1) Combine apples with lemon juice and rind. Drizzle in honey. Toss gently until uniformly coated.

(2) Sift in flour and spices. Toss again to coat. Distribute neatly into unbaked pie shell.

(3) Beat together egg and sour cream. Drizzle slowly over apples.

(4) Bake 35-40 minutes in center of oven (375°F). Serve hot or cold.

Chocolate ❧ Pudding

20-30 minutes
to prepare;
3 hours
to chill.

4·5 thorough servings.

4 oz. semisweet chocolate
3 packed Tbs. light brown sugar
2 cups milk ⤵
   (For richer-tasting pudding,
   use evaporated milk.)

a dash of salt
3 Tbs. cornstarch
½ tsp. vanilla extract
(OPTIONAL: 1 egg yolk,
   for extra richness)

(1) In a heavy saucepan, combine the chocolate, sugar, and milk. Heat very gently, whisking constantly until all the chocolate is melted, and the mixture is uniform. (You might want to use a double boiler for this, or a "waffle" heat-absorber pad underneath. Whatever precaution you use, just be sure you don't boil or burn the milk.)

(2) Combine salt and cornstarch in a small bowl. Pour in about ¾ cup of the hot mixture. Whisk vigorously until all the cornstarch is dissolved, and whisk this solution back into the saucepan. Keep whisking, and cook the pudding over very low heat about 8 - 10 more minutes, or until thick and glossy. (As pudding thickens, you can graduate from using a whisk to using a wooden spoon. Whatever you use, keep stirring.) Remove from heat.

(3) Stir in the vanilla. Beat in the optional egg yolk (or not). Transfer the hot pudding to a serving bowl, or to individual units. Chill completely before serving.

Coconut & Almond Macaroon Torte

Note: separate your eggs earlier, so they can come to room temperature. Put both yolks and whites in large bowls.

30 minutes to prepare; 30 minutes to bake.

45 minutes to cool; 15 minutes to assemble.

Butter the bottom (not sides!) of a 10-inch springform pan.

Preheat oven to 350°.

The Cake:

6 large eggs, separated and at room-temperature
½ cup (packed) light brown sugar
½ tsp. salt
1⅓ cups finely-ground almonds
1 cup shredded coconut
½ tsp. orange rind

The Filling & Topping:

½ cup red raspberry preserves
2 Tbs. butter
¼ cup semisweet chocolate chips
1 Tbs. cocoa
1 Tbs. confectioner's sugar
¼ tsp. orange rind
~extra cocoa~

(1) Using an electric mixer, beat the eggwhites until stiff.

(2) Without washing the beaters, beat the egg yolks, gradually adding brown sugar and salt. When all is added, beat 2 minutes at high speed.

(3) Stir the ground almonds and shredded coconut into the yolk mixture. Add the orange rind. Mix well.

(4) Fold the eggwhites into the mixture - carefully and quickly. Transfer the batter to your prepared pan. Bake undisturbed for 30 minutes.

(5) When the cake is completely cool, remove it from its pan, and cut it in half, using a serrated knife and a gentle sawing motion. Spread the bottom half with ½ cup raspberry preserves. Place the top half on top.

(6) In a double boiler melt together the butter and the chocolate chips. Sift in 1 Tbs. cocoa and 1 Tbs. confectioner's sugar. Stir in ¼ tsp. orange rind. Spread this mixture, while it is still warm, over the top surface, just to the edge. If desired, sift a small amount of unsweetened cocoa over the top for a nicely-finished look.

∗ Chocolate ∗ Apple ∗ Nut Torte ∗

∗ Preparation Time:
    approximately
    45 minutes.
∗ Baking Time:
    approximately
    50 minutes.

∗ Preheat oven
    to 350°F.
∗ Butter the bottom
    of a tube
    or spring-form
    cake pan.

8 eggs, separated and at room temperature
¾ cup (packed) light brown sugar
1 cup pulverized almonds
1 cup (packed) coarsely-grated tart apple
4 oz. grated (use blender or processor) semisweet chocolate

½ cup unbleached white flour ∗
½ tsp. baking powder
dash of cinnamon
½ tsp. salt
½ tsp. vanilla extract

(1) Beat together the egg yolks and the sugar. Add nuts, apple and chocolate, and beat well. (Make sure you are using a large-enough bowl.)

(2) Sift together dry ingredients.

(3) Fold dry ingredients and vanilla into the first mixture.

(4) Beat the eggwhites until stiff. Fold into the batter until well-blended (be patient, and do this gradually, so you don't deflate the eggwhites). Turn into a tube or spring-form cake pan of which only the bottom is buttered. Bake about 50 minutes, or until a knife inserted into the center comes out clean. Cool before removing from pan or slicing.

(5) Suggested topping: whipped cream with a drizzle of Amaretto.

∗ Fine breadcrumbs or matzo meal may be substituted for the flour.

Ricotta-Cherry Mousse

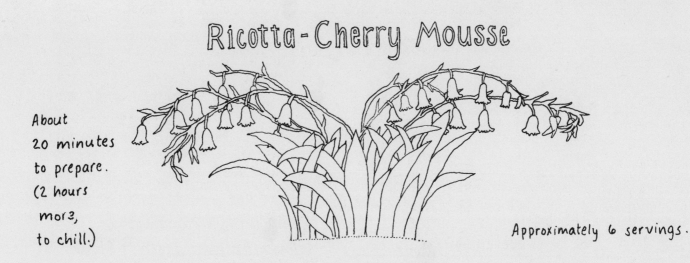

About
20 minutes
to prepare.
(2 hours
mor3,
to chill.)

Approximately 6 servings.

Unlike most other dessert mousses, this one does not involve eggs or whipped cream, so it will spare you a lot of work and expense (and even a handful of calories). What it will **not** spare: your taste buds and your sense of elegance. Ricotta cheese, modest and pure substance that it is, has a secret talent: when whipped, it is transformed texturally into a stunning white smoothness. Treat yourself to this easy recipe.

1 lb. whole milk ricotta
2 Tbs. light honey (more, to taste)
1-2 Tbs. orange liqueur
a few drops of almond extract

1/4 tsp. vanilla extract
2 cups freshly-pitted dark cherries
1/2 cup shaved semisweet chocolate
1/3 cup slivered, toasted almonds

(1) Place the ricotta in a mixing bowl, and whip with an electric mixer at high speed for about 5 minutes.

(2) Gradually add the honey, and keep beating until it is incorporated.

(3) Mix in the liqueur and the extracts. Fold in the cherries.

(4) Chill — either in individual units (parfait glasses or sherbet dishes) — or in a serving bowl.

(5) Top each serving with shaved or grated (you can use a food processor) semi-sweet chocolate and slivered, toasted almonds.

Chocolate Honeycake

25-30 minutes to prepare;
About 30 minutes to bake.

Preheat oven to 350°F.
Butter an 8-inch square pan, or
its equivalent. (You can also
use a medium-sized loaf pan.)

6 Tbs. butter
1 oz. <u>unsweetened</u> chocolate
¾ cup light honey
2 eggs
1 tsp. vanilla extract

¼ cup unsweetened cocoa
1 cup unbleached white flour
½ tsp. salt
1½ tsp. baking powder
(½ cup chopped nuts- optional)

1) Melt the butter and chocolate together over a double boiler. Let cool to room temperature.
2) Beat the honey at high speed with an electric mixer for 5 minutes. Add eggs, one at a time, beating well after each. Stir in the vanilla.
3) Sift together the dry ingredients.
4) Beat the cooled chocolate & butter into the honey mixture. Fold in the dry ingredients. Stir until just combined. Pour into prepared pan.
   Bake approximately 30 minutes
   (a loaf will take longer).

,, Jewish New Year Honeycake ,,

☾15-20 minutes
to prepare;

☾50-60 minutes
to bake.

☾Preheat oven to 350°F.

☾Butter a medium-sized
loaf pan.

☾1 cup light honey
☾1 large egg
☾3 Tbs. melted butter
☾½ cup cold black coffee

☾1 cup whole wheat flour
☾1 cup unbleached white flour
☾¼ tsp. salt
☾2½ tsp. baking powder

☾ a dash or two of : cinnamon
nutmeg
allspice

☾½ cup finely-chopped walnuts

(1)   Beat the honey at high speed with an electric mixer for about 5 minutes.
It will become frothy, white and opaque.

(2)   Add the egg, butter, and coffee. Beat well.

(3)   Sift together the dry ingredients. Fold them, along with half the nuts, into the
first mixture. Spread into prepared pan; sprinkle remaining nuts on top.

(4)   Bake 50-60 minutes (until a probing knife emerges clean).

1. TRADITIONAL TOPPING:

,, ☾1 cup dried apricots PLUS 1 cup dried prunes☾ ,,

Place these in a bowl. Pour 2 cups boiling water over them, cover & let
it stand several hours. A fruity syrup will form. Spoon fruit-plus-syrup over each
serving. This topping is traditionally called Compote (pronounce: "com-put' ").

2. NONTRADITIONAL TOPPING:

☾2 cups sliced apples   ☾1 Tbs. fresh lemon juice
☾2 Tbs. sweet butter   ☾cinnamon
☾1 Tbs. honey→,,

Sauté the apple slices in butter over low flame. Add lemon juice and some
dashes of cinnamon. Cook until the apples are soft. Remove from heat ~ add honey
Stir well, and spoon onto slices of honeycake.

20 minutes
to prepare;
1¼ hours
to bake;

About 9 hours
to cool & chill.

Amaretto Cheesecake
with Chocolate Cookie Crust

Preheat oven
to 325°F.

CRUST:

1½ cups crushed plain chocolate wafer cookies

⅓ cup ground almonds

¼ cup Amaretto liqueur

2-3 Tbs. melted butter

- Combine all ingredients. Mix well.
- Press firmly into the bottom of a 9-or 10-inch springform pan.

FILLING:

1 lb. ricotta cheese (2 cups)

8 oz. softened cream cheese (1 cup)

4 eggs

⅓ cup Amaretto liqueur

1 cup sugar

¼ tsp. salt

½ tsp. freshly-grated orange rind

- Combine all ingredients in a large bowl. Beat for at least 5 minutes with an electric mixer at high speed. Scrape the sides and bottom of the bowl often.
- Pour the batter into the crust-lined pan. Bake in the center of a 325°F oven for 1 hour. Then, turn off the oven, open the door, and leave the cake in there for another 15 minutes. Remove, let it cool, then cover the pan tightly with food-wrap and chill at least 8 hours before serving.

✱ ✱ ✱ ✱ ✱ ✱ ✱ ✱ ✱ CHEESECAKE SOUFFLÉ ✱ ✱ ✱ ✱ ✱ ✱ ✱

w/ Strawberry~Marmalade Sauce 🍓🍓

✱ ✱

Preparation Time: 2 hours   🍓🍓   6 Servings

Preheat oven to 375°F.   → Butter a large soufflé dish.

       This is an especially exciting event to plan for a small, intimate gathering. You can prepare the sauce and the ricotta mixture ahead of time (keep everything at room temperature), and midway into the evening, excuse yourself to sneak off to the kitchen, beat the eggwhites, fold everything together, and pop it into the oven. Return to your guests with a discreet smile, and one hour later, VOILÀ!!

* ✱ 1 pound whole-milk ricotta
* ✱ 6 large, separated eggs
* ✱ 5 Tbs. flour
* ✱ scant ½ tsp. salt

* ✱ 1 cup (8 oz.) sour cream
* ✱ ⅔ cup sifted confectioners sugar
* ✱ ½ tsp. pure vanilla extract
* ✱ ½ tsp. fresh lemon rind

1) After you separate the eggs, put the bowlful of whites aside (covered), to come to room temperature.

2) In a saucepan, whisk very thoroughly together the ricotta, egg yolks, flour, salt, sour cream, and sugar. Cook, whisking, over very low heat until thick and smooth (15-20 minutes). Remove from heat. Stir in vanilla and lemon rind, and let come to room temperature.

3) Beat the eggwhites until stiff. Fold these into the cooled ricotta mixture. (see the basic soufflé instructions, p.170) Turn into prepared dish. Place in preheated 375° oven, and turn the oven down to 350°. Bake one hour. Serve hot.

     → Prepare the sauce while the soufflé bakes:

* ✱ 2½ cups fresh (or frozen unsweetened) strawberries
* ✱ 1 cup orange marmalade
* ✱ ⅓ cup orange liqueur (Grand Marnier or Cointreau)

} Combine in saucepan. Cook 10 minutes. Top each serving with a few spoonsful.

Four (4) Simple & Wonderful Cookie Recipes

Mandelbrot

3 beaten eggs
6 Tbs. light honey
½ cup melted butter

1 tsp. orange rind
1 tsp. vanilla extract
2¾ cups flour
2 tsp. baking powder

¼ tsp. salt
1 cup minced almonds
½ cup minced dates
½ cup raisins or currants

Preheat oven to 375°F.

1) Beat together eggs, honey and butter until light and fluffy. Add orange rind and vanilla extract.

2) Sift together flour, baking powder and salt. Add to first mixture. Stir in nuts and fruit.

3) Divide the batter in half. Shape two parallel logs, about 2 inches wide, on a greased tray. Bake 30 minutes at 375°F.

4) Slice baked logs into ½-inch slices, place slices on the same tray, and return to same oven for another 15-20 minutes. Remove and cool.

Approximate yield: 2 Dozen

....

Wholewheat Poppyseed Cookies   Preheat oven to 375°F.

½ cup soft butter
¾ cup (packed) light brown sugar
2 beaten eggs

½ tsp. vanilla extract
½ tsp. lemon rind
⅓ cup poppyseeds

1 cup whole wheat flour
1 cup white flour
2 tsp. baking powder
¼ tsp. salt

1) Cream together butter and sugar. Beat until light. Add eggs and vanilla.

2) Add lemon rind and poppyseeds. Beat another 5 minutes.

3) Sift together dry ingredients. Add to 1st mixture and mix well.

4) Chill the dough about an hour. Roll to ¼-inch thickness. Cut into your favorite shapes. Bake on a lightly-greased tray 10-12 minutes.

Approximate yield: 4½ Dozen.

Cashew Shortbread

Preheat oven to 375°F.

1 cup soft, sweet butter	2 cups flour
½ cup (packed) light brown sugar	¼ tsp. salt
1 cup finely-chopped cashews	½ tsp. baking powder

1) Cream together butter and sugar. Add nuts; mix well.
2) Sift in dry ingredients. Work the dough into cohesiveness with your fingers. It will be crumbly. Do not refrigerate before rolling, unless you leave enough time to let it return to room temperature first.
3) Roll with Patience and Optimism.
   Keep rolling until the dough is about ¼-inch thick.
4) Cut into subtle but imaginative shapes. Place on an ungreased cookie sheet.
5) Bake 8-10 minutes at 375°F.

Approximate yield: 4 Dozen

Cheese Crescents

Preheat oven to 350°F.

Dough
1 cup soft, sweet butter
2 cups flour
1 cup firm cottage
             cheese

Filling
½ cup honey
          or fruit preserves
½ cup ground nuts } combined
2 tsp. cinnamon

1) To make the dough: Use a pastry cutter and/or electric mixer to uniformly blend together butter, flour and cheese. Divide the dough into 4; make 4 balls. Wrap well and refrigerate one hour.

2) Roll each ball out, one at a time, aspiring to a perfect circle, ⅛-inch thick. Spread with ¼ the honey or preserves, and sprinkle with ¼ the cinnamon-nuts.

3) Cut like so: (like a pizza), and roll each wedge toward its point. Place completed crescents on an ungreased tray, and bake about 25 minutes, or until nicely-browned.

Approximate yield: 4 Dozen.

Apricot Streusel Pie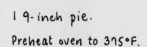

Do "Part One" in advance;
Remaining preparation
time = **40 minutes**

Baking time = **30 minutes.**

1 9-inch pie.

Preheat oven to 375°F.

 ## Part One: (Origins of the Filling)
- 2 packed cups sliced dried apricots
- ½ cup defrosted orange juice concentrate
- ⅔ cup boiling water
- (Optional: 1-2 Tbs. minced candied ginger)

- Combine everything in a bowl.
- Cover; let stand at least 2 hrs.
 (Tastiest if left for longer, like overnight, for example.)

Part Two: (Crust)
- ¼ cup cold butter
- 1 cup unbleached white flour
- 3-4 Tbs. cold water

Preheat oven to 375°F. Cut together butter and flour until uniformly blended. Gradually add enough water to hold it together, as you mix it with a fork. Roll out the dough, fit it into a 9-inch pie pan, and prebake (weight it down by placing a sheet of foil with dry beans on it) 15 minutes.
→ Remove from oven, and turn oven up to 425°F.

Part Three: (Growth & Development of the Filling)
- ¼ cup real maple syrup (or honey)
- 3 separated eggs
- ¼ tsp. salt
- ¼ tsp. cinnamon
- ½ cup slivered, toasted almonds
- The Apricots, from "Part One"

Beat together the syrup (honey), egg yolks, salt and cinnamon. Add the apricots plus their liquid; mix well. Beat the eggwhites until stiff. Fold these, plus the almonds, into the first mixture. Turn into the pre-baked crust.

Part Four: (Topping)
- ½ cup unbleached white flour
- ½ cup fine breadcrumbs - or wheat germ.
- another ¼ tsp. salt
- ¼ tsp. cinnamon, again
- 3 Tbs. butter
- 2 more Tbs. maple syrup - or honey

Combine, and mix well. Pat into place on top of the filling.

Slip the assembled pie into a 425°F oven. After 10 minutes, reduce heat to 350°F ~ and bake it 20 more minutes. Remove, and cool at least 15 minutes before slicing. Serve warm or cold.

Menu-Planning Notes

Menu-planning can be a highly creative endeavor. Even if you are following recipes, it is still an act of improvisation to group different dishes together into a Meal. There are no rules, but do consider these guidelines:

Try to achieve a balance of hot and cold dishes, as well as spicy and mild; sharp (as in something marinated) and bland (as in something soft, white, and full of soothing carbohydrates); crispy or crunchy and creamy. Pair off dishes that are complementary and harmonious at the same time. Try to avoid redundancies, for example: a cheesy casserole with a creamily-dressed salad with a cheesecake for dessert. Try to balance the varying weights of accompanying dishes. For example: if you are baking a fresh loaf of bread for dinner, serve it with lighter food (just a salad and/or a dip), so the bread, which is heavy, can be the focal point. If you find a certain rich dessert recipe compelling, plan a light meal to go before it, so the dessert will be well-noticed and appreciated (and no one will feel overstuffed afterwards).

Here are some sample menus for lunches or dinners. Try a few of these, then begin substituting other dishes. Soon you'll be creating your own menus from scratch. Suggestion: buy a new notebook for your very own Menu Diary. This will help you keep track of what you serve. You can use it to give yourself ideas on uninspired days when you have to cook, but can't think of anything.

* Vegetable Cheesecake (p.212)

* Marinated Pasta Salad (p.70)

a spinach salad with
* Creamy Mustard Dressing (p.77)

Fresh fruit

*Chilled Marinated Mushroom Soup (p.51)

*Tsimmes (p.204)

*Whole Wheat Buttermilk Biscuits (p.122)

* Spicy Gingerbread (p.259)
with whipped cream

. . . . More →

*Potato, Cheese, and Chili Soup (p.30)

* Avocado-Tofu-Egg Dip (p.246)

tortilla chips / raw vegetable sticks

*Chocolate Pudding (p.270)

* Cream of Onion Soup (p.42)

*Stuffed Artichokes (p.230)

*Freshly-baked Rolls (p.105)

a tossed green salad with
* Garlic & Herb Vinaigrette (p.77)

* Cream of Fresh Green Pea Soup (p.36)

* Cheese Blintzes (pp.154·55)
with sour cream

* Wilted Cucumbers (p.62)

* Chocolate-Apple-Nut Torte (p.272)

*Sweet Potato Pie (p.132)

*Swiss Green Beans (p.59)

*Cranberry Brown Bread (p.112)
with cinnamon butter (p.286)

* Chinese Mushroom Soup (p.28)

*Tofu-Nut Balls (p.192)

*Alfalfa-Romaino Salad (p.68)

*Sour Cream Apple Pie (p.269)

* Brazilian Stuffed Peppers (p.228)

a tossed green salad with
toasted sunflower seeds and
* Buttermilk & Cucumber Dressing (p.78)

*Yogurt & Herb Bread (p.108)
with cream cheese

There are many other menus
scattered throughout this book,
posted on scrolls for easy re-
cognition. Also, look in the index
under "Menus".

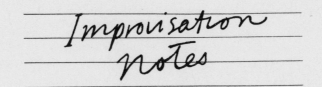

Improvisation notes

If you love to experiment in your kitchen, and cooking without recipes gives you a special feeling of satisfaction, BUT you are afraid to actually serve any of your concoctions to your gourmet friends (entertaining fantasies that they will throw their dinner on the floor... or at you....);

If you are inspired to alter a recipe, BUT you fear the heavens will punish you for deviating from the Written Word;

If you find yourself inhibited from creating a new invention because a voice from within inquires: "With 9 trillion cookbooks on the market, who am I, Jo(e) Schmo, to think I have something new to say on the subject?"

If you recognize yourself in any of the above situations, perhaps you could use a few words of encouragement. So here they are:

There is always something new to say in any expressive medium. Sure, many cookbooks have been written. Paintings are painted, and poetry is composed; people keep finding new ideas to express and new ways to re-express the timeless ones. Cooking can be a very personal statement, whether you follow a recipe, vary it, or invent your own altogether. The same recipe made by different people on different days and in different kitchens can taste new each time. There always seems to be a personal touch — a special, elusive quality — from each individual cook.

The first step toward improvisation is to read lots and lots of cookbooks. Read them without necessarily cooking the recipes; _visualize_ the food instead. You will get to the point where you understand what makes a soufflé a soufflé, a sauce a sauce, bread bread, etc. Soon you will feel so at home with these principles, you will be able to vary recipes, or even to cook without them at all.

IF YOU LOVE FOOD, YOU CAN BE A GOOD IMPROVISATIONAL COOK! All you need is a few general guidelines and some encouragement, then it's all up to you. The biggest trick is finding the courage to go ahead and try it. Let your own taste be your mentor; if you work with your favorite foods you are two-thirds of the way there. Courage has a way of becoming readily accessible when you surround yourself with ingredients you love.

. . . . . More →

Here is a chart to use as a guideline for your improvisations. It is divided according to traditional ethnic cooking styles. The first column of each section is a list of seasonings (occasionally using a vegetable as a seasoning - i.e., mushrooms or tomatoes), followed by suggested marinating ingredients, butter and/or oil, and finally, a general category of cheeses and dairy products used for each style of cooking.

Spanish

basil
bay leaf   butter
garlic   olive oil
onion
paprika (mild)   *
parsley   mild white cheeses
pepper (sweet and/or hot)
saffron

*
lemon
vinegar (cider or wine)
wine (dry red or white)

East European

caraway
dill (seed or weed)   *
horseradish   butter
mushroom
onion
paprika (mild or hot)
parsley   *
poppyseed   cottage cheese
                       cream cheese
*   sour cream, yogurt
lemon
vinegar (cider)
wine (dry red or sherry)

French

basil   tarragon
bay leaf   thyme
celery seed   *
cloves
dill weed   lemon
garlic   vinegar (wine)
horseradish   wine (dry red,
marjoram   white,
mushroom   sherry,
mustard   vermouth)
nutmeg
nuts (almonds, walnuts)   *
onion   butter
paprika (mild)   olive oil
parsley   *
pepper (sweet and/or hot)   cheddar cheese
rosemary   cream cheese
sage   swiss cheese
savory

Mexican

basil
chili powder
cilantro
cumin
garlic
onion
oregano
pepper (sweet and/or hot)
tomato

*
lemon
wine (dry red)

*
olive oil

*
cream cheese
mild white cheeses
sour cream

Italian

basil
bay leaf   butter
garlic   olive oil
marjoram   *
mushroom
onion   hard, sharp cheeses
oregano   mozzarella
parsley   ricotta
pepper (sweet and/or hot)
rosemary
saffron
thyme
tomato
     *
vinegar (wine)
wine (dry red, marsala)

Mediterranean

basil   butter
cinnamon   olive oil
cumin
dill weed   *
garlic
mint   feta cheese
onion   goat's milk cheeses
oregano   sour cream, yogurt
parsley
pepper (sweet and/or hot)
rosemary
sesame (tahini)
     *
lemon
vinegar (cider or wine)
wine (dry red)

Chinese

anise
cilantro ("Chinese parsley")
cloves
garlic
ginger
mushroom
mustard
nuts (peanuts, almonds, cashews)
onion
pepper (sweet or hot)
sesame seed
     *
soy sauce (tamari)
vinegar (dark rice wine)
wine (dry white, rice wine, sherry)
     *
peanut or soy oil
sesame oil
     *
(No cheeses or dairy products)
Tofu

Indian

cardamom   lemon
cinnamon   lime
cloves   *
coriander seed   butter
cumin (ground or seed)   peanut oil
dill (seed or weed)   *
fennel seed
fenugreek   mild curd cheese
garlic   yogurt
ginger
mustard seed
nuts
onion
pepper (sweet and/or hot)
poppyseed
saffron
sesame seed
tomato
turmeric

Detailed Pantry Notes

Here are some ideas for small, elegant touches that can enhance the soul of a kitchen, and spark an otherwise humdrum meal or snack.

seasoned salt

1) Most people keep salt shakers on the table. Most salt shakers contain salt — plain salt. But have you ever tried sesame salt? Add a tablespoon or two of crushed, lightly-toasted sesame seeds to some salt (about ½ cup) in a shaker with slightly larger-than-average holes. Also, try flavoring salt with celery seed, or with a dried herb rubbed to a fine powder (parsley, marjoram, thyme).

flavored butter

2) Every now and then serve a seasoned butter instead of plain butter. Soften it first, then mix in some freshly-minced or dried herbs. Try dill or basil. Start with a small amount, and season to taste.

Some night, serve garlic butter with freshly-baked bread. Crush a clove or two of garlic into about ½ cup soft butter.

For breakfast, try cinnamon or allspice in the butter (about 1 tsp. per ½ cup butter). Serve it with muffins, coffeecake, or toast.

spiked vinegar

3) Spike some vinegar from time to time. Use either cider or wine vinegar, and heat it first, to not-quite-boiling. Add sprigs of fresh herbs, 3 Tbs. to a quart. Recommended: tarragon, oregano, sage, thyme — or a combination. Seal it in a tightly-lidded jar, and store for 2-3 weeks in a dark place. Strain out the herbs, and use the vinegar for marinating leftover cooked beans and vegetables for salads.

For garlic vinegar: same procedure as above, only remove the garlic after 24 hours. Use 2-4 cloves garlic per quart of vinegar.

For spiced vinegar: same procedure as herbed vinegar, only use whole cloves, peppercorns, crushed red hot pepper, and/or slices of fresh ginger.

whipped honey

4) An alternative to jams and jellies: whipped honey. Use an electric mixer, and beat the honey at high speed until it turns light and opaque. Leave it plain, or add a little cinnamon and/or lemon juice. Whipped honey has a nicely-spreadable consistency.

*ginger-
in-wine*

5) After you use part of a fresh ginger root, store the unused part in a small jar of white wine or dry sherry. Keep this jar tightly-lidded and refrigerated. The ginger will preserve itself nicely this way, and the wine or sherry will acquire a gingery flavor, perfect for adding to a wokful of sautéing vegetables.

*indoor
herbs*

6) If you keep house plants, why not let some of them be potted herbs? Find the sunniest spot in your kitchen, and try growing herbs here. Chives, thyme, marjoram, tarragon, parsley, basil, and rosemary will all grow indoors. It won't yield a vast quantity (for example, you will not be able to cultivate enough basil to make a batch of pesto), but it will be plenty for frequent snippings into salads, onto soups, and even as fragrant garnishes for other dishes. Once you discover the little-known world of garnishing with sprigs of fresh herbs, your life may never be the same.

Apple Cider Jelly

If you are looking for a good jelly with no added sugar, but you don't want to use artificial sweeteners AND the prospect of making jelly from scratch seems too time-consuming, etc....... Try making jelly from apple cider. It is delicious. And all it takes is boiling.

You must use real apple cider, made with a cider press. Bring it to a boil, and boil it until it reduces to 1/8 its original volume. (So, for every 2 quarts of cider, you will get 1 cup of jelly.) After the cider is boiled down, cool it, then chill it in a tightly-lidded jar. The jelly keeps very well, if refrigerated.

Fruit Syrups

Apple juice, and other fruit juices, can also be boiled down. When the volume has reduced to 1/4 of the original, you will have a syrup, naturally-sweetened. Use this as you would any syrup, on French toast, pancakes, or waffles.

...*more*→

Dry-Roast Granola

About 25 minutes
to prepare.

Yield: about 3 cups.

Most homemade granola recipes call for a fairly heavy syrup (full of oil and honey) to be poured into the dry ingredients, and then an extended, slow baking session. Here is an alternative method. It has no oil added, so it contains many fewer calories than the syrup variety. And it is cooked quickly right on top of the stove, so you don't have to leave your oven on for a long period of time. The quick, dry sautéing gives a deep-roasted flavor to the ingredients. The brown sugar melts ever-so-slightly, gently coating each morsel.

1 cup raw rolled oats
⅓ cup chopped nuts

⅓ cup wheat germ
⅓ cup sesame seeds
⅓ cup sunflower seeds
⅓ cup shredded coconut

¼ cup (packed) brown sugar
¼ tsp. (heaping) salt

(1) Use a large, heavy skillet (preferably cast-iron). Place the oats and the nuts in the skillet, turn on the heat to medium-low, and stir them constantly for 5 minutes, as they begin to roast.

(2) Add wheat germ, sesame seeds, sunflower seeds, and coconut. Keep both the heat and the stirring action constant for 10 more minutes.

(3) Sprinkle in brown sugar and salt. Cook for 2-5 more minutes, still stirring. Remove from heat, cool, and store in an airtight container.

NOTE: This yields about 3 cups. You can double the amounts, but it is recommended that you make smaller batches more frequently instead, for greater freshness.

Baked Coated Nuts

15 minutes to prepare;
1¼ hours to bake.

Yield: ½ lb.

A nutritious nut-snack. Possibly habit-forming.

½ lb. nuts (any combination of
   whole almonds
   cashew pieces
   walnut halves, or
   pecan halves)

1 large egg
1 Tbs. tamari sauce
¼ tsp. salt

wheat germ for coating
(up to 2 cups)

(1) Preheat oven to 275°F. Lightly grease a baking tray.

(2) Beat together the egg, tamari sauce, and salt — in a medium-sized bowl.

(3) Add the nuts to the egg mixture in the bowl. Stir until they are all coated, and let them stand 5 minutes.

(4) Place the wheat germ on a flat surface, such as a plate or a large piece of waxed paper. Use a slotted spoon to scoop up the nuts, a few at a time, plop them down onto the bed of wheat germ, roll them until coated. Transfer the coated nuts to the baking tray. Continue until all the nuts are coated and evenly distributed on the tray. (It's okay if some of them are clustered together.)

(5) Bake undisturbed for 1¼ hours. Cool, and store in a tightly-lidded jar.

afterword

It is safe to assume that human beings have been involved in Eating-for-Sustenance for an immeasurably long time. There is also a good likelihood that the foods our species has ingested have been subject to some form of Preparation for a similarly long period. However, the exact date of the discovery of Deliciousness is not known. We speculate that somewhere along the way, some ancestor of ours got inspired to throw in a pinch of this with a roast leg of that, causing a sensation among the tribe. Thereafter, this person was never seen without a white chef's hat on, followed by idolaters, chanting, "XDEWRYBP! XDEWRYBP!" ("More! More!")

The art of fine cooking has been revered in many cultures. Although often shrouded in mystery, its origin has always been, and will continue to be, People. Ironically, though, the bulk of humanity feels quite excluded from "haute cuisine". If more people can feel welcome in the world of careful, expressive and healthful (not to mention, delicious) food preparation, we won't need to turn to junk food out of lack of information about anywhere else to go. We will have someplace wonderful to go, and we can all discover ourselves as artists on the way there. Trust your own tastebuds to teach you how to create delightful food for both yourself and others. The ensuing good feelings of personal and shared pleasures will be unavoidable.

I hope this book has encouraged you to feel freer and more at home in your kitchens. I hope you gain the confidence to prepare good food the way you and your close ones love it, and to fully enjoy, appreciate, and grow with it. I hope this book gets shared with children, so more people can begin earlier to discover and delight in our human nurturing powers. Last and foremost, I hope hunger of all kinds can be brought to an end in this world, so that some day all human beings will have the opportunity to know fullest physical and spiritual strength.

Note: The inclusion of a dish in a menu is indicated by *menu* after the relevant page number.

vegetable casserole 208; with poached eggs 184; stir-fried 239; and tofu 190; in vegetable dip 251; in vegetable soup 19; in vegetable strudel 140; in vegetable upside-down cake 202

BRUSSELS SPROUTS:
Pasta Sauce of 164
Soup 43

Bstilla 142 *and menu*

BUCKWHEAT (kasha), and broccoli casserole 218

Bulgarian Salad (tomato) 60, 82 *menu*

BULGHUR (cracked wheat; *Brit.* Burghul):
to cook 225

in eggplant casserole 214; in whole wheat bread 96

Burghul. *See* Bulghur

BUTTER: discussed 13; to flavor 282 *menu*, 286

BUTTERMILK:
Biscuits 122, 281 *menu*
and Cucumber Dressing 78, 282 *menu*

in bread: oatmeal-maple 112, rye 103, savory nut 107; in Bstilla (strudel) 142; in muffins: honey-bran 116, orange-date 114, pecan-oat 114; in quiche 131; with rice and peas 39; in Russian coffeecake 267; in soup: brussels sprout 43, cherry-plum 49; curried peanut 38; in vegetable upside-down cake 202

CABBAGE, GREEN:
Soup 37

in piroshki 149; stir-fried 239

CAKE (*See also* Torte):
Chocolate-Honey- 274
Cream-filled Carob Fudge Torte 260–61
Jewish New Year Honey- 275
Oatmeal Yogurt 262
Peach and Rum 258
Russian Coffee- 267
Spicy Gingerbread 259
Vegetable Upside-Down (savory) 52 *menu*, 202

CALZONE:
Dough for 148
Pesto 151
Provolone 74 *menu*, 151
Zucchini 152 *and menu*

discussion of 147

Canned foods, discussed 14

CANTALOUPE:
-Peach Soup 45
Stuffed 73, 82 *menu*

CAPERS, in eggplant salad 65

CARAWAY SEEDS, in piecrust 130

CAROB POWDER: in fudge torte 260; in pumpernickel 101; in swirl bread 102

CARROT; CARROTS:
Curry 209
Pie, Russian 133

to cut 235, 236, 237; to peel 234

in baked beans 216; in fried rice 220; in golden vegetable piecrust 130; in kugel 206; in piroshki 149; in pulao 222; in salad: cauliflower 57, rémoulade 75; stir-fried 239; in tsimmes 204; in vegetable cheesecake 212; in vegetable-flecked bread 101; in vegetable stew 213; in vegetable strudel 140; in vegetable upside-down cake 202

CASHEW NUTS:
Baked 289
Curry 209

in bread: barley 98, nut 106; in chickpea and vegetable stew 226; in enchiladas 144; in fried rice 220; in shortbread 279; with tofu: and noodles 193, sweet and sour 189; in sweet potato pie 132

CASSEROLES, 200–208, 214–19. (*See also* Kugel):
Broccoli and Buckwheat Godunov 218
Escalloped Apples 200
Frijoles con Queso 217
Humble Vegetable 208
Mushroom Mystery 201
Persian Eggplant 214
Risotto alla Milanese 219
Shepherd's Pie 203
Spicy Baked Beans 216
Tsimmes 204
Vegetable Upside-Down Cake 202

CAULIFLOWER:
Paprikash 167
Salad 57; 82, 152 *menus*
Soufflé 174

to cut 236

in confetti spaghetti 162; with macaroni 166; stir-fried 239; in vegetable soup 19; in vegetable stew 213, in vegetable cake 202

Celeriac. *See* Celery root

CELERY: to cut 236

in baked beans 216; in fried rice 220; and lentils 223; in mushroom casserole 201; in shepherd's

amaretto 276, soufflé 277, vegetable 212; in coffeecake: date-meringue 118, Russian 267; in cookies 278; in devilled egg pie 135; in fried rice 220; in kugel 168, 206, 207; in pasta dough 159; in quiche 131; in soufflé: blintz 156, savory 172–78, cheesecake 277; in soup: lemon 23, sesame-eggdrop 20, schav 48, vegetable-eggdrop 19; in strawberry mousse 263; for torte: carob fudge 272, coconut-almond macaroon 271; in tsimmes 204; in vegetable upside-down cake 202

FRIED: in broiled eggs 186; in huevos rancheros 182

HARD-BOILED: in casseroles: buckwheat 218, eggplant 214; in dip: avocado 248, avocado-tofu 246; in enchiladas 145; in piroshki 149; in salad: beet 58, tomato 73; in soup: lemon 23, mushroom 51, vegetable-barley 21; as soup garnish 21, 23; in stuffed vegetables 228, 231

Enchanted Broccoli Forest, The 229

ENCHILADA:

 Avocado and Cashew 144

 Cream Cheese 144

 Egg, Olive and Cheese 145

 Zucchini and Pepper 145

 SAUCES FOR:

  Red 146

  Salsa Verde 146

  discussion of 144

 fillings for, in stuffed vegetables 144

Entrées, eggless. See Eggless entrées

ESCAROLE (Brit. Batavia):

 Soup 40

 stir-fried 239

ETHNIC FOODS: guidelines for improvising and 284–85

 RECIPES:

 BRAZILIAN 228

 CHINESE:

  Soup 20, 28

  Entrées 189, 190, 196, 220

   Improvisations 284

 EAST EUROPEAN (see also Russian):

  Soup 21

  Salad 68, 60, 63

  Entrées 167, 218

   Improvisations 284

 FRENCH:

  Soup 31, 42

  Salad 69, 71, 75

  Entrées 131, 170–75, 178, 183, 230

  Desserts 264, 266

   Improvisations 284

 INDIAN:

  Soup 25, 38, 50

  Salad 64

  Bread 121

  Entrées 209–11, 222–23

   Improvisations 285

 ITALIAN:

  Soup 28, 40, 51

  Salad 65, 70, 74

  Entrées 151–52, 158–63, 165, 212, 219

  Dessert 276

   Improvisations 285

 JAPANESE, entrée 195

 JEWISH:

  Soup 48

  Salad 60, 63

  Bread 97

  Entrées 153–56, 168, 204–207

  Desserts 275–78

 MEDITERRANEAN:

  Soup 22, 23

  Salad 61, 62

  Entrées 139, 141, 142, 226, 232

  Nibbles 247, 250, 252

   Improvisations 285

 MEXICAN:

  Soup 30, 47

  Bread 111

  Entrées 143–46, 182, 217

  Nibble 247

   Improvisations 284

 PERSIAN, entrée 214

 RUSSIAN:

  Entrées 133, 148–50

  Dessert 267

 SPANISH:

  Soup 46

  Entrée 221

   Improvisations 284

 SWEDISH:

  Soup 37

  Bread 103

 SWISS:

  Salad 59

  Nibble 253

FARINA, in stuffed peppers 228

FETTUCINE, cutting 160. See also Pasta

in enchiladas 145, 146; in Greek pizza 141; in lasagna 165; and lentils 223; in mushroom pâté 254; in nut bread 107; in omelette 180; in pasta: with artichokes 164, with cauliflower 166, 167; in pie: carrot 133, mushroom-yogurt 134; in piecrust 128; in piroshki: cabbage-egg 149, mushroom 150; in quiche 131; with rice: risotto 219, Spanish 221; in soufflé 174; in spinach borek 139; in stew: chickpea and vegetable 226; influenced 213; with tofu: and broccoli 190, -spinach and walnut loaf 194; in vegetable cheesecake 212; in vegetable strudel 140; in vegetable upside-down cake 202

RED: in avocado soup 47; in avocado-tofu dip 246; in bread 101; in cauliflower salad 57; in curry: carrot 209, eggplant 211; in enchilada sauce 146; in raita 223

ORANGE; ORANGES:

    Chutney 223

    Muffins 114

    Salad 61

    Sesame Dressing 77

    for crêpes 266; in sweet potato pie 132; as soup garnish 35

JUICE: in bread: freshly-fruited 104, Swedish rye 103; in cake 262; in carrot curry 209; in coffeecake 118; in dip: almond-orange 245, orange-humus 247; in Hal's sauce for vegetables 240; in soup: almond 35, cantaloupe-peach 45

CONCENTRATE, in apricot streusel pie 280

Pans. See Bread, yeasted

PARSLEY:

    Chutney 222

    in cauliflower salad 57; in confetti spaghetti 162; in enchilada 144; for pesto 161; in piroshki 150; as soup garnish 21, 23, 26, 43

PARSNIP: to peel 234

    in piecrust 130

PASTA 157–68:

    with Brussels Sprouts, Mushroom and Cheese Sauce 164

    with Marinated Artichoke Hearts 164

    Primavera 158, 162

    Salad, Marinated 70; 82, 281 menus

  DOUGH:

    Egg 159

    Spinach 159

SAUCES for 163–64, 166–67

    Brussels Sprouts, Mushrooms and Cheese 164

    Cauliflower 166, 167

    Marinated Artichoke 164

    Marinated Tomato 163

    Pepper 163

    discussion of homemade 158–60

    and pesto 61 menu; shells, for salad 70

PASTRY, FILO (phyllo; strudel-leaf):

    Bstilla 142

    Cheese Tyropitas 139

    Greek Pizza 141

    Spinach Borek 139

    Vegetable Strudel 140

    discussion of 137–38

Pastry cutter, fluted 180

Pastry, strudel-leaf. See Pastry, filo

PASTRIES, MAIN DISH 125–56

    Blintzes 154–56

    Calzone 148, 151–52

    Enchiladas 143–46

    Pies 132–36

    Piecrusts 127–30

    Piroshki 148–50

    Quiche 131

    Strudel leaf (filo) 139–42

Pâté, Mushroom and Cheese 254

PEAS, FRESH GREEN:

    Soup 36, 282 menu

    in curry 210; with pasta primavera 162; in potato salad 66; in shepherd's pie 203; and rice: 39, risotto 219; in soup: garbanzo 34, Inspiration 44, sesame-eggdrop 20, vegetable 18

PEACH; PEACHES:

    Soup, with Cantaloupe 45

    in blintzes 156; in pudding cake 258

PEANUT; PEANUTS:

    Dip, with Tofu 250

    Soup, Curried 38–39

    with tofu: and broccoli 190, and noodles 193

  BUTTER: in dip 250; in soup 38–39; with tofu: and broccoli 190, and noodles 193

PECAN NUTS:

    Baked 289

    Muffins, with Oats 114

    in eggplant curry 211; in nut bread 107; in sweet potato pie 132; in piecrust 133; in stuffed pears 71

PEARS, Fancy Stuffed 71

PEPPERS, BELL (if not specified, green and sweet red peppers are interchangeable). See also Chilies, canned green; Pimiento

WATER CHESTNUTS 14; in Chinese mushroom soup 28; in vegetable stir-fry 240

WHEAT BERRIES, in bread 96

Wheat, cracked. *See* Bulghur

WHEAT GERM:

Bread 104

Muffins 116

for baked nuts 289; in granola 288; in kugel 168, 206, 207; in mushroom pâté 254; in orange-date muffins 114; in pie: apricot streusel 280, sweet potato 132; in piecrust 129; in piroshki 150; in stuffed artichokes 230; with tofu 191, 194; in tsimmes 204; in vegetable strudel 140; in vegetable upside-down cake 202

WINE, DRY WHITE, in fried rice 220; in mushroom soup 51; in rarebit 253; in stuffed artichokes 230

YAMS, to peel 234

YEAST, active dry (B*rit.* Dried) 86

action of 89; in coffeecake 117; compared with cake 90; in dough for piroshki and calzone 146

YOGURT, UNFLAVORED (B*rit.* Natural):

Bread 108, 282 *menu*

Muffins 113

Sauce (raita) 39, 223

discussed 13

in buckwheat and broccoli casserole 218; in chutney 222; in coffeecake 117; in corn bread 111, 217; in curried eggs 186; in soup: apple 25, potato 50; with curry 209; in dip 245, 248; in frijoles con queso 217; in enchiladas 144; in gingerbread 259; in oatmeal-yogurt cake 262; in nut bread 107; for pasta sauce 167; in pie: mushroom 136, sour cream and onion 134; sweet potato 132; in salad: asparagus 69, beet 58, broccoli 56, cucumber 62, eggplant 64, rémoulade 75; as soup garnish 23; in stuffed cantaloupe 73; in torte: carob fudge 260, coconut-almond macaroon 261; in vegetable strudel 140

ZUCCHINI (B*rit.* Courgette):

Bread 110

Salad 74, 82 *menu*

to cut 236, 237; to peel 234

in bread 101; in calzone 152; in enchiladas 145; in frijoles con queso 217; in frittata 185; in kugel 206; with pasta 162; in soup: green noodle 29, vegetable 19; stir-fried 239; in vegetable cheesecake 212

Zuppa Alla Pavese 19

Notes

Notes

Notes

Notes

Notes

Notes

Notes

Notes

Notes

Notes

Notes

Photo: Jeffrey Black   Broccoli Embroidery: Patricia Dustan

ollie Katzen was born in 1950 in Rochester, New York. She was educated at the Eastman School of Music, Cornell University, and the San Francisco Art Institute. Although her formal training was as an artist and musician, she exhibited natural cooking inclinations from a very early age, and cooked professionally — in restaurants and as a caterer — for ten years. In 1973 she was one of the founders of the Moosewood Restaurant in Ithaca, New York, and during her five years of cooking there, she compiled, illustrated and handlettered the **Moosewood Cookbook.** (Ten Speed Press, 1977.)

In addition to her writing and illustrating, Mollie is a committed student of classical piano. She now resides in Berkeley, California, where she is at work on her first children's book.